POPULATION AGEING FROM A LIFECOURSE PERSPECTIVE

Critical and international approaches

Edited by
Kathrin Komp and Stina Johansson

First published in Great Britain in 2015 by

Policy Press
University of Bristol
1–9 Old Park Hill
Bristol BS2 8BB
UK
+44 (0)117 331 4054
tpp-info@bristol.ac.uk
www.policypress.co.uk

North America office:
Policy Press
c/o The University of Chicago Press
1427 East 60th Street
Chicago, IL 60637, USA
t: +1 773 702 7700
f: +1 773 702 9756
sales@press.uchicago.edu
www.press.uchicago.edu

British Library Cataloguing in Publication Data
A catalogue record for this book is available from the British Library.

Library of Congress Cataloging-in-Publication Data
A catalog record for this book has been requested.

ISBN: 978 1 44731 071 6 hardcover

Cover design by Policy Press
Front cover: image kindly supplied by iStock
Printed and bound in Great Britain by CPI Group (UK) Ltd,
Croydon, CR0 4YY
Policy Press uses environmentally responsible print partners

Contents

List of tables and figures

Tables

Figures

Notes on the contributors

Sofia Aboim is a research fellow at the Institute of Social Sciences, University of Lisbon. Her research interests include family and the lifecourse, social inequalities, gender, feminisms, masculinities studies and social theory. She has published several articles in Portuguese and international journals as well as a number of books, including *Plural masculinities: The remaking of the self in private life*. She is working on other book projects and undertaking research on masculinities and gender. Currently, she coordinates the project TRANSRIGHTS – Gender citizenship and sexual rights in Europe, financed by the European Research Council.

J. Scott Brown is an associate professor and director of graduate studies in the Department of Sociology and Gerontology and research fellow with Scripps Gerontology Center at Miami University (USA). His research interests are focused on wealth and health inequalities across the lifecourse with particular emphasis on gender and race differences in physical and mental health. He has authored or co-authored over two dozen articles and book chapters across multiple research areas including mortality and disability, mental-health trajectories across age, variation in race and ethnic measurement and its social and health implications, and cross-national investigation of welfare state policies.

Zhen Cong is an associate professor in the Department of Human Development and Family Studies at Texas Tech University (USA). Her research focuses on the influences of cultural expectations and norms in the process of how social changes and intergenerational interactions influence older adults' well-being. Her research also advocates for taking an extended family perspective in studying intergenerational interactions, especially in cultures where complicated interactions and social exchanges are carried out within an extended family.

Annette Franke is professor for health promotion and methods in social work at the Protestant University of Applied Sciences in Ludwigsburg (Germany). She holds a first degree in social sciences and received her doctoral degree at the Department for Social Gerontology and Life Course Research at the Technical University of Dortmund. She is also chair of the section for behavioural and social gerontology in the German Society of Gerontology and Geriatrics. Her main research interests are retirement planning, lifecourse perspectives on health and work, older workers, reconciliation of work and care, and social networks.

Ilkka Haapola is a senior researcher in the Palmenia Centre for Continuing Education at the University of Helsinki (Finland). He has a broad experience on empirical social research, targeted on unemployment, poverty, and social exclusion. His most recent field of study is that of ageing research, in particular the longitudinal and cohort analysis of ageing. His research interests include quality of life, person-environment relations, and the use of social and health services in later life.

Stina Johansson is professor emerita in social work at Umeå University, Sweden and associate professor in sociology at Uppsala University. Her research interests are social care, social gerontology, gender, diversity and comparative social policy. Johansson has directed several research projects and has published together with researchers from the Scandinavian countries, China and Australia. She has also been chief editor of the *Swedish Journal of Social Research*, and is one of the authors of *Gendered citizenship in Western Europe* published by Policy Press.

Antti Karisto is professor of social gerontology at the Department of Social Research, University of Helsinki. Recently he has studied on the baby boomers, retirement migration and lifestyles of older people. He has written extensively on health and well-being, social policy, urban topics, and everyday life (see http://blogs.helsinki.fi/akaristo/).

Kathrin Komp is assistant professor at the Department of Social Research at Helsinki University, Finland. She also is chair of the Research Network on Ageing in Europe. Her research focuses on population ageing, life-courses, social policies, and the 2008 economic crisis. She has presented her findings in more than 40 publications, and in 2011 she was named a 'Future Leader of Ageing Research in Europe'.

Daniel Larsson is a senior lecturer, researcher and director of studies at the Department of Sociology, Umeå University (Sweden). His research interests are among else social policy, social exclusion, poverty and the labour market. He is the PI of a research project on self-employment and member of a research project on welfare service provision in transition. He has also published research on white-collar crime.

Scott M. Lynch is a professor of sociology and director of the Demography of Aging Training programme in the Population Research Institute at Duke University. His research interests are in demographic and statistical methods for studying lifecourse processes and in the relationship between socioeconomic status, race, and health in the US. He has published two books and numerous articles and book chapters in these and other areas. He is currently completing a book on handling missing data in social science research and investigating regional differences in health and mortality in the US.

Patrik Marier is professor of political science at Concordia University and currently holds a Canada Research Chair in comparative public policy. He is also the scientific director for the *Centre de recherche et d'expertise en gérontologie sociale* (CREGÉS). The CREGÉS regroups more than 50 experts and researchers originating from 14 different academic disciplines in social gerontology. His research focuses on socio-political and policy challenges related to an aging population. He has published extensively on multiple facets of pension policies. This includes comparative analyses on the pension reform process, pension outcomes, and the role of civil servants in pension reforms.

Timothy S. Melnyk is a PhD student in sociology at the University of Nevada, Las Vegas, USA. His research has examined the experiences of problem gamblers in a Las Vegas-based recovery programme. He is a co-investigator of several gaming-related research projects in Canada.

Shannon M. Monnat is an assistant professor of rural sociology, demography, and sociology and a research associate with the Population Research Institute at Pennsylvania State University. Her research focuses on the demography of children, youth, and families in rural and urban areas of the US with a particular focus on social and spatial inequalities and social determinants of health.

Andreas Motel-Klingebiel is a professor in ageing and later life at the National Institute for the Study of Ageing and Later Life, Linköping University, Sweden. He has undertaken research in major lifecourse and ageing studies at the German Centre of Gerontology, Freie Universität Berlin and the Max-Planck-Institute for Human Development. A sociologist and gerontologist, he has taught sociology at Humboldt-Universität of Berlin and gerontology at the University of Vechta. Research interests include lifecourses, social inequalities, social change and later life in/exclusion as well as welfare systems and policy interventions in ageing Europe.

Jolanta Perek-Białas is statistician and economist but her scientific interest is mainly gerontology. She works at the Warsaw School of Economics and also in the Institute of Sociology of the Jagiellonian University in Kraków, Poland. She has publications related to socio-economic consequences of population ageing in Poland, and in selected Central and Eastern European countries, active ageing policy, reconciliation of work and care, social exclusion/inclusion of older people and long-term care.

Jennifer Reid Keene is professor of sociology and associate dean of the College of Liberal Arts at the University of Nevada, Las Vegas. As a social gerontologist, Dr Keene studies family caregiving across the lifecourse, the intersection of work and family life and social thanatology. She is co-author of *Death and dying in America* (Polity, 2009).

Anna C. Smedley is an assistant professor in residence with the Department of Sociology at the University of Nevada, Las Vegas (UNLV). Her research has focused on women's racial and ethnic variation in STEM and STEM-skilled fields. She has been heavily involved in diversity initiatives at UNLV and is an active member of the Minority Serving Institution task force. Dr Smedley is also currently working on several projects related to student learning outcomes.

Mikael Stattin is associate professor in the Department of Sociology, Umeå University, Sweden. Mikael have for several years worked on issues about labour market participations and exit among older workers. He has been responsible for a national longitudinal survey with the aim of mapping living conditions among older people in Sweden. He is also co-leading the Swedish part of the comparative study Survey of Health, Ageing and Retirement in Europe (SHARE). Recently he launched a research project that will study the importance of work place characteristics and human resources policies in relation to employees' attitudes towards the timing of retirement.

Justyna Stypińska is a researcher and lecturer in sociology at the Department of Sociology at the Free University in Berlin. Her research expertise focuses on ageism, reconciliation of work and care, legal aspects of age discrimination in the labour market, and intersectional analysis of age, gender and migration status. Her newest research project poses a question about destandardisation of professional lifecourses, taking older entrepreneurs as an empirical example.

Fleur Thomese is an associate professor at the Department of Sociology, VU University in Amsterdam. She is associated with the Longitudinal Aging Study Amsterdam, and is director of the Talma Institute, an interdisciplinary institute focusing on sustainable care systems. She is especially interested in how grandparental investments in child care are related to societal contexts on the one hand, and evolutionarily relevant outcomes on the other hand. She also publishes on how neighbourhoods and living environment affect social integration and social participation.

Konrad Turek is a sociologist, labour market researcher and analyst in the Centre of Evaluation and Public Policy Analysis at Jagiellonian University, Poland. He is engaged in the biggest labour market research project in Poland (Human Capital Balance), conducted since 2010. He is also a co-author of the governmental strategy for improvement of economic activity of people aged 50+ for the years 2013–20. His research expertise covers the sociology of economy, labour market research, social gerontology and statistics. Most of his work focus on ageing, the impact of population ageing on economy, labour market relations and lifelong learning.

Karin Wall is a research professor at the Institute for Social Sciences at the University of Lisbon. Her areas of expertise are sociology of families and comparative social policy. She coordinates the Observatory on Families and Family Policies at ICS and works as an expert on family policies in Europe. Her research interests include family forms and interactions, family and the lifecourse, family and care policies, migrant families, gender and work–life balance. She is currently coordinating a cross-national study of family trajectories and social networks across three generations and conducting comparative research on parental leave policies and men's changing family roles.

Jeni Warburton holds the John Richards Chair in Rural Aged Care Research at La Trobe University, Australia. She has 25 years' experience of research into social policy, particularly relating to issues associated with an ageing population, volunteering and community. Her research has played a key role in the development of practice and policy around volunteering and social inclusion, particularly relating to older people.

Rachel Winterton is a research fellow with the John Richards Initiative at La Trobe University, Australia. Her programme of research investigates the influence of rurality on healthy ageing, with a specific focus on social and civic participation among diverse groups of rural older people. Her recent work explores how rural communities and local agencies are managing and responding to challenges posed by local population ageing through systems of governance, health and social infrastructure.

Takashi Yamashita is an assistant professor of sociology at University of Nevada, Las Vegas. His primary research interests are geographic access to health resources (for example, healthy foods, health care services) in older populations, subjective well-being over the lifecourse, and ageing in place. He teaches medical sociology, social gerontology and statistics.

Foreword

Judith Phillips

Kathrin Komp and Stina Johansson draw together an edited collection which revisits the central theme of this series: ageing and the lifecourse. Interrogating this theme, they take a critical gerontological perspective on the lifecourse, acknowledging its diversity, fluidity, complexity and connectedness with other phases of life and generations. Given its shifting parameters, 'some fixed, some malleable', how this concept is incorporated into policy is difficult, yet the book provides a global snapshot of how this can be accomplished. Ways in which ageing and old age as a category are constructed and structured by the society and culture in which it takes place are illustrated through examples in Europe, China, the US, Canada and Australia. The message throughout the book, conveyed by internationally renowned authors on ageing, is that ageing has to be viewed within the lifecourse framework, if we are to address the health and social care needs of older people and the inequalities of ageing. *Population ageing from a lifecourse perspective* contributes significantly to the literature on critical gerontology and is a vital resource for academics, students and professionals interested in ageing and later life.

ONE

Introduction

Kathrin Komp and Stina Johansson

When demography and lifecourse research meet

On Pentecost Sunday, Dr Juvenal Urbino tried to save his parrot from a mango tree. He climbed a ladder, slipped and fell, ending his life at the age of 81 years. His grieving widow, the 71-year-old Fermina Daza, set up a wake the same evening. After the guests had paid their respects, the president of the riverboat company, 76-year-old Florentino Ariza approached the widow. To her dismay he declared: 'I have waited for this opportunity for more than half a century, to repeat to you once again my vow of eternal fidelity and everlasting love' (Garcia Marquez, 1989, p 50). Needless to say, the widow threw him out.

Ariza's out-of-place behaviour is the starting point for Gabriel Garcia Marquez's world-renowned novel *Love in the time of cholera*. In this book, Garcia Marquez sends the reader on a journey with Florentino Ariza, starting with his first encounter with Fermina Daza in their teens. After a short period of courtship, Fermina rejected Ariza's advances and instead married the well-situated Doctor Urbino. While Ariza moved on with his life, he could not forget about Fermina and used the first opportunity that presented itself to reiterate his devotion to her. Unfortunately this was decades too late, at her deceased husband's wake. We will not spoil the book by telling what happened next, but instead would like to draw your attention to the fact that it is much easier to understand Ariza's impromptu declaration after learning about his history with the widow. This is what scholars call a 'lifecourse perspective'.

The lifecourse perspective looks at the activities and situations of individuals over time. In its most extensive form, it follows them from the cradle to the grave. The sequence of activities and life situations from birth to death is called the *lifecourse*. The rationale behind the lifecourse perspective is that experiences do not only have immediate effects, but can also affect lives years or even decades into the future (Elder, 1994; Grenier, 2012). For example, the education that youths receive affects their labour market careers when they are of mid-age, the timing of their retirement, and how much pension benefits they receive when they are old (Strandh and Nordlund, 2008; Komp et al, 2010; Vignoli and De Santis, 2010). Thus, the situation during one's youth can already set the tracks for one's later life. In other words, if we want to understand the situation of older people, we need to look at their lifecourses. Moreover, if we want to influence what our lives will be like when we are old, we need to start planning early. If we only start making changes when we are old, the effects will be limited. However, if start when we are young or middle-aged, the effects are bigger (Morel et al, 2012).

Nowadays, scholars and the public are increasingly focusing attention on people of old age because of population ageing. Population ageing occurs when the share of older people in a population increases (Thorslund and Parker, 1995). The share of people aged 65 years and older in the global population increased from 5% in 1950 to 8% in 2010. In Europe, the oldest continent in the world, the share reached even 16% in 2010 (United Nations, 2013). This demographic shift changes societies. Individuals have to revise their life-plans, families have to rethink their care arrangements, and policy makers need to reform pension policies and health care services, and labour markets and entire economies shift along with these demographic changes (Komp and Aartsen, 2013). Thus, population change causes social change.

Demography helps us to better understand the process of population ageing. Demography is the branch of science that studies populations (Daugherty and Kammeyer, 1995). Predominant topics in today's demographic research are population ageing, as well as its root causes and consequences (Christensen et al, 2009; Morgan, 2003; Van Oyen et al, 2010). The main explanations for the process of population ageing are that people in developed nations nowadays live longer and that they have fewer children. A small role is also attributed to migration flows between countries (Christensen et al, 2009; Daugherty and Kammeyer, 1995). According to the demographic transition theory, population ageing is the fate of all countries that undergo modernisation (Kirk, 1996; Lesthaeghe and Neels, 2002).

While demography and lifecourse research have different starting points, their perspectives on old age complement each other. Lifecourse research starts from the micro-level perspective of individuals, arguing that a person's lifecourse connects all life-events. Among these life-events are childbearing, the decision to migrate, and death. Demographers aggregate the information on childbearing, deaths and migration to make statements about the macro-level of populations. They then build a bridge between lifecourses and the process of population ageing. At the same time, lifecourse scholars underline that characteristics of the macro-level population influence the lives of individuals. The population composition affects the worldviews, habits and culture in a country, and also shapes social institutions such as families, workplaces and pension schemes. These social institutions, in turn, structure lifecourses. Thus, lifecourses and the process of population ageing are interconnected through a feedback-loop (see Figure 1.1).

Figure 1.1: The interconnection between lifecourses and population ageing

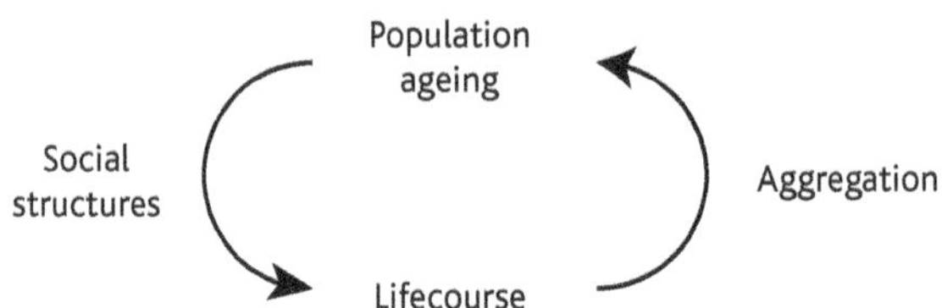

This text combines findings from lifecourse research and demography to better understand the causes and consequences of population ageing. This combination highlights that the process of population ageing that we witness today is a result of developments in the past. Consequently, there are no quick fixes to slow down this process. Today's policy and cultural interventions into population ageing will only show results years, maybe even decades, into the future. Moreover, the combination of lifecourse research and demography underlines that population ageing stems from complex changes in people's lives. Most events in a person's life are interrelated, and many of these events condition or exclude each other. Therefore, intervention into population ageing might have unintended side-effects.

Different lifecourses – different contributions to population ageing

Individuals differ in their characteristics as much as their lifecourses. Therefore, studies of lifecourses and of demography examine the variety of ways in which the lives of people unfold. For example, existing research demonstrates that women live longer than men, and that people with a high educational level have fewer children than their counterparts with a lower educational level (Joffe and Li, 1994; Van Oyen et al, 2010). Because of these social differences, we cannot make a universal statement on how lifecourse developments drive population ageing. Instead, we need to adopt a differentiated view that compares the situation of individuals within and between countries. This idea is at the heart of critical perspectives on the lifecourse (Grenier, 2012).

Lifecourse differences within countries

People differ in many ways, be it in their characteristics, preferences or life goals. These characteristics, preferences and life goals influence how their lives progress. Thus, differences between people translate into differences between lifecourses. Such lifecourse differences have been documented in respect of, for example, gender and generational membership. Interestingly, lifecourse differences entail that people contribute to population ageing in different ways and to differing degrees. Moreover, such differences suggest that intervention into population ageing needs to identify which subpopulation it wants to target, and then design the intervention according to the lifecourse patterns of this subpopulation.

Important lifecourse differences stem from generational membership, gender, socioeconomic status, ethnicity, and place of residence. Generational membership and place of residence point to external influences on the lifecourse. Generational membership denotes when people were born, which historical events they witnessed and what values they hold (Mannheim, 1928/1997). Place of residence is often characterised according to the degree of urbanisation and national infrastructure, which indicates the access people have to, for example, health care services that can prolong lives (Smith et al, 1995; Keating, 2008). Gender, socioeconomic status and ethnicity, in contrast, point to traits of individuals that shape lifecourses. These three characteristics influence, on the one hand, which logics people use when making decisions, in addition to how people are affected by social structures and historical events. For example, men and women react differently to the demands of the labour market and to care needs within their families (Komp and Aartsen, 2013; Perek-Bialas and Schippers, 2013); people with high socioeconomic status might have better access to health care services (Shaw et al, 2007); and ethnicity can be the basis for discrimination and exclusion from society (Andersen and Collins, 2013).

Significantly, some characteristics that shape lifecourses are fixed at birth, while others might change over time. Characteristics that are fixed at birth are, for example, gender, ethnicity, and generational membership. Characteristics that might change over time are socioeconomic status and place of residence. Socioeconomic status denotes the relative position an individual holds within society, based on educational level, income and prestige (Shaw et al, 2007). This status might change when individuals, for example, go on to further education or get a promotion at work. Place of residence changes when people migrate. They might do this within a country, for example between rural areas and cities. In this case, the process of population ageing might be indirectly affected, because the logic according to which that individual's life unfolds changes. However, individuals might also migrate between countries. In this case, the process of population ageing is directly affected, because the age structure of the population changes (Daugherty and Kammeyer, 1995).

The existence of lifecourse inequalities raises an interesting question: do social structures determine lifecourses, or do people have the possibility to determine their own fate (Alesina and Glaeser, 2008)? If lifecourses depend on characteristics that are fixed at birth, like gender or ethnicity, then a determinist view of lifecourses might prevail. Then again, the degree to which individuals have agency to shape their own lives is also debated (Marshall, 2005). Researchers have not yet established whether structure or agency dominates our understanding of lifecourses, although the answer to this question may itself differ across social groups.

Lifecourse differences between countries

As intriguing as the ideas of lifecourse differences is, grasping it proves challenging. This chapter has already established that lifecourses are heterogeneous, and they therefore cannot be grasped with one single model. One might now assume that lifecourses group together in a small number of clusters. Instead of one universal lifecourse model, there might be three, four, maybe five models existing side by side. This idea of a small number of lifecourse models is more complex than the one of a universal lifecourse model. Instead of one statement on lifecourses, one would now need to make several statements. Instead of one description of lifecourse changes, one would now need to give several descriptions. Instead of one explanation of how lifecourse changes drive population ageing, one would now need to give several explanations. Unfortunately, the heterogeneity between lifecourses is bigger than this explanation suggests. The new layer of heterogeneity stems from differences between countries.

Anyone who has travelled internationally knows that countries differ on many levels. It is warmer in some countries than in others; in some countries, you can easily take the train, while in others you need a car; and in some countries, you can be sure to find a doctor when you have had an accident, while in others you might not be so lucky (such variations can also be found among different regions within countries). Scholars from across the social sciences have tried to capture these differences between countries, and to relate them to lifecourses and to the process of population ageing. The idea of lifecourse regimes proves particularly helpful in explaining country differences in the structure of lifecourses (Mayer, 2005). This idea suggests that countries produce specific lifecourse patterns. This idea builds on the work of the political scientist Esping-Andersen (1990), who identified ideal types of welfare states, which he called 'welfare regimes'. He described these welfare regimes and determined which countries correspond to which regime. Mayer (2001, 2005) took the idea of the welfare regimes one step further, by identifying the more encompassing lifecourse regimes. He describes these lifecourse regimes according to, for example, their welfare state design and labour market structure, and he identified which typical lifecourse patterns they produce. For example, he emphasised that the deregulated labour market in the United Kingdom leaves some leeway for social inequalities to unfold over the lifecourse, whereas the strong state intervention in Sweden largely evens out social inequalities across the lifecourse. The country clusters that Mayer describes resemble the ones suggested by Esping-Andersen (1990).

The demographic transition theory, on the other hand, proves particularly helpful in explaining how population ageing comes about (Kirk, 1996). It states that industrialisation and the accompanying processes of modernisation and urbanisation lead to falling death rates and birth rates. These changes together cause population ageing (Kirk, 1996). The demographic transition theory is particularly important for this book, because it implies that the question that the book pursues is not a global one. Countries differ in how far the demographic transition has progressed in them, with developed countries being further along in the transition process than developing countries (Mason, 2005). Due to this, the discussions in this book are mainly an issue in modern developed countries. The country examples for this book are, therefore, taken from this group of countries. The connection between lifecourses and population ageing in other countries and at other historical times might follow a different logic.

The reflections on country difference in lifecourses point to another interesting question: what happens when societies transition into a late modernity? Beck and Lau (2005) argue that such a transition brings about changes in social institutions. In our case, social institutions such as families and pension schemes adapt to ageing populations, and therefore – intentionally and unintentionally – start to influence lifecourses in a new way. The mechanisms and structures we will describe in this book might, therefore, no longer apply. Giddens (1990, 1991), moreover, argues that extant institutions and ideas lose some of their structuring function over time. This development opens up more room for social differences, and it changes influences on lifecourses. Lifecourse influences stemming from earlier experiences in a person's life will now be stronger, compared to weakening influences of social structures on lifecourses.

We talk the talk, let's walk the walk

A lifecourse perspective on population ageing renders important insight – for scholars, policy makers, practitioners and every interested single individual. On the one hand, it points to questions of timing. Intervention into population ageing needs a long time horizon, because it does not simply serve to perform a quick fix of the situation of today's older people. Instead, it needs to enact additional changes in the behaviour of youths and middle-agers, which affect the progression of lifecourses and, therewith, the situation of tomorrow's older people. Medical advances are examples of such agents of change.

On the other hand, the lifecourse perspective entails that older might be more heterogeneous than a quick glance suggests. Even though some older people are in similar situations, they might have reached these circumstances via different life paths. Therefore, they might have different views on life, different preferences and different needs for help. Anybody thinking about their own old age or interaction with older people could benefit from keeping these two insights in mind. For example, individuals who want to plan for their own old age might want to start doing so at an early age. However, they nevertheless need to keep their planning flexible, because there might be extensive social and environmental changes during their lifetime. Care providers, who want to help older people, can set up more tailored support and care services if they look into the lifecourses of the older people and consider that patterns are changeable. Employers, finally, could maintain and further develop the skills of their employees if they intervened at an early age, which would make it easier for older employees to participate in the workforce. The lifecourse perspective can, therefore, help to meet more effectively the social changes brought about by ageing populations.

Overview of the book

This book utilises the lifecourse perspective to shed new light on population ageing. It does this in a country-comparative way to highlight national differences in population ageing and in lifecourse effects. The remainder of this book is structured in four parts.

Part I, entitled 'Theoretical framework', summarises theories on population ageing and on the lifecourse perspective. Scott Brown and Scott Lynch (in Chapter Two) adopt a demographer's view of population ageing. They explain mechanisms that lead to population ageing, and how ageing populations affect lifecourses. Then they suggest how demographic reasoning can be incorporated into lifecourse research. Andreas Motel-Klingebiel, on the other hand, takes the opposite approach in Chapter Three. He starts out by explaining the central theories and concepts of lifecourse research. Then, he argues that changes in the lifecourse affect population ageing, and that population ageing represents social change which, in turn, can affect lifecourses.

Part II is dedicated to critical perspectives. Critical perspectives on the lifecourse stress the variation in individuals' experiences and developments. They call for a differentiated view on lifecourse developments that compares the situation of individuals. Due to such lifecourse inequalities, social groups influence the progression of population ageing in different ways. The chapters in this part, therefore, focus on social inequalities, on how these inequalities lead to differences in lifecourses, and on the implications for population ageing. In Chapter Four, Antti Karisto and Ilkka Haapola explore generations in Finland. Generations are groups of people who were born at the same historical time, who experienced historical events at similar ages, and who consequently developed a shared identity. Karisto and Haapola show that generations have characteristic lifecourses. Karin Wall and Sofia Aboim focus on gender differences in Portugal in Chapter Five. The lives of men and women differ drastically due to biological and social influences. Because only women can become pregnant, women especially have to consider how to balance work and family obligations. Wall and Aboim demonstrate that, for this reason, women have more diverse lifecourses than men. In Chapter Six, Konrad Turek, Jolanta Perek-Bialas and Justyna Stypinska investigate differences in socioeconomic status in Poland. Socioeconomic status describes the position that a person occupies within society on grounds of wealth, educational level and occupational prestige. As lifecourses progress, social inequalities due to socioeconomic status deepen. Moreover, the meaning of socioeconomic status depends on social context. When Poland transformed from a communist to a post-communist society, lifecourses and inequalities between lifecourses were transformed. Takashi Yamashita, Timothy Melnyk, Jennifer Keene, Shannon Monnat and Anna Smedley describe ethnic differences in the United States (Chapter Seven). Ethnic groups have common ancestry and they share a distinctive culture. Yamashita and colleagues demonstrate that ethnic groups also have typical health risks, lifestyles, work biographies and overall lifecourses. Finally, Jeni Warburton and Rachel Winterton explore in Chapter Eight the urban–rural split in Australia. People in urban areas and in rural areas live and age differently. For example, people in rural areas typically have more conservative values, but fewer social and health care services at their disposal. Warburton and Winterton outline how place of residence influences lifecourses, and the progression of population ageing – leading to older populations in rural areas than in urban areas.

Part III of this volume explores the practical implications of a lifecourse approach to population ageing. It does this by dedicating each chapter to one actor that is affected by population ageing. Annette Franke (Chapter Nine) discusses how the self-employed in Germany can plan for their old age. Individuals nowadays live longer than their parents and grandparents did. At the same time, the increasing number of older people challenges existing support mechanisms, such as pension schemes and care arrangements. Consequently, individuals might need to plan for their own old age. Such planning is crucial for the self-employed, who have more possibilities to shape their working careers and often less support from public and occupational social insurances. Fleur Thomese and Zhen Cong take a closer look in Chapter Ten at families in the Netherlands and China. Families are the primary locus of intergenerational exchanges, and the lives of their members are intrinsically linked. As populations age, family structures change. Nowadays, families consist of more generations, and they have more older family members and fewer younger family members than before. Moreover, grandparents can nowadays spend more years with their grandchildren. As a result, opportunities for intergenerational support increase. In Chapter Eleven, Stina Johansson focuses on social care provision in Sweden. Ageing populations comprise many frail individuals who need care and support. However, the challenges that these people face differ, which often results from differences in their previous lifecourses. Johansson uses the example of migrants to illustrate that social care providers need a deeper understanding of lifecourses to design care services that can easily be understood and accepted by the older individuals. Mikael Stattin and Daniel Larsson discuss the Swedish labour market (Chapter Twelve). Population ageing goes hand in hand with an increasing number of healthy years of life, which individuals can use for various activities. Policy makers encourage individuals to spend at least some of these years on paid work, because such a step would boost the economy and consolidate the financial basis of pension schemes. Stattin and Larsson argue that a combination of lifecourses, workplace characteristics and social policies decides whether people use their later life for work. Finally, in Chapter Thirteen, Kathrin Komp and Patrik Marier investigate ageing in Canada. Due to population ageing, old-age policies have gained increasing attention over the last few decades. Komp and Marier underline that policies dealing with population ageing cannot focus on older people alone. Instead, they need to account for lifecourse effects and, therefore, tackle the situation of individuals of all ages.

The book concludes with a discussion section in Part IV. This section summarises the findings of the book and reflects on their implications. It expands and further develops the idea that lifecourse changes and population ageing affect one another. It thereby gives a more detailed indication of how the lifecourse perspective and demography can be merged.

References

Alesina, A. and Glaeser, E. (2008) *Fighting poverty in the US and Europe: A world of difference*, Oxford: Oxford University Press.

Andersen, M.L. and Collins, P.H. (2013) *Race, class & gender: An anthology*, Belmont, CA: Wadsworth Cengage.

Beck, U. and Lau, C. (2005) 'Second modernity as a research agenda: theoretical and empirical explorations in the "meta-change" of modern society', *The British Journal of Sociology*, 56, 4, 525-57.

Christensen, K., Doblhammer, G., Rau, R. and Vaupel, J.W. (2009) 'Ageing populations: The challenges ahead', *The Lancet*, 374, 9696, 1196-208.

Daugherty, H.G. and Kammeyer, K.C.W. (1995) *An introduction to population*, New York: The Guilford Press.

Elder, G.H., Jr (1994) 'Time, human agency, and social change: Perspectives on the life course', *Social Psychology Quarterly*, 57, 1, 4-15.

Esping-Andersen, G. (1990) *The three worlds of welfare capitalism*, Cambridge: Polity Press.

Garcia Marquez, G. (1989) *Love in the time of cholera*, London: Penguin.

Giddens, A. (1991) *Modernity and self-identity. Self and society in the late modern age*, Cambridge: Polity Press

Giffens, A. (1990) *The consequences of modernity*, Cambridge: Polity Press.

Grenier, A. (2012) *Transitions and the lifecourse: Challenging the constructions of 'growing old'*, Bristol: Policy Press.

Joffe, M. and Li, Z. (1994,) 'Male and female factors in fertility', *American Journal of Epidemiology*, 140, 10, 921-9.

Keating, N. (2008) *Rural ageing: A good place to grow old?*, Bristol: Policy Press.

Kirk, D. (1996) 'Demographic transition theiry', *Population Studies: A Journal of Demography*, 50, 3, 361-87.

Komp, K. and Aartsen, M. (2013) 'Introduction: Older people under the magnifying glass', in K. Komp and M. Aartsen (eds) *Old age in Europe. A textbook in gerontology*, Dordrecht: Springer, 1-14.

Komp, K., Van Tilburg, T and Broese van Groenou, M, (2010) 'Paid work between age 60 and 70 years in Europe: a matter of socio-economic status?', *International Journal of Ageing and Later Life*, 5, 1, 45-75.

Lesthaeghe, R. and Neels, K. (2002) 'From the first to the second demographic transition: an interpretation of the spatial continuity of demographic innovation in France, Belgium and Switzerland', *European Journal of Population*, 18, 4, 325-60.

Mannheim, K. (1928/1997) 'The problem of generation', in M.A. Hardy (ed) *Studying ageing and social change: Conceptual and methodological issues*, London: Sage, pp 22-65.

Marshall, V.W. (2005) 'Agency, events, and structure at the end of the life course', in R. Levy, P. Ghisletta, J.-M. le Goff, D. Spini and E. Widmer (eds) *Towards an interdisciplinary perspective on the life course. Advances in life course research*, 10, Amsterdam: Elsevier.

Mason, A. (2005) *Demographic transition and demographic dividends in developed and developing countries*, United Nations Expert Group Meeting on Special and Economic Implications of Changing Population Age Structures, Mexico City.

Mayer, K.U. (2001) 'The paradox of global social change and national path dependencies: Life course patterns in advanced societies', in A.E. Woodward and M. Kohli (eds) *Inclusions and exclusions in European societies*, London: Routledge, 89-110.

Mayer, K.U. (2005) 'Life courses and life chances in a comparative perspective', in S. Svallfors (ed) *Analyzing inequality: Life chances and social mobility in comparative perspective*, Palo Alto, CA: Stanford University Press, 17-55.

Morel, N, Palier, B. and Palme, J. (eds) (2012) *Towards a social investment welfare state: ideas, policies and challenges*, Bristol: Policy Press.

Morgan, A.P. (2003) Is low fertility a twenty-first-century demographic crisis? *Demography*, 49, 4, 589-603.

Perek-Bialas, J. and Schippers, J.J. (2013) 'Economic gerontology: Older people as consumers and workers', in K. Komp and M. Aartsen (eds) *Old age in Europe. A textbook of gerontology*, Dordrecht: Springer, 79-96.

Shaw, M., Bruna Galobardes, D.A., Lawlor, J.L., Wheeler, B. and Smith, G.D. (2007) *The handbook of inequality and socioeconomic position. Concepts and measures*, Bristol: Policy Press.

Smith, M.H., Beaulieu, L.J. and Seraphine, A. (1995) 'Social capital, place of residence, and college attendance', *Rural Sociology*, 60, 3, 363-80.

Strandh, M. and Nordlund, M. (2008) 'Active labour market policy and unemployment scarring: A ten-year Swedish panel study, *Journal of Social Policy*, 37, 3, 357-82.

Thorslund, M. and Parker, M.G. (1995) Strategies for an ageing population: Expanding the priorities discussion, *Ageing and Society*, 15, 2, 199-217.

United Nations (2013) *World population prospects: the 2012 revision*. http://esa.un.org/unpd/wpp/Excel-Data/EXCEL_FILES/1_Population/WPP2012_POP_F09_1_PERCENTAGE_OF_TOTAL_POPULATION_BY_BROAD_AGE_GROUP_BOTH_SEXES.XLS

Van Oyen, H., Cox, B., Jagger, C., Cambois, E., Nusselder, W., Gilles, C. and Robine, J.-M. (2010) Gender gaps in life expectancy and expected years with activity limitations at age 50 in the European Union: Associations with macro-level structural indicators, *European Journal of Ageing*, 7, 4, 229-37.

Vignoli, D. and De Santis, G. (2010) Individual and contextual correlates of economic difficulties in old age in Europe, *Population Research and Policy Review*, 29, 4, 481-501.

Part I

THEORETICAL FRAMEWORK

TWO

A demographer's view: population structures tell a story about lifecourses

J. Scott Brown and Scott M. Lynch

Introduction

Demography is the study of populations, with populations commonly defined as: persons living within a geographic boundary who tend to share a common language and culture. Traditionally, demographers have focused on the three sources of change – the 'population dynamics' – that influence the size and growth or decline of populations. Change in the components of population dynamics, at least as observed in human populations, inevitably lead to population ageing and have tremendous consequences for the lifecourse of individuals. In this chapter, we describe population dynamics and explain how they lead to population ageing, illustrating the complex and varying means by which populations age. We then discuss the consequences for the individual lifecourse, and we offer suggestions for incorporating demographic reasoning into micro-level lifecourse research.

Population dynamics

Population size is influenced by three factors: births into the population, deaths out of the population, and net migration, where net migration is the sum of migration into the population (immigration) and migration out of the population (emigration). The fundamental 'balancing equation' in demography demonstrates how population change occurs:

$$P_t = P_{\{t-k\}} + B_{\{t-k,t\}} - D_{\{t-k,t\}} + NM_{\{t-k,t\}}, \tag{1}$$

where P_t is the population size at time t, $P_{\{t-k\}}$ is the population size at time $t - k$, $B_{\{t-k,t\}}$ is the number of births in the population between t-k and t, $D_{\{t-k,t\}}$ is the number of deaths in the population between $t - k$ and t, and $NM_{\{t-k,t\}}$ is the net migration into the population between $t - k$ and t. If $P_t > P_{\{t-k\}}$, then the population is growing over time; if $P_t < P_{\{t-k\}}$, then the population is declining; if $P_t = P_{\{t-k\}}$, then the population is stable (Preston et al, 2000).

Historically, most populations in the world have grown over time because births have tended to outpace deaths, and this is especially so in societies prior to the 20th century. Eventually, as countries become more developed, via agricultural and industrial revolutions, most countries experience a demographic transition (Thompson, 1929). A demographic transition is marked by declining death rates, followed by declining fertility rates, inevitably leading to both rapid population growth and a change in the population's age structure. The decline in death rates leads to population growth because more persons survive to later ages than before – in particular, at least initially, more persons survive beyond one year of age.

We can conceptualise pre-transition populations' age structures as pyramids, with a broad base of younger persons and a top that tapers, reflecting fewer and fewer persons at older and older ages. When both fertility and death rates decline, the population pyramid 'rectangularises', reflecting a more uniform distribution of the population into age ranges.

Figures 2.1 and 2.2 illustrate rectangularisation and the population ageing process at different stages of the demographic transition. Figure 2.1 shows the population pyramid for Benin in 2013, a country that has not yet experienced a demographic transition. Benin's population pyramid is very triangular in shape, with the majority of the nation's population being in the younger age groups. Indeed, there are more persons in Benin under six years of age than there are persons over the age of 50. Figure 2.2, in contrast, shows the population of the United States (US) in 2013, a nation that completed its demographic transition in the early 20th century. This population pyramid is much more rectangular in shape except for the very oldest age groups. For example, the US population has about the same number of persons in the age groups nearing retirement

Figure 2.1: Population of Benin by gender, 2013

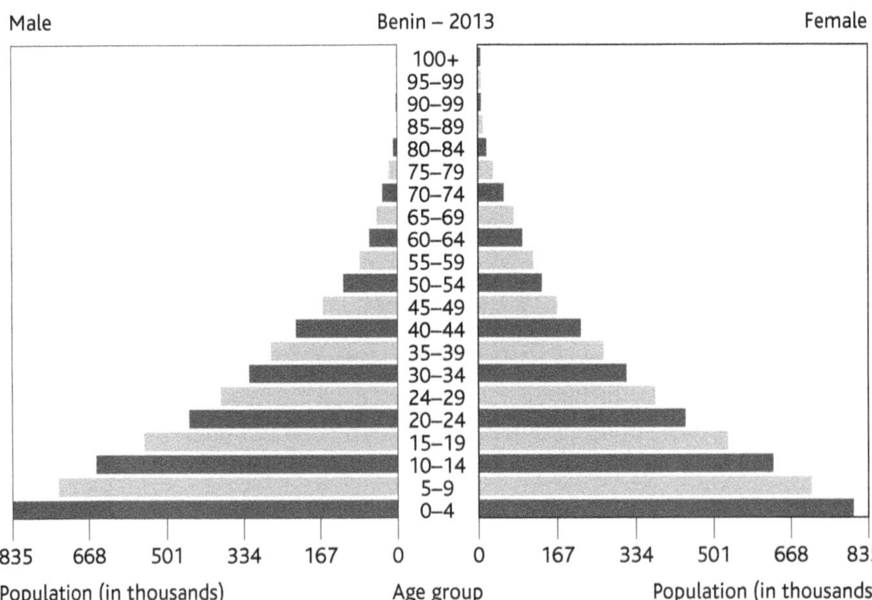

Source: Central Intelligence Agency, 2013

Figure 2.2: Population of the United States by gender, 2013

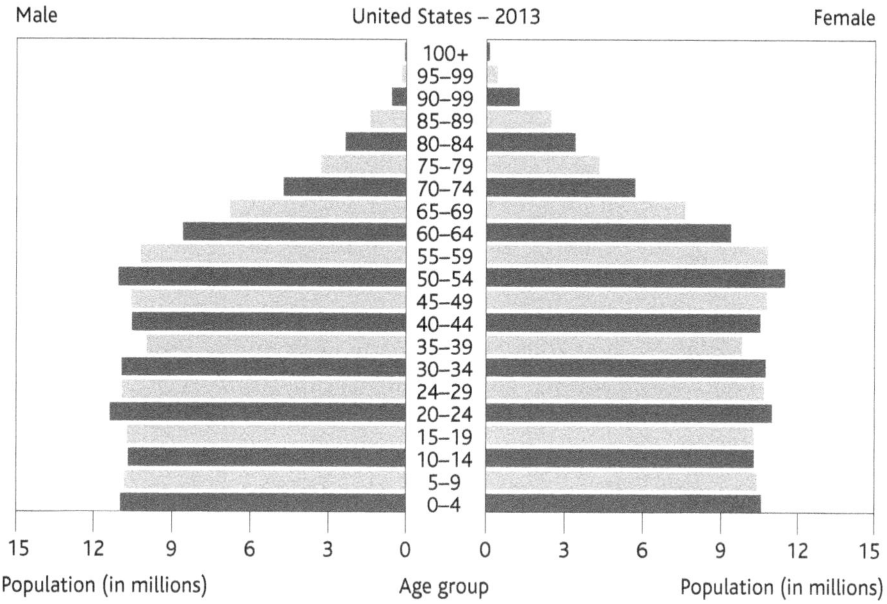

Source: Central Intelligence Agency, 2013

(meaning in their 50s and early 60s) as the number of persons who are children and adolescents.

Population dynamics and population ageing

The consequence of declining mortality and fertility is population ageing, and it is often illustrated in one of two ways: (1) as an increase in the mean and/or median age of persons in the population; and/or (2) as an increase in the proportion of the total population that falls in an arbitrarily defined 'old' age group, such as above age 60, 65 or even 85. While these two measures of population ageing appear to reflect the same process, they do not. They may stem from very different combinations of the dynamics underlying the balancing equation.

Most, if not all, developed societies are ageing, but the population dynamics underlying population ageing are complex and varied across societies. Population ageing can result from changes in any of the three components of the balancing equation, as well as combinations therein. Most, if not all, developed societies, for example, have experienced an 'epidemiologic transition' following their general demographic transition. Epidemiologic transitions are marked by fundamental changes in the relative incidence of different causes of death (Omran, 1971). Early on within developed societies, there is a transition from predominantly agriculture-based economies to predominantly industrial economies, and fertility rates fall but death rates remain relatively constant. At that stage, deaths stem from infectious and related acute causes as well as accidents (especially for males working in industrial locations). Such causes may be relatively evenly distributed across the age range, or they may hit the ends of the age distribution the hardest, that is, the youngest and the oldest. Infant and child mortality are often high, and few persons live long enough to die from 'old-age' diseases that require accumulation of exposure, such as heart disease, cancer and stroke. Eventually, however, with implementation of widespread public health measures like waste removal, sewage treatment, water purification and vaccination, along with advances in medical practice, including, for example, the development and use of antibiotics, most acute causes of death decline in incidence. Additionally, work-related deaths also decline somewhat as these societies impose workplace safety practices and regulations. Individuals, therefore, become more likely to live well into middle and late adulthood, and chronic disease death rates increase. The net result is that the population grows mostly at older ages, because fertility rates continue to decline while death rates in old age remain relatively flat or decline slightly (see McKeown, 2009, for a detailed discussion of the theory of epidemiologic transition and its critiques). A second epidemiologic transition has tended to follow the first in many developed societies in which death rates due to chronic conditions have fallen as such diseases have been pushed off to later and later in life (for example Lamb and Myers, 1993). Thus, fertility rates remain low and death rates at older ages plummet, thereby accelerating population ageing.

In short, population ageing can occur due to change in mortality at either end of the age distribution, and with or without changes in fertility, although most societies experience both significant fertility decline and reductions in mortality throughout the age range. Reductions in fertility increase the average age in the population by reducing the proportion of the total population in younger age groups. In that situation, the proportion of a population that is in older age groups increases, but only relatively, because of the reduction in the numbers of persons at younger ages, and the average age of the population increases as well. Reductions in childhood mortality increase the average age of the population, because of the survival of persons into older – but still young – age groups. Thus, in that situation, the average age increases, while the proportion of the population in the oldest age groups may be unaffected. Reductions in old age mortality may increase the average age of the population, but they do not have to, if fertility increases. For that matter, such reductions do not necessarily imply an increase in the proportion of the population in the oldest age groups. In other words, population ageing may be measured in different ways, but measures are not necessarily correlated, because ageing may occur in very different fashions, and therefore have very different implications for the lifecourse, as we discuss later.

In addition to changes in fertility and mortality dynamics, migration can – and does – play a substantial role in population ageing, and its influence is even more complex across societies. Of the three elements of demographic change, migration is often the least emphasised in terms of population ageing. Nevertheless, migration between populations can have a tremendous effect on the age structure of populations receiving migrants as well as on the age distribution of those nations from which individuals emigrate. This is largely due to the tendency for migrants to be working-age adults. Indeed, the United Nations estimates that almost 75% of all migrants worldwide in 2010 were of any adult working age (meaning between 18 and 65), and more than 50% of all migrants were between age 20 and age 50 (United Nations, 2011). This age pattern of migration results in a slowing of population ageing in the receiving country, while at the same time accelerating population ageing within the sending nation. For example, Germany is a relatively old country, with about 20% of its population over the age of 65 in 2011. Turkey on the other hand is a relatively young country, with an age 65+ population of only about 7% in 2011. However, migration between these two nations has been substantial, with Germany receiving a large number of typically young adult Turkish immigrants over the last three to four decades such that around three million persons of Turkish descent now reside in Germany (more than 3%). Given that these immigrants were overwhelmingly working-age adults, this migration has resulted in a somewhat younger age structure in Germany than there would have been otherwise and a somewhat older age structure in Turkey. In other words, the difference in population ageing between these two nations would be more substantial except for the migration between their populations.

Similarly, in the US, a society which is ageing rapidly, both in terms of the mean age increasing and the proportion of the total population in the oldest age groups, the influx of Mexican migrants has served to slow the rate of population ageing. Although debates over immigration policy have often mentioned the potential negative consequences of both legal and illegal Mexican migration in terms of reducing wages and consuming health care and social assistance resources, such migration has, in fact, served to slow the rate of population ageing, because migrants tend to be of working ages. Despite the fact that migrants tend to help 'anchor' illegal immigrants' families in the US, and some family members are elders who may draw social security and Medicare benefits, the net result is a larger working-age population. At the same time that immigration from Mexico into the US reduces the rate of ageing for the US, it simultaneously increases the rate of ageing in Mexico. More insidiously, most migration, regardless of location, tends to involve movement of healthy persons (Palloni and Arias, 2004). As a result, Mexican migration into the US has served to reduce ageing and improve the health of the US population, while simultaneously increasing ageing and worsening the health of the Mexican population.

This migration effect on population health and ageing is not limited to migration that crosses national borders. Indeed, the same process is occurring within national boundaries, as migration from rural to urban locations is common. For example, in Thailand, due in large part to economic reasons, Bangkok draws substantial immigration from the rural countryside. Much like the international migration shown in the examples of Mexico and Turkey mentioned earlier, these migrants are predominantly working-age adults. Thus, this internal migration tends to slow population ageing in the urban areas of Thailand, while at the same time accelerating ageing in Thai rural areas – a migration and ageing pattern that is fairly common among developing nations. This internal migration pattern also occurs in developed nations, but with the added complexity of retirement migration. That is, in developed nations like the US, it is not uncommon for individuals, on retiring, to migrate. In the US, this migration is often unidirectional to southern states that offer a warmer climate and commonly a lower cost of living. Thus, this migration can alter the age structure of these areas that receive migrating retirees. But this is only one part of the story. It is also common in these developed nation contexts for retirees who have migrated, should they become significantly ill, to return to their native area to receive care (and perhaps caregiving from family that still live in those areas). In other words, internal migration has a very complex relationship with population ageing, where it can slow ageing in some areas, increase ageing in other areas with only modest effects on health, and increase ageing in yet other areas while also worsening the overall population health of those areas.

Population ageing and lifecourse implications

Changes in fertility, mortality and migration patterns like those discussed, while macro-level phenomena, both result from and inform individual lifecourse processes. Certainly, births, deaths and moves are individual-level events, and their aggregation is what produces population rates. And, of course it requires individual-level change to produce macro-level change: indeed, Ryder (1965) defined the birth cohort – the collection of persons born in the same year – as the fundamental vehicle for producing social change. However, individuals' behaviours are also largely shaped by social structures and cultures that exist long before their birth. From that perspective, it is easy to see how demographic processes – especially population ageing – may shape individual lifecourses. As such, the demographer and the lifecourse scholar often study the same social issues surrounding ageing, but they may do so from different initial vantage points. A fundamental difference in understanding population ageing from the perspective of a demographer and from the perspective of a lifecourse scholar is that the demographers typically are more experienced in working with and thinking about macro-level, aggregate patterns, while lifecourse scholars often limit themselves to analysing data on individuals and thinking at the micro level.

The implications of large-scale population change for the individual lifecourse are easy to see. For example, the effects of the demographic transition and the epidemiologic transition can be seen in an examination of how individual lives are structured across the lifecourse. Figure 2.3 shows two hypothetical lifecourse sequences: a lifecourse sequence from before the demographic transition typical of hunter-gather and early agrarian societies; and a lifecourse sequence from after the demographic and epidemiologic transitions typical of the current developed world. The sequences list standard stages and transitions in the lifecourse, including childhood, education, work, marriage, childbearing, retirement and death.

Figure 2.3: Hypothetical lifecourse sequences and durations

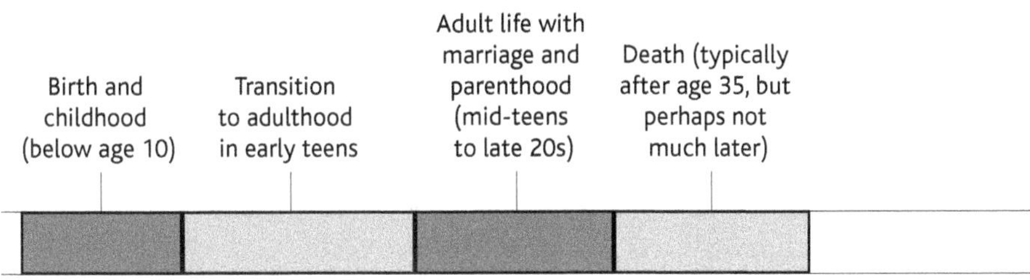

Pre-transition life course

Post-transition life course

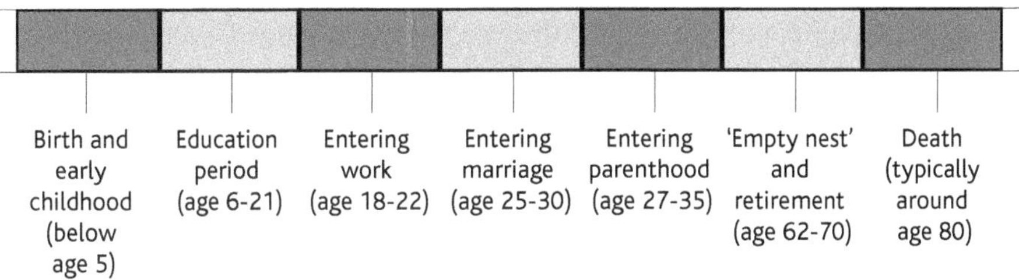

The differences between these two hypothetical lifecourse sequences are substantial. The pre-transition sequence shows a brief childhood that is somewhat deceiving, because most children in such societies are usually working, typically in subsistence agriculture, for most of this period. That is, working in this pre-modern sequence does not necessarily signify a transition into adulthood as it does in many modern societies. This pattern also shows very early entry into adulthood with relatively early transitions into marriage and parenthood. Notably, the pre-transition lifecourse is typically very short with median life expectancy often in the mid-30s, and living into a fifth or sixth decade of life being relatively rare (for example Knapp, 1998). The post-transition sequence, on the other hand, is longer and more complex. Early childhood is brief, but this period is typically without social obligations beyond the family. This stage is followed by an extended period for education, in which the growing child is prepared for the transitions of adulthood. Transitions into the workforce, into marriage and into parenthood follow rapidly over the decade following the education stage, with adulthood (possibly including multiple work, marriage and child-rearing transitions) extending into the fourth and fifth decades of life. The post-transition lifecourse also includes a late-life transition typically occurring in the sixth or seventh decade, in which an individual leaves the workforce. This transition is followed by death after the individual has lived well into old age, often spending as many years in retirement as in childhood.

For a lifecourse scholar who ignores demography, these are merely two different lifecourse sequences that typify the cultural contexts from which they are hypothetically drawn. However, viewing them as such would lead a scholar to examine these patterns independently. For the demographer, however, these two sequences are necessarily linked by the demographic (and epidemiologic) transition. To illustrate this, we can examine the individual elements of the balancing equation in relation to pre- and post-transition lifecourses.

As previously discussed, a key aspect of demographic work in population ageing actually, and perhaps surprisingly to non-demographers, involves issues surrounding fertility. Fertility affects population age structures in multiple ways, and these effects also have direct relevance for the lifecourse of individuals. For example, the epidemiologic transition resulted in a shift from deaths being mostly due to acute, infectious diseases in early life to a dominance of death by late-life chronic diseases. The effect on population ageing is fairly straightforward – more people now live through childhood, thus ageing the overall population. This shift in disease has also had a tremendous effect on fertility, because families no longer need to be as large to ensure that at least some children live into adulthood. With this reduced need for multiple children, the fertility rates in post-transition societies drop to replacement level[1] or even lower. For example, Singapore's current fertility rate is about 0.8 children per woman (Central Intelligence Agency, 2013), and most Western countries have either experienced, are currently experiencing, or have approached fertility levels below replacement (Morgan, 2003).

This drop in population-level fertility rates also reflects a fundamental change in individual-level fertility behaviour. Reduced childhood disease and death rates translate into longer life for potential parents. Faced with a longer life expectancy for themselves and their offspring, many individuals choose to delay various lifecourse transitions related to fertility. They may delay marriage and the timing of their first child, because they have more time to prepare for entering and completing these lifecourse statuses. Indeed, it could even be the case that, compared to the pre-transition parent, modern individuals may delay such transitions not only as a result of having fundamentally more time over which to experience these social events, but also to increase their ability to invest in their now limited number of offspring. Such a linkage between fertility, population ageing and lifecourse transitions is at the heart of lifecourse theories in demography like the Easterlin Hypothesis (Easterlin, 1975; Macunovich, 1998) and reflects a fundamental change in the structure of the individual lifecourse.

Compared to fertility, the end of life is often more closely associated with ageing in the literature, and as such, mortality demography may more readily be seen as relevant to lifecourse work. For the demographer, mortality is the ultimate exit from a population – an 'absorbing state' – and understanding mortality has been at the heart of demographic work from its very beginning (Gompertz, 1825). A demographer's primary focus might be on understanding the role of the demographic transition in facilitating the change between the lifecourse sequences illustrated earlier in Figure 2.3. Yet, this fundamental shift in when and where mortality occurs as a result of the demographic transition is of great importance to the lifecourse scholar as well. Most obviously, the extension of the lifespan with individuals now living, on average, more than twice as long as they did prior to the demographic transition produces fundamental changes in the way the lifecourse is structured and in how individuals view their own lifecourses.

The addition of a retirement phase in the post-transition lifecourse in Figure 2.3 demonstrates a substantial change in how the individual lifecourse is structured and in how lifecourse scholars articulate how we age. For example, it has been suggested that a new period (phase or stage, even) of life has now emerged for individuals in developed societies for the time that is spent in relative good health following retirement. This new period is often referred to as the 'Third Age' (of life), and although it has now been extensively discussed in recent lifecourse literature, it has seen only limited influence from demographic work (Carr and Komp, 2011). Specifically, the existence of a 'Third Age' is predicated on the assumption that longevity, health and leaving the workforce coincide, yielding a universal period of potentially productive, but untapped, life in contemporary populations. However, a demographer would note that life expectancy, as well as other state expectancy measures, are averages, and it is possible that no individual in a given society actually experiences all three of these statuses simultaneously.[2]

A demographically informed view of longevity may also be relevant to lifecourse work on how we define old age. Research has shown that even individuals from similarly developed societies can have different views on how old one must be to be considered of old age (for example Westerhof and Barrett, 2003). The lengthening of life due to the demographic and epidemiologic transitions defines the contexts in which we age, and thus, is also likely to be an important factor in determining how we define the old-age period of the lifecourse.

The demography of migration can also inform lifecourse research. As previously discussed, migration into and out of different populations can have a significant effect on the overall age structure of populations. However, demographic forces such as the demographic transition also impact on individual lives via migration directly. The industrialisation that drives the demographic transition and influences fertility trends also creates an environment conducive to substantial migration. The rural agrarian communities in post-transition societies no longer have the large families to work farmland manually for surplus harvests; and, given the increasing automation from industrialisation, such large families are far less needed for manual labour. At the same time, industrialisation requires an increasingly dense population of workers near factories to maintain levels of production resulting in a strong pull for rural residents to move to these areas. This results in a highly mobile population during the transition and the post-transition period compared to pre-transition populations. Such population-level migration forces necessarily structure and change the way individuals live their lives. For example, some may delay child-bearing until after a move, and some may alter their entrance into work life pending a subsequent move.

The need for a demographic view to fully understand the lifecourse

Clearly, the overlap between population ageing and lifecourse scholarship is substantial. Much of the work on ageing and the lifecourse in recent decades has recognised this fact and has made great strides in incorporating demographic ideas into lifecourse discussions (just as much demographic work in population ageing has appealed to lifecourse concepts to explain the micro-level processes underlying the aggregate patterns being observed). However, a lack of an in-depth understanding of population ageing and the demographic perspectives and tools used to describe it can lead to completely fallacious misconceptions about how we are ageing. It is imperative that lifecourse researchers have an understanding of the basics of demography and population dynamics to fully understand the structures that shape the lifecourses we observe. Understanding basic concepts, such as mortality rates, fertility rates and net migration rates, and how these interact with each other to affect the lifecourse, is fundamental. Becoming familiar with demographic methodology is also important, as is having a basic understanding of the balancing equation.

First, being able to translate the aggregate nature of some demographic concepts appropriately into the micro-level context of much lifecourse research is a necessity. For example, the basic demographic concept of life expectancy is often stated in individualistic terms when reported (meaning the life expectancy at birth is often equated to how long one can expect to live at birth). However, life expectancy is not an individual measure: in its most common construction, it is produced from an amalgam of age-specific mortality rates in which the rates are all observed simultaneously (usually in a single year). Thus, the measure is not constructed using information from any single lifecourse, and it therefore does not apply to any one individual or sub-group that might be the direct subject of lifecourse research. Indeed, as an average value, it may be used to misconstrue as common a life experience that no individual from the population actually experiences! For example, if half a population lives for 50 years and the other half lives for 100 years, the calculated life expectancy at birth would be about 75 years despite the fact that no individual experiences anything close to that life expectancy.

Even more problematic is that change in life expectancy can be very deceptive.[3] In the US in 1900, life expectancy at birth was roughly 47 years of age. By 2000, life expectancy at birth was about 77 years. Does this change reflect that the typical age at death has increased substantially over the last century? The answer is: not necessarily. In fact, most early gains in life expectancy at birth in the US were due to large reductions in infant mortality, a consequence of – or evidence of – the epidemiologic transition. In 1900, for example, life expectancy at age 1 was approximately 54 years. Thus, if an infant lived through their first year of life, then they 'gained' an additional seven years of expected life, in addition to the one they had just survived. Furthermore, if they lived through their second and third year of life, they gained another year of expected life each year. Thus, a child surviving to age 3 could expect to live to another 55 years, for a total of 58 years. In contrast, a century later, life expectancy at age 1 was about 76.5.

Clearly, today's life expectancy at birth is much more interpretable as a true measure of the length of an individual's lifecourse, whereas the same measure in 1900 was heavily influenced by infant mortality. However, even estimates of life expectancy today are inaccurate reflections for any particular person, because they are generally constructed from age-specific rates that apply to members of different birth cohorts. As a result, given our continued increases in longevity, estimates are too low to represent what anyone except perhaps the very oldest can expect.

Perhaps a better measure of expected individual lifecourse length is the age at which midlife occurs. In 1900, age 34 was the first age at which expected life remaining was less than life lived: 32 more years could be expected. In 2000, age 40 was midlife: a survivor to age 40 could expect to live an additional 38 years. Thus, in 1900, 64 years of age might be considered old, while in 2000, 78 might be considered old. The shifting of midlife by roughly six years over the last century, and life expectancy at midlife by another six years, encourages a more stable perspective on population ageing: population ageing is not a new phenomenon. It is a long-term, ongoing process that has been occurring for some time. It is being driven primarily by falling fertility – which has dropped in part due to declining infant mortality – and by a larger proportion of the population living beyond midlife.

In addition to understanding basic demographic measures, it is important that lifecourse scholars understand aggregate-level causal mechanisms for the demographic outcomes that are of interest. As we have just discussed, drastic life expectancy increases have, at their root, been caused substantially by falling infant mortality. A counterintuitive process was also involved in producing the Baby Boom in the US. For example, the Baby Boom, which is the name given to the unusually large number of children born in the birth cohorts from 1946 to 1964, is often attributed by non-demographers exclusively to families having more children – a very micro-level explanation. However, this belief is a misconception. The number of families with three or more children has generally declined throughout the 20th century. Among the ultimate causes of the Baby Boom are second-parity births (that is, families having a second child) and fertility momentum from changes in timing of first births. Specifically, a fair portion of the boom can be attributed to the two-child family becoming the normative fertility behaviour during this period. Additionally, a major causal factor of the boom is a result of the women who reached adulthood during the end of the Great Depression and during World War II delaying their first child birth, while the women reaching adulthood during the boom period experienced a first birth very soon after becoming adults (Ryder, 1980; Cherlin, 1981). In other words, much of the Baby Boom is due to an aggregate-level demographic effect rather than to individual choices to have larger families over the lifecourse.

Migration processes can also result in counterintuitive findings for ageing outcomes. Perhaps the most unusual ageing-related finding affected by migration is the Hispanic Paradox. Briefly stated, the Hispanic Paradox refers to persons of Latin American descent living in the United States having longer life expectancies than their non-Hispanic, white age-peers despite also having lower socioeconomic status (Markides, 1983). This finding is paradoxical because considerable research over the last several decades has shown that lower socioeconomic status is linked to poorer health and earlier death in general. Several hypotheses have emerged to explain the paradox, including a cultural hypothesis (that is, Hispanic cultural practices, including reduced propensity to smoke, has some protective effect) and the suggestion that data artifacts (like reporting errors in age and/or ethnicity) result in incorrect death rate calculations for the Hispanic subpopulation (Palloni and Arias, 2004). Two migration-related hypotheses have also emerged: the healthy migrant hypothesis and the salmon-bias hypothesis. The healthy migrant hypothesis states that healthy individuals are more likely to move or are more capable of moving, while the salmon-bias hypothesis states that individuals have a tendency to return to, and perhaps die in, their native country after becoming significantly ill. Palloni and Arias' findings suggest that a small portion of the Hispanic mortality advantage may be due to some limited data artifact effects, but it is in large part the result of salmon-bias effects – Latin American migrants who become significantly ill often return to their native country, artificially lowering the death rate of Hispanics in the US.

Important for our discussion here, ultimately understanding this paradox, then, necessarily has required an understanding of non-demographic perspectives (the cultural hypothesis), demographic perspectives (healthy-migrant and salmon-bias effects) and demographic measurement (how data artifacts affect rates).

Counterintuitive findings and misconceptions about population ageing and the processes that underlie it are potential hazards for all researchers who study ageing. This is especially true for lifecourse scholars, whose focus is especially on individual lifecourse patterns and transitions. Translation of population trends into terms of individual lives and aggregation of individual lives into population level trends are complex processes. Understanding population-level processes and the tools used to measure them is a necessity for lifecourse scholars to fully understand trajectories and transitions within individual lives.

Conclusion

Demography is a field that has historically focused on macro-level rates and trends to understand how populations change across space and time. The increase in the proportion of elders in many developed populations, as well as the rise in the average age of many populations, has resulted in a strong demographic interest in population ageing and has led to an extensive body of research on the topic. At the micro level, individual lives have changed substantially in the ways they are lived over the last century in no small way as a result of the same extension of the lifespan that has produced population ageing. Many scholars working at this micro level have adopted the lifecourse paradigm to anchor their work. In more recent decades, lifecourse study and the demography of ageing have become more commonly integrated, and this integration continues in research today.

A solid knowledge of demographic perspectives on, and methods for investigating, population ageing is required for lifecourse scholars to fully understand the relationship between population and individual ageing. The interplay of fertility, mortality and migration, highlighted by demographic tools like the balancing equation, facilitate learning how demography can influence individual lifecourses. Yet, fully understanding how macro-level changes impact on individual lives is far from straightforward.

Integrative work is extremely important given the prominence of social and historical context, which are at the heart of the lifecourse paradigm (Elder and Johnson, 2002). Demography in general, and the subfield of population ageing specifically, is essential to understanding the context within which any individual ages. Whether it is the more obvious relationship between ageing and mortality or the less obvious roles of fertility and migration in the ageing process, population ageing in many ways shapes the lives that individuals live. The demographic transition provides an easy 'jumping off' point for linking population ageing and lifecourse processes. Demographers have already extensively described the transition processes and outcomes in ways that can inform lifecourse research about how lifecourse patterns change across time. Likewise, lifecourse work enhances our understanding of the effects of the transition on individual lives, a nuance that is important for articulating the underlying forces that produce macro-level demographic trends. Thus, a demographically informed view of ageing and the processes that lead to population change are essential for understanding what demographic change means for the lifecourse.

Notes

[1] Replacement-level fertility is the fertility rate at which the population replaces itself. In other words, a child is born for each potential mother and father. This rate, however, is not a total fertility rate of 2. Rather, because about 10% of individuals worldwide are unable to have children or die before reaching childbearing ages, the replacement level rate is about 2.1 children per woman.

[2] This brief example presentation of the 'Third Age' is admittedly oversimplified. The original formulation of this proposed new stage of the lifecourse is considerably more complex (Laslett, 1989), and the exploration of the mechanisms that might underlie it have been quite nuanced (for example, see Gilleard and Higgs, 2002). Nevertheless, as we have noted elsewhere, theoretical and empirical work on the 'Third Age' from a precisely demographic perspective is extremely limited (Brown and Lynch, 2011), a critique that is not entirely new (for example, see Siegel, 1990).

[3] The data on life expectancy discussed here come from the Berkeley Mortality Database and the Human Mortality Database (University of California, Berkeley and Max Planck Institute for Demographic Research).

References

Berkeley Mortality Database. http://demog.berkeley.edu/~bmd

Brown, J.S. and Lynch, S.M. (2011) 'Demographic approaches and their potential application in third age research', in D.C. Carr and K.S. Komp (eds) *Gerontology in the era of the third age: Implications and next steps*, New York: Springer, 89-105.

Carr, D.C. and Komp, K.S. (eds) (2011) *Gerontology in the era of the Third Age: Implications and next steps*, Springer: New York.

Central Intelligence Agency (2013) *The World Factbook 2013-14*, Washington, DC: Central Intelligence Agency. https://www.cia.gov/library/publications/the-world-factbook/index.html

Cherlin, A.J. (1981). *Marriage, divorce, remarriage*, Cambridge, MA: Harvard University Press.

Easterlin, R.A. (1975) 'An economic framework for fertility analysis', *Studies in Family Planning,* 6, 3, 54-63.

Elder, G.H. Jr and Johnson, M.K. (2002) 'The life course and aging: Challenges, lessons, and new directions', in R.A. Settersten (ed) *Invitation to the life course: Toward new understandings of later life*, Amityville, MA: Baywood Publishing Co, 49-84.

Gilleard, G. and Higgs, P. (2002) 'The third age: Class, cohort, or generation?', *Ageing and Society*, 22, 3, 369-82.

Gompertz, B. (1825) 'On the nature of the function expressive of the law of human mortality, and on a new mode of determining the value of life contingencies', *Philosophical Transactions of the Royal Society of London*, 115, 513-85.

Knapp V.J. (1998) 'Life expectancy, infant mortality and malnutrition in preindustrial Europe: A contemporary explanation', *Nutrition and Health*, 12, 2, 89-95.

Lamb, V.L. and Myers, G.C. (1993) 'Theoretical perspectives on healthy life expectancy', in J.M. Robine, C.D. Mathers, M.R. Bone and I. Romieu (eds) *Calculations of health expectancies*, Montrouge: John Libbey Eurotext, 109-19.

Laslett, P. (1989) *A Fresh Map of Life: The Emergence of the Third Age*, Weidenfeld and London: Nicolson.

Macunovich, D.J. (1998) 'Fertility and the Easterlin hypothesis: An assessment of the literature', *Journal of Population Economics*, 11, 1-59.

Markides, K.S. (1983) 'Mortality among minority populations: A review of recent patterns and trends', *Public Health Reports*, 98, 252-60.

McKeown, R.E. (2009) 'The epidemiologic transition: Changing patterns of mortality and population dynamics', *American Journal of Lifestyle Medicine*, 1, 3, 19s-26s.

Morgan, S.P. (2003) 'Is low fertility a twenty-first century demographic crisis?', *Demography*, 40, 4, 589-603.

Omran, A.R. (1971) 'A theory of the empidemiology of population change', *Milbank Memorial Fund Quarterly*, 49, 509-38.

Palloni, A. and Arias, E. (2004) 'Paradox lost: Explaining the Hispanic adult mortality advantage', *Demography*, 41, 3, 385-415.

Preston, S.H., Heuveline, P. and Guillot, M. (2000) *Demography: Measuring and modeling social processes*, Oxford: Blackwell.

Ryder, N.B. (1965) 'The cohort as a concept in the study of social change', *American Sociological Review*, 30, 6, 843-61.

Ryder, N.B. (1980) 'Components of temporal variations in American fertility', in R.W. Hiorns (ed) *Demographic patterns in developed societies*, London: Taylor & Francis, 15-54.

Siegel, J.S. (1990) 'Book review of *A Fresh Map of Life: The Emergence of the Third Age*', *Population and Development Review*, 16, 2, 363-7.

Thompson, W.S. (1929) 'Population', *American Journal of Sociology*, 34, 6, 959-75.

United Nations (2011) *Trends in international migrant stock: Migrants by age and sex* [Database]. http://esa.un.org/MigAge/.

University of California, Berkeley and Max Planck Institute for Demographic Research. *Human mortality database.* www.mortality.org

Westerhof, G. and Barrett, A.E. (2003) 'Forever young? A comparison of age identities in the United States and Germany', *Research on Aging*, 25, 366-83.

THREE

A lifecourse scholar's view: lifecourses crystallise in demographic structures

Andreas Motel-Klingebiel

Introduction: changing population structures and the lifecourse

The ageing of societies is one of the social megatrends in the Western world, China, India and other major societies (United Nations, 2001). Population ageing is the change of the demographic structure towards an increase in absolute numbers and relative share of older people. It is mainly due to prolonged lifespans, with mortality increasingly moved into the later life phases, as well as declines in fertility rates. It takes place jointly with other changes in society, like economic growth, de-industrialisation, and shifts to a service sector economy, educational expansion, increasing uncertainties in life and the development of social security. At the same time, there are substantial shifts at the level of individuals and their lifecourses, including the expansion of the lifespan with the postponement of mortality risks into later life, prolongation of educational phases, increasing conditionality of partnership and parenthood, growing regional mobility and an overall flexibilisation, pluralisation and individualisation.

All three of these trends – population ageing, other changes in society and the transformation of the lifecourse – are closely intertwined. This connection is this chapter's subject of interest and it is approached from the perspective of lifecourse research.

The prolonged lifespan

At the beginning of the 21st century, a long lifespan has come to be taken for granted by individuals in the majority of societies as well as in societal discourses. The life expectancy at birth significantly increased over the 20th century. It is now on average twice as high as it was about a hundred years ago in the majority of European countries. Nevertheless, life expectancy at birth varies between men and women and between societies. This is also true for the healthy life expectancy as well as for the remaining life expectancy of those who have already reached later life. These increases in life expectancy go hand in hand with a shift of mortality risks into the older age groups. These changes are a great success for modern society. Simultaneously, they also are one of the major sources of the ongoing demographic change which implies a structural change of society as a whole –

and therefore not only a demographic matter but even more a sociological and political issue. Nowadays, more than half of the new-born children in Western Europe have the chance of becoming 90 years of age and even much older, if the overall trend of the past continues in a similar way in the future (United Nations, 2004; Schnabel et al, 2005). This has a major impact on individual lifecourses, on life planning and on the social institution of the lifecourse as such.

Diminishing fertility

The prolongation of human life emerges together with decreases in fertility rates, the extent of which differ substantially between European societies. Within the European Union (EU), fertility rates vary from 1.2 children per woman in Latvia and 2.1 children per woman in Ireland. Even the differences between the larger EU member states are immense, with about 2.0 in France, Sweden and the United Kingdom and only about 1.4 in Germany, Poland, Italy and Spain (World Bank, 2010; Statista, 2013). Fertility declines result both from conscious decisions against parenthood and from fertility postponements that may result in unintentional childlessness. Together with the growing number of older people, diminishing fertility is sometimes labelled a threat to society, because it leads to shrinking workforces, falling productivity, increasing welfare state transfers and shrinking potentials for innovation in production or in the political field. However, diminishing fertility can also be considered the expression of a fundamental societal achievement to postpone death and to leave parenthood to individual or partner-like life planning as a major decision in the lives of men and women.

Altered migration patterns

Besides the changes in mortality and fertility patterns, migration also shapes the demographic structure of modern societies. While it is typically international migration-relocation over national borders that attracts attention, focus must also be directed towards internal migration, for example from rural to urban or from deprived to more advantaged regions, which substantially impacts on local developments and exacerbates or cushions overall national trends within regions or municipalities.

Even before World War II, nearly all European societies were shaped by international or internal migration, but reasons behind migration decisions, their destinations and the structure of migrant populations vary over time and differ between societies. As a result, the effects of migration decisions on demographic patterns are widely inconsistent. But as migrants are more often younger people than older people – even if this substantially depends on the motivations for migration – immigration has the tendency to postpone population ageing. But as migrants also age and participate in the prolongation of the lifespan as well as in the individualisation of fertility-related decisions, it only alters but does not reverse the overall trend of population ageing.

Linking population structures with lifecourse patterns

All of these three core demographic aspects – mortality, fertility and migration – are closely related to the human course of life, but it is basically ongoing social change that brings about substantial changes in the lifecourse. Hence, in this perspective, demographic change is an adjustment related to the transformation of societies (macro-level) mediated by the lifecourses (micro-level). However, it is also lifecourses as a series of intended and meaningful individual decisions that manifest in changing demographic structures – even if they emerge within constraining institutional and social contexts. But what exactly is the connection between the lifecourse on the one hand and social and demographic patterns on the other hand? The fundamental questions are how changing social conditions influence lifecourses and in how changes in lifecourses have an impact on demographic patterns of society. The answers to these questions are relevant for the sociological understanding of modern society as well as for the formulation of social policies that target social risks and that strive to moderate demographic structures.

To tackle the question of relevance of lifecourse changes to demographic change and vice versa, this chapter will look first of all at the conception of the lifecourse in different perspectives. It will then put population ageing into a framework of social change and discuss the relationship between lifecourse patterns and the ongoing transformation of society. Having arranged the tools of the trade, this chapter will then outline the accomplishment of demographic transformation by discussing several lifecourse events, such as the foundation and dissolution of families, fertility decisions, educational participation, employment, retirement and migration. In conclusion, it will discuss how lifecourse policies may contribute to social policy efforts to change demographic patterns and will stress the long-term perspective – or even inefficacy – of such approaches. It will be argued that lifecourse patterns cannot be changed (if at all) with single political decisions or acts. Instead, they require substantial changes in ideas, habits, norms and values as well as institutional and biographical contexts of rational short-term lifecourse decisions regarding lifestyles, partnership and family as well as mobility in an increasingly dynamic and demanding context.

On the lifecourse: what are we talking about?

Human ageing is a universal process, but ...

The ageing of human beings is a universal fact and it covers the whole lifespan. At the same time it is a widely open biological and social process that can be shaped. In this sense it shows the impact and the weight of social conditions. Becoming, being and passing away can be observed as a biological fact. But the lifecourse needs some comprehensive interpretation and social construction to untangle it as an ordered and conceivable process. It simultaneously takes place over individual and social time.

Even though the ageing process can be influenced, the individual lifecourse is also constrained. On the one hand it is restricted by its biological preconditions, personal resources and the simple fact that life is limited through losses and its universal ending in death. On the other hand, and sociologically more crucially, the lifecourse is specifically shaped by the social-regional conditions and the societal embeddedness that are fundamental to the ageing process.

Lifecourses: time and social developments

The 'lifecourse' is a multi-faceted concept in current social sciences and social policy that allows us to merge the aspects of time and society in a comprehensive concept. It is a heterogeneous but appealing theoretical perspective or model that mainly emerged from the mid-20th century onwards.

It was in the early 1960s that Glen Elder started to develop a lifecourse model from childhood studies. In this, he initiated and coined lifecourse theory with his analyses of the life paths of the children of the Great Depression (Elder, 1974). Here the starting point was human development – a merely psychological concept. But Elder added substantial social science value to it by looking at the impact of the obviously momentous historical circumstances of the American birth cohorts of the 1930s on various areas of life, such as family and network structures, educational participation and employment (Hutchison, 2003).

Taking into account these beginnings, but also following next steps by Hareven (2001), Mayer (2009) and many others, lifecourses and lifecourse research are closely related to the angle of cohorts and generations, hence to the historical and the socio-structural perspective (Alwin and McCammon, 2006). In the thorough analysis of consecutive cohorts and generations over historical time, the impact of social change on individual life can be traced – and vice versa, lifecourses mirror the transformation of social institutions in a way that allows us to deduce social developments from changes that can be assessed at the individual micro level (Mayer, 2004).

Age and ageing as characteristics of society

Elder's early works point to the fact that the course of human lives is substantially bound to political, cultural and economic issues of societies (Elder, 1974). Thus, the process is only superficially one of individual nature, and as a whole and in its specific stages, a property of society and social structure (Dannefer and Settersten, 2010: 4). Research has shown that in modern societies the lifecourse is developed to a significant social institution, as it was described by Martin Kohli in the concept of the institutionalisation of the lifecourse (Kohli, 1985). Because trends of flexibilisation, individualisation and de-standardisation were noticed since the 1970s, researchers assumed that there is now a tendency towards de-institutionalisation of the lifecourse (Kohli, 2007; Scherger, 2007). Nevertheless, the role of the lifecourse was controversially discussed over the years and there was a key critique that the lifecourse has given way to a less determinate life project in late modernity (Joas and Knöbl, 2011). But it seems that age is a relevant feature of social structure in general (Settersten, 2006) and the lifecourse basically still expresses a set of features that structure individual lives.

However, some argue that the lifecourse as a sequence of situations and transitions over time directly links the macro level of society and the micro levels of individuals' lifestyles, living situations, planning and decision making without being an institution in its own right (Mayer, 2004; Mayer, 2009). Changes in these fields lead to changes in trajectories and the configuration of life phases like childhood and later life as well as to changes in their societal conceptions. They also affect family structures and living arrangements, which depend strongly on individual fertility, on housing and migration decisions based on individuals' changing resources and preferences, as well as on shifting institutional challenges with which individuals are confronted.

The causal system of the lifecourse and its interdependencies over time

From a purely micro-level perspective of the lifespan and human development, earlier events and decisions have an impact on later ones, deriving from resources, constraints and experiences in those previous phases (Elder and Shanahan, 2006). Dale Dannefer (2003) underlines that (dis)advantages can accumulate over the lifecourse, a theory that was later adapted and further developed as cumulative inequality by Ferraro et al, 2009. This perspective was influential and was applied in numerous analyses on later-life inequality (for example by Prokos and Keene, 2012). Also, related approaches such as lifecourse epidemiology (Ben-Shlomo and Kuh, 2002; Kuh et al, 2003) are inspired by the idea that later-life outcomes, such as morbidity or mortality patterns, may relate to the interaction between previous, current and future situations over the lifecourse. However, some age-specific tendencies, such as the overall decline in health or the transition into retirement, can also reduce inequalities in the process of ageing (Motel-Klingebiel et al, 2009). Consequently, both trends may overlap and result in a more complex picture of intra-cohort inequality patterns and their dynamics over the lifecourse (Schöllgen et al, 2010).

In another perspective, individuals' lives are linked or synchronised with other people's lives, for example partners, parents or children, but also social networks of non-relatives like friends, workmates and others – with families playing a dominant role in lifecourse research of this kind (Hareven, 1996). This leads to the perspective of linked lives beyond the joint embeddedness in common structural contexts of history or society (Macmillan and Copher, 2005).

Lifecourses as biographies

In addition, lifecourses gain relevance from being biographies. Biographies are individuals' life stories and represent the respective individual's understanding of these series of events. Hence, the term does not just include more or less objective facts (Kohli, 2009); it describes life history as a planned, experienced and interpreted journey through life, and it highlights individual agency.

Lifecourses in the sense of biographies are based on individual expectations and proposals that may change over historical time, but they nevertheless have a high degree of autonomy against institutional structures. Therefore biographies are significant units of analysis for a biography-oriented lifecourse and ageing research as such (Öberg et al, 2004). The concept of biography gains in significance if one considers biographical disruptions and their consequences in individual lives (for example Bury, 1982). Critical life events, especially unwanted ones like illnesses, loss of partners or friends, involuntary migration and unexpected crises, mark breaks in biographies and have far-reaching effects (for example Halleröd, 2013). The subjective representation of life history and risks may be more defining in furthering an individual's decision-making and life planning than objective markers. Hence, there is substantial relevance of this perspective for the reflection on demographic phenomena.

Summary: perspectives on the lifecourse

All this condenses into four prototypical, more or less distinct perspectives on the lifecourse that can be applied to discuss the interconnection between lifecourses and demographic structures:

- Lifecourses merely reflect institutional arrangements in society and their changes over time.
- The lifecourse is a social institution by itself, with distinct outcomes and dynamics.
- Lifecourses express individual ageing processes as objective conditions, and they are cumulative and self-referential.
- Lifecourses are biographies that indicate proposals and subjective representations of events and life planning.

The impact of changing lifecourses on demographic trends – and vice versa

To discuss this properly, the ongoing demographic developments must be put into a framework of overall social change that relates to individual lifecourses. The demographic transition is consistently discussed as a result of societal development over time – mostly in terms of modernisation (Kelly and Cutright, 1980; Kirk, 1996). But population ageing is at the same time a driver of social change, and societal ageing influences the resources and chances in life of individuals of different age groups and birth cohorts – in other words, the decision-making of individuals on the backgrounds of their available resources and present constraints.

Demographic developments are part of the ongoing process of social change, and the link between them is mediated by institutionalised lifecourse patterns, by individual lifecourses as trajectories of minor or major life events, and by individual biographies as planned and experienced life. This interplay of the different aspects of social change and individual lifecourses also concerns decisions that have a direct impact on demographic patterns and vice versa. To exemplify this, it is necessary to capture the complexity and to take a more detailed look at specific aspects of the lifecourse in the fields of family and partnership, fertility, education, employment, retirement and migration.

Family foundation and dissolution

Families can be understood as a social institution as well as being social networks that tie individual lives together (Blossfeld and Dronic, 2009; Huinink, 2009; Leigh, 1982). In both perspectives, as institution and network, family is constantly (re)produced by individual decisions and activities in various and varying social contexts and it is also a context for individual life (Bengtson et al, 1976). Lifecourse decision-making, however, is not only affected by changing institutional contexts like the labour market or social security. It is also related to demographic change, which leads to changes in size and structure of the family of origin as well as increases in shared lifetimes and family models in society – with effects, for example, on housing issues as well as social role models, norms and desirability. Hence, population ageing is relevant to assumptions on contemporary change of the family (Bumpass, 1990).

Consequently, data for recent birth cohorts show: a postponement of family foundation and dissolution; increasing childlessness and shrinking numbers of children; the emerging dominance of living arrangements without own children in certain stages of life; and less stable partnerships that seem to be oriented more towards emotional attachment and less towards parenthood as a long-term project in most developed countries. On the one hand, all this exacerbates the demographic challenge resulting from decreases in birth rates over time. On the other hand, both aspects may also have an impact on the problems deriving from the growing need for help and care due to increasing longevity with fewer children and less committed or less available partners at the end of life.

Fertility patterns

While from a historical perspective parenthood was mostly more a matter of duty, burden and failure in most societies, things changed substantially over the 20th century, with women's liberation as part of the modernisation process and the availability of contraceptives. Only since then did childbearing become a real matter of choice – hence, largely intended and planned behaviour (Morgan and Bachrach, 2011) under the condition of (changing) constraints for most people.

The conditions for such decisions changed successively since the 1980s, as European societies took extensive action to increase female educational and labour participation, affecting individual preferences and life ambitions. A main policy goal was the assimilation of male and female labour force participation, with a more or less unaffected male lifecourse as a basic model. Thus, the male-breadwinner model was insufficiently questioned, meaning solely from the perspective of female employment – and in many societies without adequate backing by measures that allow a compatibility of family and work for both genders. The traditional division of labour within the family was maintained through dominant family policies that were still based on the commitment of women to family work. At the same time, it was also female work orientation – and not so much male family orientation – that experienced substantial changes over time. Hence, both empirical trends went hand in hand, while family policies only partly followed – with significant effects on decisions about parenthood in female and male lifecourses resulting in low birth rates.

Education and early employment

Youth as a preparatory phase – in terms of Martin Kohli's (1985) concept of the institutionalised lifecourse – became more and more important in most people's lives during the last century. While education beyond compulsory schooling was an exception until the mid-century for males too, the educational sector was substantially extended in most Western societies. This went hand in hand with the increased market demand for skilled work in the Golden Age of post-war capitalism (Hobsbawm, 1994) and led to a prolongation of primary education, the emergence of further education in mid-life and the extended coverage of an increasing proportion of the population.

From the perspective of the lifecourse, more and more competing options emerged and more complex decisions were required (Kwiek, 2012). Due to the increased number of options, the choice of a life path was successively personalised, which led to an individualisation (Beck, 1983; Macmillan, 2005) and pluralisation of living situations. Decisions on educational pathways became directly related to those in the sphere of family formation, partnership and child bearing. Both spheres proved to provide new constraints for each other. On the one hand, child bearing and parenthood still limit educational participation and job opportunities in the transition into employment mainly for women. But young women have, over the last 30 years, been closing the gap and are now even outperforming young men in education (Beck, 1983; Macmillan, 2005), while noteworthy gaps in employment still remain (Misra et al, 2011). On the other hand, it is higher education that in turn reduces the likelihood of long-term stable institutionalised partnership and increases the constraints on fertility decision (Friebel, 2008).

Late employment and retirement

Employment in later life and retirement choices do not in most cases directly interfere with people's fertility decisions as such. But labour market policies aimed at increased labour market participation by people aged 55 and older, and a postponement of the standard retirement age to a cut-off at 67, 70 or beyond this (Taylor, 2010), may nevertheless interact with population patterns and the challenges of population ageing. This is mainly due to the interconnectedness of people's lives in partnerships, families and social networks, but is also due to commonly assumed connections between retirement age and longevity (Litwin, 2007).

Because of delaying retirement through changes in institutional regulations and incentive structures – but probably also due to shifts in needs and new attitudes regarding paid work in recent birth cohorts (Mermin et al, 2007) – employment may increasingly interfere with family work or further private engagement. Even though this is not introduced here as a sound political argument against prolonging working life, it must nevertheless be stressed that a shift in labour market activities affects decisions and constraints on family support, unpaid work and other social activities – hence, productivity outside the labour market.

Migration

As previously stated, migration shapes population size, structures and distributions. From a lifecourse perspective, migration is also part of individual life planning and decision-making, based on choices and constraints in the respective context of societies on both sides of the migration process: the society of origin and the destination society, at least in its subjectively anticipated form. While migration increasingly became part of the modern lifecourse and touches several social science disciplines, it is mainly discussed from a singular angle only; migration research, demography, ageing research, cultural studies, inequality research or human geography, while overarching approaches, are rare (Baykara-Krumme et al, 2012). Furthermore, it is typically international migration – meaning relocation over national borders – that attracts the attention of social scientists and policy makers.

Nevertheless, in the context of population ageing, internal migration must also be considered, because it impacts substantially on social change and national demographic developments at the local levels. During recent decades (and even during the most recent centuries, most of Europe was shaped by numerous waves of migration. But reasons for migration decisions, their destinations and the structure of migrant populations vary over time and differ between societies. Even if this depends substantially on the motivations for migration, migrants are more often younger people and, hence, immigration postpones population ageing. However, migrants participate in prolonging the lifespan in their new societal context, and they age too, of course. Therefore, migration does not reverse the overall trend of population ageing, but alters it. As a consequence, the effects of migration on demographic patterns are broadly inconsistent. However, migration is an issue on the agenda of population policies, but measures to regulate migration by national or supranational schemes are rare and are tricky to deal with.

Summary and conclusions

So, what can we conclude from these brief considerations? First of all, the lifecourse in modern societies is an multi-faceted issue. It can be considered as a social institution, as a trajectory over time with a series of positions and transitions, as an endogenous micro-structural condition affecting further development, as well as an individual interpretation of past, present and future developments. From the perspective of ongoing social change in an ageing society, it seems to be an entity that mediates between socio-structural changes and individual behaviour on the one hand and demographic patterns on the other.

Second, population ageing must be grasped as a complex issue that is embedded in the wider processes of social change and the transformation of people's lifecourses, which in turn may influence demographic outcomes. Third, the 'lifecourse' as a term of analysis has been dissected and described according to several specific views of sociological lifecourse research and from institutional, as well as gerontological and biographical, perspectives. It is argued that lifecourse changes that occur in different life domains – and life phases that are intertwined with processes of social change in general – must be seen from these different angles to understand their relevance for ongoing demographic developments. The domains and phases selectively mentioned in this chapter are: family foundation and dissolution, fertility, education, employment and retirement as well as migration. In all these areas, changes in lifecourses have implications not only for the demographic configuration of societies but also beyond this for their social structure and social inequality patterns. This holds true for the intergenerational perspective or the relations between age groups and also – if not overwhelmingly – for the disparities within generations and age groups, for example for inequalities between genders, social classes or strata, working and unemployed people, healthy and sick people, regions, ethnicities or cultures.

Finally, this raises the issue of social policies dealing with the question of inequalities and equity – and even sustainability – that accompanies the recent transformations in the lifecourse. In contemporary welfare states, these can be targeted by redistributive measures, but also by lifecourse policies, which include the aspect of individual and historical time. But contrary to primarily short-term redistributive instruments, the truly long-term perspective of lifecourse policies or even their potential inefficacy must be stressed. Lifecourse patterns are intricately embedded in societal and biographical contexts and cannot simply be changed by individual political decisions or measures. Instead, approaches to stabilise population patterns must allow the compatibility of concurrent (or even competitive) goals. What is called for are increasing options within institutional and biographical contexts of rational short-term lifecourse decisions on lifestyles, partnerships, family and mobility, as well as substantial changes in ideas, habits, norms and values, under the increasingly dynamic and demanding conditions of contemporary societies.

References

Alwin, D.F. and McCammon, R.J. (2006) 'Generations, cohorts, and social change', in J.T. Mortimer and M.J. Shanahan (eds) *Handbook of the life course*, New York: Springer, 23-49.

Baykara-Krumme, H., Motel-Klingebiel, A. and Schimany, P. (eds) (2012) *Viele Welten des Alterns. Ältere Migranten im alternden Deutschland [Many worlds of ageing. Older migrants in ageing Germany]*, Wiesbaden: Springer VS.

Beck, U. (1983) 'Jenseits von Stand und Klasse' ['Beyond status and class'], in R. Kreckel (ed) *Soziale Ungleichheiten, Soziale Welt [Social inequalities, social world], Sonderband 2*, Göttingen: Schwartz, 35-74.

Ben-Shlomo, Y. and Kuh, D. (2002) 'A life course approach to chronic disease epidemiology: conceptual models, empirical challenges and interdisciplinary perspectives', *International Journal of Epidemiology*, 31, 285-93.

Bengtson, V.L., Kasschau, P.L. and Ragan, P.K. (1976) 'The impact of social structure on aging individuals', in J.E. Birren and K.W. Schaie (eds) *Handbook of the psychology of aging*, New York, Academic Press, 327-53.

Blossfeld, H.-P. and Dronic, S. (2009) 'Theoretical perspectives on couples' careers' in W.R. Heinz, J. Huinink and A. Weymann (eds) *The life course reader. Individuals and societies across time*, Frankfurt/New York: Campus Verlag, 338-69.

Bumpass, L.L. (1990) 'What's happening to the family? Interactions between demographic and institutional change', *Demography*, 27, 483-98.

Bury, M. (1982) 'Chronic illness as biographical disruption', *Sociology of Health & Illness*, 4, 167-82.

Dannefer, D. (2003) 'Cumulative advantage/disadvantage and the life course. Cross-fertilizing age and social science theory', *The Journals of Gerontology Series B: Psychological Sciences and Social Sciences*, 58B, S327-37.

Dannefer, D. and Settersten, R.A. (2010) 'The study of the life course: implications for social gerontology', in D. Dannefer, and R.A. Settersten (eds) *The SAGE handbook of social gerontology*, London: Sage, 3-19.

Elder, G.H. (1974) *Children of the Great Depression: social change in life experience*, Chicago: University of Chicago Press.

Elder, G.H. and Shanahan, M.J. (2006) 'The life course and human development', in R.M. Lerner (ed) *Handbook of child psychology*, New York: Wiley, 665-715.

Ferraro, K.F., Shippee, T.P. and Schafer, M.H. (2009), 'Cumulative inequality theory for research on aging and the life course', in V. Bengtson, M. Silverstein, N. Putney and D. Gans (eds) *Handbook of theories of aging*, New York: Springer, 413-33.

Friebel, H. (2008) 'The children of the educational expansion era in Germany: Education and further training participation in the life-course', *British Journal of Sociology of Education*, 29, 479-92.

Halleröd, B. (2013) 'Gender inequality from beyond the grave: intra-household distribution and wellbeing after spousal loss', *Ageing & Society*, 33, 1-21.

Hareven, T.K. (1996) *Aging and generational relations over the life course: A historical and cross-cultural perspective*, Berlin/New York: W. de Gruyter.

Hareven, T.K. (2001). 'Historical perspectives on aging and family relations', in R.H. Binstock and L.K. George (eds) *Handbook of aging and the social sciences*, San Diego: Academic Press, 141-59.

Hobsbawm, E. (1994) *'The age of extremes. A history of the world, 1914–1991*, London: Abacus.

Huinink, J. (2009)'Linked lives, families, and intergenerational relations' in W.R. Heinz, J. Huinink and A. Weymann (eds) *The life course reader. Individuals and societies across time*, Frankfurt/New York: Campus Verlag, 303-10.

Hutchison, E.D. (2003) 'A life course perspective', in E.D. Hutchison (ed) *Dimensions of human behavior: The changing life course*, New York: Sage, 3-38.

Joas, H. and Knöbl, W. (2011) *Social theory: Twenty introductory lectures*. Cambridge, New York: Cambridge University Press.

Kelly, W.R. and Cutright, P. (1980) 'Modernization and the demographic transition: Cross-sectional and longitudinal analyses of a revised model', *Sociological Focus*, 13, 315-29.

Kirk, D. (1996) 'Demographic transition theory', *Population Studies*, 50, 361-87.

Kohli, M. (1985) ‚Die Institutionalisierung des Lebenslaufs – Historische Befunde und theoretische Argumente' [The institutionalisation of the life-course – historical findings and theoretical arguments], *Kölner Zeitschrift für Soziologie und Sozialpsychologie*, 37, 1-29.

Kohli, M. (2007) 'The institutionalization of the life course: Looking back to look ahead', *Research in Human Development*, 4, 253-71.

Kohli, M. (2009) 'The world we forgot: A historical review of the life course' in W.R. Heinz, J. Huinink and A. Weymann (eds) *The life course reader. Individuals and societies across time*, Frankfurt/New York: Campus Verlag, 64-90.

Kuh, D., Ben-Shlomo, Y., Lynch, J., Hallqvist, J. and Power, C. (2003) 'Life course epidemiology', *Journal of Epidemiology and Community Health*, 57, 778-83.

Kwiek, M. (2012) 'The growing complexity of the academic enterprise in Europe: A panoramic view', *European Journal of Higher Education*, 2, 112-31.

Leigh, G.K. (1982) 'Kinship interaction over the family life span', *Journal of Marriage and the Family*, 44, 197-208.

Litwin, H. (2007) 'Does early retirement lead to longer life?' *Ageing & Society*, 27, 739-54.

Macmillan, R. (2005) *The structure of the life course. Standardized? Individualized? Differentiated?*, Amsterdam: Elsevier JAI.

Macmillan, R. and Copher, R. (2005) 'Families in the life course: interdependency of roles, role configurations, and pathways', *Journal of Marriage and Family*, 67, 858-79.

Mayer, K.U. (2004)'Whose lives? How history, societies, and institutions define and shape life courses', *Research in Human Development*, 1, 161-87.

Mayer, K.U. (2009) 'New directions in life course research', *Annual Review of Sociology*, 35, 41333.

Mermin, G.B.T., Johnson, R.W. and Murphy, D.P. (2007) 'Why do boomers plan to work longer?', *The Journals of Gerontology Series B: Psychological Sciences and Social Sciences*, 62, S286-94.

Misra, J., Budig, M. and Boeckmann, I. (2011) 'Work-family policies and the effects of children on women's employment hours and wages', *Community, Work & Family*, 14, 139-57.

Morgan, S.P. and Bachrach, C.A. (2011) 'Is the theory of planned behaviour an appropriate model for human fertility?', *Vienna Yearbook of Population Research*, 9, 11-18.

Motel-Klingebiel, A., Romeu Gordo, L. and Betzin, J. (2009) 'Welfare states and quality of later life: distributions and predictions in a comparative perspective', *European Journal of Ageing*, 6, 67-78.

Öberg, B.-M., Närvänen, A.-L., Näsman, E. and Olsson, E. (eds) (2004) *Changing worlds and the ageing subject. Dimensions in the study of ageing and later life*, Aldershot: Ashgate.

Prokos, A.H. and Keene, J.R. (2012) 'The life course and cumulative disadvantage', *Research on Aging*, 34, 592-621.

Scherger, S. (2007) *Destandardisierung, Differenzierung, Individualisierung. Westdeutsche Lebensläufe im Wandel [De-Standardisation, differentiation, individualisation. Changing West-German lifecourses]*, Wiesbaden: VS.

Schnabel, S., Von Kistowski, K.G. and Vaupel, J.W. (2005) ,Immer neue Rekorde und kein Ende in Sicht. Der Blick in die Zukunft lässt Deutschland grauer aussehen als viele erwarten' [Always new records and no end in sight. A look into the future makes Germany look greyer than many expect], *Demografische Forschung aus Erster Hand*, 2, 3.

Schöllgen, I., Huxhold, O. and Tesch-Roemer, C. (2010) 'Socioeconomic status and health in the second half of life: Findings from the German Ageing Survey', *European Journal of Ageing*, 7, 17-28.

Settersten, R.A. (2006) 'Age structuring and the rhythm of the life course', in J.T. Mortimer and M.J. Shanahan (eds) *Handbook of the life course*, New York: Springer, 81-98.

Statista (2013) *Fertility rates in the Member States of the European Union 2010*. http://de.statista.com/statistik/daten/studie/200065/umfrage/geburtenziffern-in-ausgewaehlten-laendern-europas

Taylor, P. (2010) 'Cross-national trends in work and retirement', in D. Dannefer and R.A. Settersten (eds) *The SAGE handbook of social gerontology*, London: Sage, 540-50.

United Nations (2001) *World population ageing: 1950-2050*, New York: United Nations.
United Nations (2004) *World population to 2300*, New York: United Nations.
World Bank (2010) *World development indicators*, Washington: World Bank.

Part II

CRITICAL PERSPECTIVES

FOUR

Generations in ageing Finland: finding your place in the demographic structure

Antti Karisto and Ilkka Haapola

This chapter introduces a specific approach to demographic change, namely a generational perspective. Generations are groups of people born around the same time, who share a common identity and lifestyle because they have experienced the same historical events at similar points in their lives and have similarities in their lifecourses (Mannheim, 1928/1997). Generations differ in their size and also therefore contribute to population ageing to different degrees.

This chapter uses Finnish data on the baby boomers in order to investigate possible changes in post-retirement lifestyles. In Finland, the baby boom was exceptionally strong, and since birth the baby boomers have been highly visible in society. Now most have retired and are on the threshold of old age. There has been speculation that a new kind of 'third age' will emerge when the baby boomers are reaching retirement age, but still have, according to estimates of healthy life expectancy, a considerable number of active years ahead of them and have, on average, rather good opportunities for making life choices according to their tastes and preferences – which are expected to be different from those of earlier generations.

But is this really so? Are the baby boomers really forerunners or crucial drivers of what old age will look like in the near future? This chapter studies this with the help of longitudinal cohort survey data from the years 2002 and 2012, which allow age-adjusted comparisons between generations. Our study compares the activity-based wellbeing of mid-60-year-old baby boomers (born in 1946-50) with that of the preceding cohort, born 10 years earlier (1936-40), when they were at the same age.

The chapter consists of four sections. First, there is a description of the Finnish baby boom generation. Second, it discusses the concept of the third age, which is often used when new post-retirement lifestyles are explored. This is followed by an empirical section that starts with an analysis of whether the baby boomers are better positioned to live an active and satisfactory life than the previous generation at the same age. This is followed by an investigation of differences in activeness between the two generations. The last section summarises some of our findings and makes conclusions.

The baby boom in Finland

Although the post-World War II baby boom was a universal phenomenon, at least in the Western world, demographics differ between countries. The Finnish baby boom has specific features that make it an interesting case (Karisto, 2005; Karisto, 2007).

Everywhere the baby boom was connected with recovery from the war, but the first peculiar feature in Finland was that it occurred so rapidly, just as soon as was possible. The war against the Soviet Union ended in September 1944, and the majority of soldiers were demobilised at the end of that year. It took nine months from their homecoming for the first baby boomers to be born, and in the first post-war summer the birth rate climbed to a level never seen before or since (Karisto, 2005). While this looks natural and intelligible, the meteoric increase in the birth rate is slightly surprising given the loss of married men in the war and the way the war had impeded the mating of young people. In many European countries, the peak of fertility was reached somewhat later, as was also the case in the US (see Chapter Seven).

Differences in the timing of the baby boom apply not only to its beginning but also to its duration (Bonvalet and Ogg, 2011). In the US, the baby boom lasted until the mid-1960s, as it did in Great Britain, where it was a twin-peak phenomenon, with the first increase in the birth rate in the late 1940s followed by a later rise in the early 1960s. In Finland, the baby boom started early and was also over fairly soon. Although, the birth rate remained relatively high in the 1950s and 1960s, a marked decline had already begun in the late 1940s. While it is a little difficult to determine the last birth year of the baby boom, it is most frequently set at the year 1950. Figure 4.1 displays the numbers of births in Finland between 1940 and 2013.

The second special characteristic of the Finnish baby boomers is their number, for nowhere else does their relative size differ as much from the prior and succeeding cohorts (Valkonen, 1990). In Great Britain, for instance, the annual birth rate curve climbed only about a quarter above the prior and succeeding level (Falkingham, 1997), but in Finland it almost doubled.

Due to their numbers, the baby boomers are highly visible in Finnish society. Figure 4.2 describes the absolute sizes of different age groups from 1900 until 2050. We can observe how the same peak is repeated: each time the baby boomers are represented in a particular age group, their numbers are unprecedented. These demographic waves have not been without consequences. When the baby boomers were children, new childcare services were needed and school institutions had to be expanded. Classrooms were packed, and schools often operated in two shifts, with children attending school like shift workers. When the baby boomers were in their teenage years, there were more teenagers than ever. Shouts from the streets were heard, and a new youth culture was born.

Now the baby boomers are prominent as 'senior boomers'. The Finnish labour force is diminishing, and during the next two decades the old-age dependency

Figure 4.1: Number of births in Finland by the year, 1940-2003

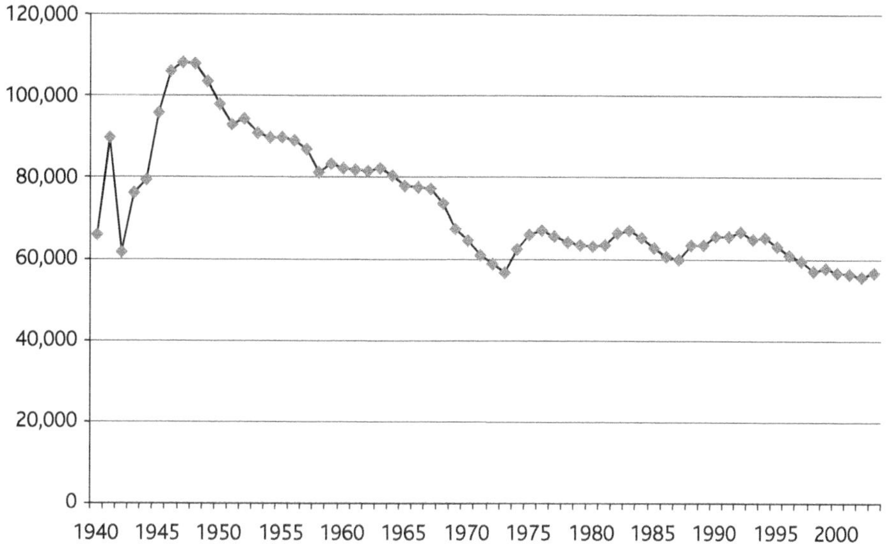

120,000
100,000
80,000
60,000
40,000
20,000
0
1940 1945 1950 1955 1960 1965 1970 1975 1980 1985 1990 1995 2000

Source: Statistics Finland (2014)

Figure 4.2: Past and predicted changes in the absolute sizes of different age groups in Finland, 1900-2050

1.8
1.6
1.4
1.2
1.0
0.8
0.6
0.4
0.2
0
1900 1915 1930 1945 1960 1975 1990 2005 2020 2035 2050
80+ y
65–79 y
50–64 y
35–49 y
20–34 y
0–19 y

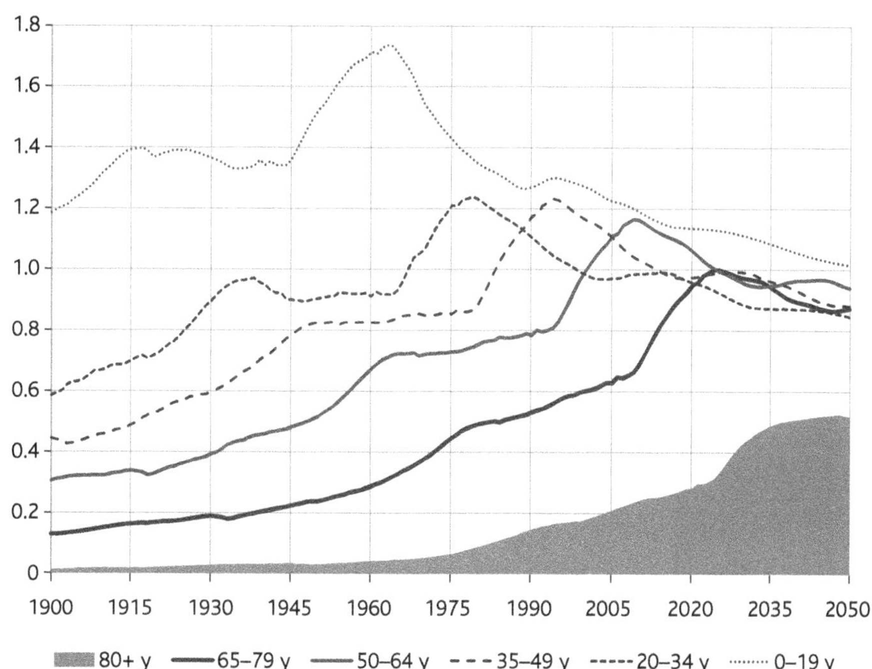

Source: Parkkinen, 2005: 302

ratio will weaken faster than in any other EU country because of the baby boomers (European Commission, 2009). On the one hand, gloomy scenarios have thus been presented of the burden of the ageing boomers represent to the rest of society. On the other hand, the baby boomers also have the reputation of being an avant-garde generation, who have introduced all kinds of novelties. Therefore, it is believed that they will change the practice of post-retirement lifestyles. Behavioural changes are often exaggerated, but even if there is no lifestyle revolution on the way, small qualitative changes can also have an impact, because of the quantitative cohort effect that certainly exists.

The exceptional size of the Finnish baby boom, as well as its timing and duration, relate to its third specific characteristic: its generation-making effect. The Finnish baby boom was strong enough and long enough, but yet not too long a phenomenon, for these birth cohorts to be considered a generation of their own. This is not self-evident, because generation is a sociological, not only a demographic, concept. A generation is 'a cohort which constitutes itself a cultural identity and as a collective one has social significance' (Eyerman and Turner, 1998: 7). According to Karl Mannheim (1928/1997) – the founding father of the sociology of generations – the decisive factor in the formation of a generation from a cohort is what happens in society during the formative years of the group concerned. Many things happened when the Finnish baby boomers were young. The 1960s was a decade of economic change, rapid urbanisation, cultural modernisation, the rise of political radicalism, the rise of consumer society and the emergence of youth culture.

The Mannheimian idea that generational consciousness is produced by key experiences during their formative years (Mannheim, 1928/1997) implies that consciousness weakens in time when the memories of youth gradually fade away. However, a cohort's generational consciousness and public image can also become intensified over the years, if they are renewed and reproduced in public, as has been the case with the Finnish baby boomers. Current public discourses on population ageing have been strongly linked to them.

Contrary to conventional theories, we also believe that the common experiences behind generation formation need not be only on the scale of wars and political turmoil in order to have an effect. Minor events may also matter, because generational consciousness has a tacit dimension related to minor everyday experiences. There are minor but still significant memory traces that help people recognise their generational peers, and on which generational styles are also based: the music that was listened to, the clothes that were worn and so on. We could talk about 'generational gaze', implying that people of the generation share preferences and tastes. For example, environmental preferences and architectural and aesthetic likes and dislikes are structured not only according to gender and social class but also, to some extent, according to generation.

Generational consciousness does not arise automatically from certain life experiences, but has to be produced. According to Semi Purhonen (2007: 136), the birth of a generation requires 'a discursive breakthrough', and only afterwards can people fit their own personal experiences and memories with this articulation. Furthermore, it is not a uniform process; rather, in the light of Pierre Bourdieu's theory, it may more accurately be seen as a battlefield (Purhonen, 2007). The elite of a generation tries to make its own articulation generally accepted, and members of the 'mass generation' then more or less adopt these images or labels. All this is visible among the Finnish baby boom generation, whose public image and reputation have spread from its educated elite (or part of it), for example when the baby boomers have been characterised as being 'a radical generation'. It is true, on the one hand, that the boomers were active in the left-wing political mobilisation of university students in the late 1960s and early 1970s, but, on the other hand, only a few were involved, as only a tiny minority of baby boomers were university students. Nor is it to be expected that a comprehensively new kind of post-retirement lifestyle is emerging among the whole generation.

Generations are not homogeneous. There are fractions and internal divisions among them, even among their elites. However, just about every baby boomer in Finland is aware of belonging to the boomer generation. This is not a trivial fact, because in many other countries boomers are primarily a phenomenon recognised by demographers and statistical experts, and in an obscure way by the media and marketing. In Finland, the generational consciousness of boomers is strong, much stronger than among younger Finnish birth cohorts, even though all kinds of generational symbols have been publicly imposed on them (Purhonen, 2007). Consequently, if any post-war cohort can be called a generation, it is the baby boomers.

The third age

The discourse around the third age is one way to conceptualise lifecourses and the changes to come (Carr and Komp, 2011). It is suggested that traditional taxonomies of the lifecourse are no more valid. People do not become 'old' immediately after retirement; rather the early years of retirement form a unique life period of their own, different from proper old age. Retired people are not economically active, but they are active in many other ways: they do voluntary work, help their parents and support their younger relatives. But, first and foremost, the third age is believed to be devoted to personal interests. Its emergence is seen as a positive development that can make old age pleasant and desirable, and alluring visions of the pleasures of the third age may function as a factor for increasing the attraction of retirement years. The concept of the third age contains a promise of wellbeing, a kind of prime of one's life. Peter Laslett (1996), who introduced the concept, stressed that the third age is a period dedicated to one's own wellbeing. Finally, people can devote themselves to hobbies and interests for which they had insufficient time while working.

This is a very welcome counter view to the 'grand narrative' of ageing, which sees ageing as nothing more than a decline (Powell, 2006). The perspective of the third age offers an alternative model for what it is to grow old. Unlike old age proper, the third age is not framed by the inevitable decline of the body, disengagement and structural restraints and dependencies; rather, it is framed in terms of agency, choices and opportunities, second chances and new beginnings (Giddens, 1991; Gilleard and Higgs, 2005).

However, is this kind of third age a reality or just a cultural illusion? And if it is a reality, is it being ushered in by the baby boomers? In order to answer the first question, the concept of the third age has to be deconstructed. When approached demographically, we can see that the life expectancy at the age of 65 – which had hardly increased in Finland since the late 18th century – has greatly lengthened in recent decades and is now growing by almost two years in every decade(for example Myrskylä et al, 2013). The lifespan has been prolonged at this very juncture, and most of the new retirement years are relatively healthy years – especially for the educated, although socioeconomic differences in (healthy) life expectancy are great. The compression of morbidity theory (Fries, 1980), which suggests that illnesses are compressed to the last years of life, irrespective of life expectancy, has gained strong, although not comprehensive, support.

Another demographic fact is that an exceptionally large number of people are now reaching early retirement years. These two driving forces of the third age – the unprecedentedly large numbers of people entering this age, and the prolonged duration of this life period – are the indisputable facts constituting its demographic framework. The third component, however, is vaguer. It suggests that the baby boomers as Finland's first youth generation may well also be the first generation to lead a new kind of life during retirement. The baby boomers are reaching retirement age with different expectations and orientations from those of previous generations, and thus they are the first generation to display a distinctive third-age lifestyle. However, this is an open question, and therefore the orientations, preferences, choices and activities of the baby boomers need to be studied empirically.

The third-age discourse may also be biased towards lifestyle choices. Max Weber already concluded that lifestyles should not be conceived merely within the framework of life choices, but also within the framework of life chances (Cockerham et al, 1993). Consequently, the post-retirement life phase should be approached in its socio-historical context. The whole concept of the third age is less valid in circumstances where there is an extreme scarcity of resources. Moreover, even in affluent societies the emergence of new lifestyles is dependent on the possession of resources. There may be financial, medical and other barriers, which can turn the dreams of an energetic and eventful life after retirement into castles in the air.

Doing as a part of wellbeing

According to the Finnish sociologist Erik Allardt (1976 and 1993), wellbeing consists of three or four broad domains: *having* refers to the material standard of living; *loving* refers to social relations; and *being* refers to people's self-actualisation.

Doing, participating in meaningful activities, is a part of being, and is the target here. Since the formulation of the activity theory (Havighurst, 1961), its importance is well understood in gerontology.

In recent discourses on productive ageing, work-like activities are emphasised most. Productive ageing, however, is too economistic a concept for our taste. A more fruitful way of thinking is to value activities according to their perceived meaningfulness and their benefit to individual wellbeing. Meaningful activities are rewarding in themselves, by giving joy and immediate social rewards, but they are also beneficial in the long run. It is well known that physical activity, along with other health-related lifestyles, may prevent the emergence of many diseases, but there is also widespread evidence that cultural activity and participation may decrease morbidity and mortality, and may increase wellbeing in many ways (for example, Glass et al, 1999; Hyyppä and Mäki, 2001; Konlaan, 2001; Agahi and Parker, 2008; Adams et al, 2011).

Functional capacities are something that people have to 'use or lose'. Using them reproduces them, and a positive circle of activeness may emerge. This has an effect on the societal impact of population ageing, too. Care costs are age dependent, but if older people are active and able to live independently, service needs will be postponed and costs do not necessarily increase in relation to the number of retired people. Therefore, there is also a strong societal interest in studying how active people are, and how they are using and reproducing their functional capacities. Through activeness and participation, ageing citizens can also contribute to the common good, for instance by volunteering. Participation in civic activities is also a sign that ageing people are still autonomous and competent members of society and are not disengaged and excluded.

The data

The data used in this chapter come from the longitudinal GOAL-study (Good Ageing in the Lahti region a.k.a. Ikihyvä Päijät-Häme), which has been in progress since 2002. The region of Päijät-Häme – the geographical target of the GOAL-study – lies in southern Finland, 100–150 km north of Helsinki, and its population is typical of the Finnish population living outside the most advanced urban centres. In the GOAL-study, people belonging to three five-year birth cohorts (born in 1926-30, 1936-40 and 1946-50) were followed from 2002 until 2012, with assessments also in 2005 and 2008. The data concentrate on health and health behaviour, but also include living conditions, lifestyles and ageing experiences (Fogelholm et al, 2006; Haapola et al, 2013).

The original sample consisted of 4,272 individuals, of whom 2,814 (66%) participated at the baseline and 1,679 (51% of the prevailing sample) in the last study wave. In addition to the panel, a new parallel cross-section survey on the same cohorts was conducted in 2012 (N=1343, participation rate 56%), in order to control panel conditioning. Here these datasets have been merged to create a bigger and more representative sample for the year 2012.

The data are first used to give an overall picture of age-dependent activeness or to test the idea that 'new beginnings' are typical of the third age. The activeness of the baby boomer generation will then be compared to the generation born 10 years earlier keeping age constant (see the bold row in Table 4.1).

Table 4.1: The respondents of the GOAL-study in 2002 and 2012, by age group

Age group	Year 2002	Year 2012
82-86 y	–	617
72-76 y	883	1063
62-66 y	**1,023**	**1,091**
52-56 y	908	269

New beginnings

Closely related to the concept of third age is the idea of 'new beginnings', which was operationalised here by asking the respondents if they had found a new interest or hobby during the last three or four years (since the previous enquiry). Generational comparisons cannot, however, be made in this respect, because the question was first posed in 2005. Gender differences among the baby boomer generation were evident, as it was found that women are more capable of adopting new behaviours than men: in 2012, half (47%) of the women had taken up a new hobby or interest during the last four years, while among the men only a quarter (26%) had acquired a new interest.

Norms regulating what is appropriate and acceptable for senior citizens have become more flexible. This became evident when the respondents were asked if it was appropriate for a senior citizen to dress youthfully, have an active sex life, visit pubs and restaurants and so on. From their answers we could see that the climate had become more liberal or tolerant, especially when they were compared to opinions presented in the late 1970s (Jyrkämä, 1995). Even if respondents themselves did not go to pubs or dress youthfully, they were happy for others to do so, and there were hardly any remnants of the sharp gender and regional differences noted by Jyrkämä (1995; see also Karisto and Konttinen, 2004).

Thus, ageing people are 'allowed' to do things that were earlier considered inappropriate, and they also engage in new activities during their mature years. Nevertheless, ageing, of course, also forces people to give up activities. However, Figure 4.3 shows that among those in early old age there are more who have found a new interest or hobby than those who have abandoned one. Everyday life is enriching after retirement in this respect. It is not until the age of 75 that the net change curve – the difference between those who have acquired a new hobby and those who have given one up – falls below zero. This moment or intersection constitutes, roughly speaking, a kind of threshold, after which the third age begins to turn into old age. Women adopt new activities more than

Figure 4.3: Participation in leisure activities in Finland, by age

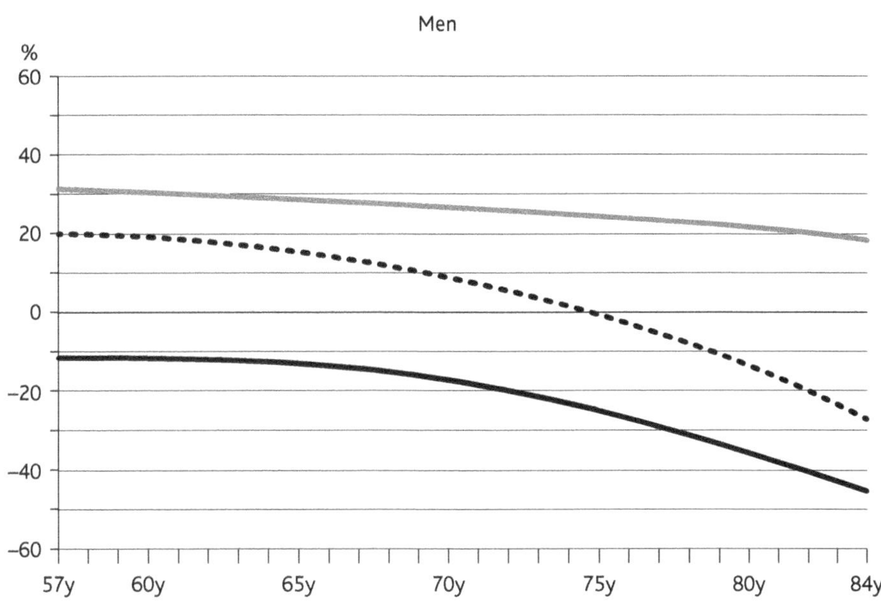

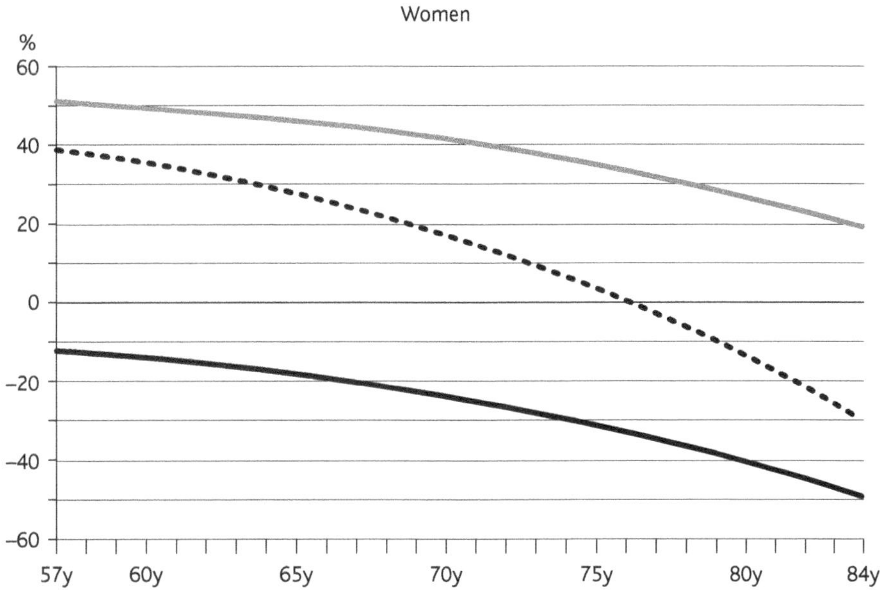

Note: The proportion of those who have found a new interest or hobby (grey line), the proportion of those who have had to give up a hobby or an interest due to ageing (black line) and the difference between the groups (net change, dotted line). Combination of the results of the GOAL cohort study from the years 2005, 2008 and 2012.

men, but they do not 'turn old' later, because they also give up activities more than men.

Possibilities for living an active life

We started the cohort comparisons by investigating people's opportunities for living an active life in terms of their resources. The Finnish pension system was reformed in 2005, establishing a flexible retirement age (63–68 years) and introducing new incentives for participating longer in the labour market. The average age of retirement started to increase, and this is also reflected in our data: in 2002 only 11% of 62–66 year olds were working, but in 2012 more than a quarter (27%) of the baby boomers were working at the same age. The educational level of the boomer generation is also markedly higher than that of the preceding generation, although much lower than among subsequent cohorts. Among the boomers, 56% attended school for at least 10 years, whereas among the cohort born in the late 1930s the corresponding figure is 33%.

According to Table 4.2, the economic situation of the baby boomer generation at the age of 62–66 years was better than that of the preceding cohort 10 years earlier in light of objective and subjective indicators. This is partly due to more active participation in the labour market, but income levels have also increased among retired people. Health is another important resource affecting ageing people's activities. Fewer of the baby boomers suffer from certain chronic diseases than those of the preceding generation, and more remarkable still is the difference in self-rated health. The last indicator in Table 4.2 is an item taken from the RAND-36 Item Health Questionnaire (Aalto et al, 1999). Here it is interpreted

Table 4.2: Indicators describing the economic situation and the health status of the two cohorts at the age of 62-66

	Cohort born 1936-40	Cohort born 1946-50
Working (at least part-time)	11%	27%
Education: at least 10 years in school	33%	56%
Median disposable income, in fixed prices (euro/OECD consumption unit/month)	1256€	1667€
Subjective financial well-being: respondent has managed to cover regular outlays very or fairly well	61%	70%
Perceives own health as very or fairly good	46%	66%
Prevalence of		
– coronary heart disease	10%	4%
– neck or shoulder pain	47%	30%
– diabetes mellitus	8%	8%
– asthma	7%	6%
Respondent felt full of life 'most of the time' over the past month	44%	54%

as being an indicator of vitality or 'energy capital', and it shows that the baby boomers feel slightly more energetic. All in all, they seem to have somewhat better resources than the preceding generation for living an active and gratifying life. But how are people using these opportunities? This will be studied next, with a special emphasis on possible gender differences.

From physical to spiritual: different activity domains

The data include detailed qualitative information on people's favourite activities. It is not possible to report the whole spectrum here, but there is a huge variety of activities – from t'ai chi, bailatino, esperanto, calligraphy, violin-making, motor-cycling, ice swimming and gold mining to meeting up with friends in a café. The data provide so much information on activities that they cannot be thoroughly analysed. We have therefore concentrated the analysis on broader activity domains, which could be identified either *a priori*, on the basis of the existing literature on older adults' lifestyles, or empirically, by using techniques like factor analysis. As Kathryn Bett Adams and her colleagues (2011) state, both of these methods have their merits and limitations. The classification that follows was based on their literature review, but we also tested it by means of principal component analyses and cluster analysis, which chiefly yielded the same result. The following activity domains were distinguished, and each of them was measured with one to three items:

- *physical activities:* physical exercise and outdoor recreation (at least weekly);
- *utility-oriented activities:* doing handicrafts (at least weakly), gardening (at least weekly);
- *cultural or intellectual activities:* reading books (at least weekly), going to art exhibitions, theatre or movies (at least once a month), painting, playing a musical instrument, singing in a choir (at least once a month);
- *spiritual activities:* participating in religious events (at least weekly), doing voluntary work (at least once a month);
- *experience-oriented activities:* participating in spectator sports (at least weekly), dancing (at least once a month).

We allowed the items to become part of just one domain, although in reality they could be interpreted as being measures of several activity domains. For instance, voluntary work could also be a measure of utility-oriented activities, which would then give a stronger finding for 'productive ageing'. In Finland, however (among the generations examined, especially), voluntary work is closely related to religious or spiritual activities and is often performed through church organisations. Gardening is another example of a multipurpose activity. Growing vegetables creates economic utility and was therefore regarded as a utility-oriented activity. However, it is also a physical activity and could even be included in the domain of spiritual activities, because it also gives contemplative and aesthetic pleasure.

Table 4.3 describes participation inactivity domains. It measures the share of those who regularly participate in at least one activity in the domain. Gender differences are evident. Utility-oriented, intellectual and spiritual activities are distinctly more common among women than men and, among the baby boomers, women are also more active in the domain of physical activities. Experience-oriented activities are more typical of men, because men are more involved in spectator sports.

It was quite surprising that participation rates decreased in every domain between 2002 and 2012. Contrary to expectations, the baby boomers are *less* active than the late 1930s cohort was at the same age, and the difference is statistically significant in all domains except cultural or intellectual activities.

The content of some of our measures, however, makes this unexpected result understandable. Secularisation has led to a downward trend in participation in religious events, and possible new forms of spirituality are not covered by our measure. Although gardening and handicrafts are even trendy hobbies, they may mainly be associated with past lifestyles, and again it is possible that the baby boomers pursue utility-oriented activities that our measure does not cover. The

Table 4.3: Participation rates in different activity domains by gender in 2002 and 2012 (%)

Activity domain	The cohort born in 1936-40 (year 2002)	The cohort born in 1946-50 (year 2012)	Statistical significance of the difference
Physical activities			
Men	92	87	*
Women	95	94	
All	94	91	*
Utility-oriented activities			
Men	43	33	**
Women	66	53	***
All	55	43	***
Cultural or intellectual activities			
Men	43	43	
Women	59	55	
All	52	49	
Spiritual activities			
Men	16	13	
Women	25	20	*
All	21	17	*
Experience-oriented activities			
Men	87	76	***
Women	75	64	***
All	81	70	***

Note: $^{*}p \leq 0.05$; $^{**}p \leq 0.01$; $^{***}p \leq 0.001$

downward trend in experience-oriented activities is mainly due to the fact that spectator sports have lost their popularity, but possibly other sources of new experiences have become more popular. One example is travel, as the next section shows.

Nevertheless, the main finding remains that the baby boomers are not more active than the earlier cohort after retirement. This compels us to rethink this generation once more and, perhaps, also to re-evaluate the concepts of active ageing and the third age.

The age, period and cohort effects of travel

Taking travel or tourism as the last empirical example, we can more closely approach age, period and cohort effects, which are intertwined (see Yang, 2011). In 2002, only tiny differences between age groups appeared in the share of people who had never travelled abroad, as well as in the share of long-distance travellers (people who had travelled to continents other than Europe). In all age groups the majority of respondents had made their 'grand tour' – the trip to the most distant place they had ever visited – quite recently, typically during the last 10 years. This meant that people belonging to different cohorts had made this trip at a different age: the baby boomers in their fifties, the middle cohort in their sixties and the oldest cohort in their seventies. Therefore, travelling abroad seems not so much an age-dependent or cohort-dependent phenomenon as a time-dependent phenomenon, typical of modern times (Karisto and Konttinen, 2004).

The longitudinal data used in the Table 4.4, however, confirm the intuitive assumption that travelling is also dependent on age. The figures among the older age groups are so high that there is probably also a time-effect in travelling along with the obvious age-effect. We do not have comparable figures from earlier decades, but it is evident that before the age of mass tourism only a tiny share of pensioners, let alone those in their seventies or eighties, travelled abroad. Now every second 72–76 year old has travelled abroad during the last year. During recent years, travelling has become even more popular and can be considered a typical third-age activity.

It seems evident that time-dependent changes in travelling have happened cohort-wise. The baby boomers (especially women) travel more than the previous generation at the same age, and, respectively, the cohort born in the late 1930s travels more than the late 1920s-born cohort did when they were in their seventies. When looking at the baby boomers, we can see that in 2012 women travelled more than they did in 2002, when they were 10 years younger and still working.

Conclusions

The discourses on active ageing, engaged lifestyles and the third age offer a welcome alternative to the dominant 'burden discourse', where population ageing is regarded as a societal disaster, leading only to increasing costs and the

Table 4.4: The proportion (%) of people who have travelled abroad during the last year, by gender and age group in 2002 and 2012

	2002	2012
Men		
82-86 years	–	24
72-76 years	38	48
62-66 years	48	52
52-56 years	52	–
Women		
82-86 years	–	20
72-76 years	35	48
62-66 years	51	64
52-56 years	56	–
All		
82-86 years	–	21
72-76 years	36	48
62-66 years	49	59
52-56 years	54	–

reduced sustainability of public economy. This discourse very easily blames the victim, holding ageing people responsible for being so numerous and causing societal problems.

However, these counter-discourses are neither innocent nor without subtle side-effects. The discourse on the third age, for instance, may give rise to new cleavages in old age. The more cheerful a picture we paint of life after retirement, the gloomier we see old age proper, which does not fit into this construction.[1] A sharp demarcation line is appearing between the third age and the fourth age, and those in later old age are easily excluded.

An active life is usually a good life, but the wellbeing of senior citizens cannot be conceptualised solely in terms of activeness. Nor can the activeness of senior citizens be taken as a given. Here activeness was studied by comparing 62–66 year old baby boomers with the preceding generation at the same age. On average, the baby boomers are relatively well-to-do and can expect more active years ahead compared to the earlier generations. They are healthier, more energetic and also have more financial resources to participate in different activities. In some respects, for example as tourists, they also participate more actively, but on the whole they do not manifest greater activeness than the preceding cohort. This is contrary to the hypothesis that it is the baby boomers who are heralding in the third age and its active life.

Along with the analysis presented here we also made comparisons between cohorts born in the late 1920s and 1930s at two points in time, when both groups were 72–76 years old. We noticed that in this age group, activeness had increased between 2002 and 2012. This could imply that active lifestyles had become more common *before* the baby boomers were of retirement age.

On the other hand, there are also indications that new post-retirement lifestyles have been adopted among cohorts born *later* than the baby boomers. For instance, in a qualitative study connected to the GOAL study, the authors strongly emphasised continuities in the orientations and lifestyles of the baby boomers, and concluded that their attitudinal and behavioural patterns more closely resemble those of older cohorts than those of younger cohorts. They noticed, for instance, that free-time exercise has become popular among the children of the baby boomers rather than among the boomers themselves (Häkkinen et al, 2013).

The current literature on the baby boomers often presents them as a generation born in the new consumer society. They have engaged in consumer lifestyles and new recreational practices and have learnt to seek self-expression and pleasure in consumption (for example Gilleard and Higgs, 2005; Gilleard et al, 2005). The consumer behaviour of the Finnish baby boomers has not been widely studied, but we prefer to term them 'a bridging generation', who have a hand in both past and present societies (Karisto, 2005 and 2007; Leach et al, 2013). Over three quarters of the baby boomers were born in rural areas, far away from modern consumer society, but now the majority live in an urban environment. They live in a post-industrial consumer society, but they still have a life-historical connection to traditional society.

The bridging nature of the generation, or its twofold connectedness to the past and present, is reflected, for example, in physical activities. In a study of sports in the life of different generations (Zacheus, 2008), it appeared that those baby boomers who played sports often practised both old, traditional sports (for example cross-country skiing) and new, modern ones (for example going to the gym). Traces of life-historical layers were also present in our data, for instance when the respondents were asked to name their favourite places. Even with city people, and more among the baby boomers than among preceding generations, they were close to nature, and were often historically charged: a summer cottage and a childhood home in the country, a sauna on the shore of a lake and a forest were typical answers; shopping centres, cafés and other urban locations and amenities were rarely mentioned (Karisto and Konttinen, 2004).

Our data also show that a large number of baby boomers (especially men with a working-class or small-farming background) are somewhat dismissive of the messages of modern health promotion and retained old unhealthy habits: eating fatty food, smoking, drinking excessively, not exercising (Karisto, 2006). In this way they are also sticking to 'the old school' or representing a kind of 'culture of contestation' in changing times (Lomabardi-Satriani, 1974).

Two conclusions can be made. First, topics like the third age or baby boomer lifestyles are not universally applicable, as often seems to be implied in health-oriented studies of old age, where associations between variables are sought and considered to be as important, regardless of the society in which they originate. Baby boomers in different societies are different, and studies inspired by forward-looking visions emphasising change should also be grounded in their socio-historical contexts or made comparatively. This is also what the sociological concept of generation implies. For instance, the simple fact that the Finnish baby boomers were born slightly earlier than their peers in some other countries, and in a society which was not so modern and urban, is significant.

The second conclusion – which we dare to make without the necessary further studies – is that because generations are far from homogeneous, new lifestyles are adopted unevenly. The characterisations of the young Finnish baby boomers as 'a radical generation' were based on the observations of a small fraction of that generation. Similarly, the notion that new lifestyles are arising now, when the baby boomers are retiring, is often based on the behaviour of fractions of the generation. The educated elite of the generation may also be the forerunner here. Our analysis was only made according to gender. It proved that women are distinctly more active than men and more open to different kinds of new beginnings. In general, new lifestyles may first emerge among some subgroups and only afterwards spread to mass generation.

The main finding of this study shows that, on the whole, the baby boomers do not seem to be more active than the earlier generation at the same age. This warns us not to become too excited about vivid third-age visions presented in the media.

Notes

[1] Old age is full of ambiguities which are reflected in language or constructed by it. Retired people dislike being called 'old', and this term has become politically incorrect. But there is a scarcity of accepted alternatives. The respondents of the GOAL-study were asked how adequate the terms 'old', 'elderly', 'senior citizens' and so on are, when describing retired people in general and the respondents personally. None of the terms was considered really adequate (Karisto, 2007). The term 'third age' used in this chapter is not so familiar to ordinary people in Finland, although it is widely used in Great Britain, France (*le troisième âge*) and Spain *(la tercera edad)*.

References

Aalto, A.M, Aro, A.R. and Teperi, J. (1999) *RAND-36 terveyteen liittyvän elämänlaadun mittarina: Mittarin luotettavuus ja suomalaiset väestöarvot* [*The RAND-36 health related quality of life scale: Reliability of the scale and its values for the Finnish population*], Helsinki: Stakes.

Adams, K.B., Leibbrandt, S. and Moon, H. (2011) 'A critical review of the literature on social and leisure activity and wellbeing in later life', *Ageing and Society*, 31, 683-712.

Agahi, N. and Parker, G. (2008) 'Leisure activities and mortality', *Journal of Aging and Health*, 20, 855-71.

Allardt, E. (1976) *Hyvinvoinninulottuvuuksia* [*Dimensions of wellbeing*], Helsinki: WSOY.

Allardt, E. (1993) 'Having, loving, being: An alternative to the Swedish model of welfare research', in Nussbaum, M. and Sen, A. (eds) *The quality of life*, Oxford: Clarendon Press, 88-94.

Bonvalet, C. and Ogg, J. (2011) *Baby boomers: A mobile generation.* Oxford: The Bardwell Press.

Carr, D.C. and Komp, K. (2011) 'Introduction', in D.C. Carr and K. Komp (eds) *Gerontology in the era of the third age. Implications and next steps*, New York: Springer, 1-10.

Cockerham, W., Abel, T. and Lüschen, G. (1993) 'Max Weber, formal rationality and health life styles', *Sociological Quarterly*, 34, 313-4.

European Commission (2009) *Demography report 2008: Meeting the social needs in an ageing society*, Luxembourg: Office of Official Publications of the European Communities.

Eyerman, J. and Turner, B. (1998) 'Outline of a theory of generations', *European Journal of Social Theory*, 1, 91–106.

Falkingham, J. (1997) 'Who are the baby boomers? A demographic profile', in M. Evandrou (ed) *Baby boomers. Ageing in the 21st century*, London: Age Concern Books, 15-40.

Fogelholm, M., Valve, R., Absetz, P., Heinonen, H., Uutela, A., Patja, K., Karisto, A., Konttinen, R., Mäkelä, T., Nissinen, A., Jallinoja, P., Nummela, O. and Talja, M. (2006) 'Rural-urban differences in health and health behaviour: A baseline description of a community health-promotion program for the elderly', *Scandinavian Journal of Public Health*, 34, 632-40.

Fries, J.F. (1980) 'Aging, natural death and the compression of morbidity', *The New England Journal of Medicine*, 303, 130-5.

Giddens, A. (1991) *Modernity and self-identity. Self and society in the late modern age*, Cambridge: Polity Press.

Gilleard, C. and Higgs, P. (2005) *Context of ageing. Class, cohort and community*, Cambridge: Polity Press.

Gilleard, C., Higgs, P., Hyde, M., Wiggins, R. and Blane, R. (2005) 'Class, cohort, and consumption: The British experience of the third age', *The Journals of Gerontology, B Series*, 60, 6, 305-10.

Glass, T.A., Mendes de Leon, C., Marottoli, R.A. and Berkman, L.F. (1999) 'Population based study of social and productive activities as predictors of survival among elderly Americans', *British Medical Journal*, 319, 478-83.

Haapola, I., Karisto, A. and Fogelholm, M. (2013) *Vanhuusikä muutoksessa: Ikihyvä Päijät-Häme -tutkimuksen tuloksia 2002–2012* [*Old age in transition: Results from the GOAL-study 2002–2012*], Lahti: Päijät-Hämeen sosiaali- ja terveysyhtymän julkaisuja, 72.

Häkkinen, A., Ojajärvi, A., Puuronen, A. and Salasuo, M. (2013) *Sosiaalinen albumi: Elämäntavat sukupolvien murroksissa* [*The social album: Lifestyle changes between generations*], Helsinki: Nuorisutkimusverkosto.

Havighurst, R.J. (1961) 'Successful aging', *The Gerontologist*, 1, 8-13.

Hyyppä, M.T. and Mäki, J. (2001) 'Why do Swedish-speaking Finns have longer active life? An area for social capital research', *Health Promotion International*, 16, 55-64.

Jyrkämä, J. (1995) '*Rauhaisasti alas illan lepoon? Tutkimus vanhenemisen sosiaalisuudesta neljässä paikallisyhteisössä*' [*Down to rest peacefully tonight?Studying social ageing in four municipalities*], Tampere: Acta Universitatis Tamperensis.

Karisto, A. (2005) 'Suuret ikäluokat kuvastimessa' [Baby boomers in the mirror], in A. Karisto (ed) *Suuret ikäluokat* [*The baby boomers*], Tampere: Vastapaino, 17-58.

Karisto, A. (2006) 'Terveydelle viileän elämäntyylin jäljillä'. [Tracing a cool lifestyle: disobedience to health promotion messages], *Kansanterveys*, 2, 14-15.

Karisto, A. (2007) 'The Finnish baby boomers and the emergence of the third age', *International Journal of Ageing and Later Life*, 2, 2, 91-108.

Karisto, A. and Konttinen, R. (2004) *Kotikatua, kotiruokaa, kaukomatkailua. Tutkimus ikääntyvien elämäntyylistä* [*Kidneypie, Emmerdale, Holidays on the Canary Islands. A study of lifestyles among the elderly*], Helsinki: Palmenia-kustannus.

Konlaan, B.B. (2001) *Cultural experience and health: The coherence of health and leisure time activities*, Umea: Umeå University.

Laslett, P. (1996) *A fresh map of life. The emergence of third age* (2nd edn), London: Macmillan Press.

Leach, R., Phillipson, C., Biggs, S. and Money, A. (2013) 'Baby boomer, consumption, and social change: The bridging generation?', *International Review of Sociology: Revue Internationale de Sociologie*, 23, 1, 104-22.

Lombardi-Satriani, L. (1974) 'Folklore as culture of contestation', *Journal of the Folklore Institute*, XI, 1-2.

Mannheim, K. (1928/1997) 'The problem of generation', in M.A. Hardy (ed) *Studying ageing and social change: Conceptual and methodological issues*, London: Sage, 22-65.

Myrskylä, M., Leinonen, T. and Martikainen, P. (2013) *Life expectancy by labor force status and social class: Recent period and cohort trends and projections for Finland*, Helsinki: Finnish Centre for Pensions.

Parkkinen, P. (2005) 'Vaikutukset vanhuusmenoihin' [Effects on old age spendings], in Karisto, A. (ed.) *Suuretikäluokat* [*The baby boomers*], Tampere: Vastapaino, 298-318.

Powell, J.L. (2006) *Social theory and aging,* Lanham, MD: Rowman & Littlefield.

Purhonen, S. (2007) *Sukupolvien ongelma: Tutkielmia sukupolven käsitteestä, sukupolvitietoisuudesta ja suurista ikäluokista* [*The problem of generations: Studying the concept of generations, generational consciousness, and the baby boomers*], Helsinki: Helsingin University.

Statistics Finland (2014) 'Live births by sex 1751–2013'. Retrieved from http://bit.ly/1tKspGF.

Valkonen, T. (1990) 'Väestönkehitys' [Demographic trends], in O. Riihinen (ed) *Suomi 2017* [*Finland 2017*], Helsinki: Keskinäinen henkivakuutusyhtiö Suomi & Gummerus, 227-46.

Yang, Y. (2011) 'Aging, cohort and methods', in R.H. Binstock and L.K. George (eds) *Handbook of aging and the social sciences*, London: Academic Press, Elsevier, 17-30.

Zacheus T. (2008) *Luonnonmukaisesta arkiliikunnasta liikunnan eriytymiseen. Suomalaiset liikuntasukupolvet ja liikuntakulttuurin muutos* [*From natural to differentiated exercise. Finnish sports generations and changes in sports cultures*]. Turku: Turku University.

FIVE

Gender in ageing Portugal: following the lives of men and women

Karin Wall and Sofia Aboim

Introduction

Seeking to account for the complex sequencing of states and events that span individual lives from birth to death, sociologists have looked primarily to historical and institutional factors. The degree to which and the manner in which societies are socially and spatially differentiated, the impact of institutions such as the educational system, the family, the labour market and the welfare system, and the historical circumstances which shape the opportunity structure and institutional fabric of society have all been seen as the most important mechanisms framing the regularities (or discontinuities) of lifecourses.

Within this approach, one would expect gender regimes[1] to be crucial in documenting the diversity of life paths. Strikingly, however, gender, along with education, class and ethnicity, has largely been put forward as just one more social variable, rather than as a major institution defining a fundamental social order that creates specific biographical contingencies. The gender perspective has played a marginal role in lifecourse research (Krüger and Lévy, 2001; Grunow, 2006; Widmer and Ritschard, 2009).

This is not to say that it is absent. Although male and female biographies are often seen to follow the same incorporated timetable of the life stages which provide individuals with continuity commitment, the frictions between gender, family and the employment system have been shown to impose constraints on female life trajectories both in the past and in the present (Hareven, 1982; Rossi, 1985; Hochschild and Machung, 1989; Moen, 2001; Pfau-Effinger, 2004). Gender has been especially highlighted as an important life marker in early and middle adulthood, in particular in the transition to parenthood and while children are young, and for both younger and older cohorts (Billari, 2001; Shanahan, 2000). Recent analyses of the connections between the gender divide and de-standardisation of the lifecourse in some European countries also point in the same direction (Lévy et al, 2013; Elzinga and Liefbroer, 2007; Grunow, 2006; Widmer and Ritschard, 2009). Men in the first part of adult life, both in younger and older cohorts, have fairly stable and linear occupational trajectories, while women's are more diverse. Contemporary female de-standardisation during adulthood stems mainly from moving between full-time, part-time and unpaid work in the family, suggesting that women are required to be more adaptable than men, and face greater uncertainty. In contrast, family trajectories emerge as less embedded in gender inequalities than occupational paths, at least for cohorts born in the 1950s (Widmer and Ritschard, 2009).

This chapter addresses three key questions on the gendering of lifecourses and ageing. The first is whether flexibility is also required of women in other life stages beyond early and middle adulthood. Drawing on a lifecourse approach that considers retirement and later life as a 'process that occurs over time' (Moen, 2004: 269), this chapter will examine male and female life paths at a new life stage, midcourse between the years of career-family building and old age. Described by some scholars as an emerging 'midcourse life stage' spanning the fifties, sixties and even seventies (Moen, 2004), it may be defined as the period when many midlife adults begin shifting gears and contemplating a new life stage (Arber and Ginn, 1995).

Retirement has generally been regarded as an institutionalised and homogeneous transition, increasingly possible for individuals as pensions became accessible in the second half of the 20th century. However, this new life path may not be available to everybody. Moreover, it reflects the disadvantages of earlier life stages, because especially those in poor health, those with physically demanding or precarious jobs, those without social insurance or those without children experience the midcourse years more as an accumulation of risk than a time of opportunity. The midcourse years may be increasingly a time of uncertain, uneven or unscripted transitions, strongly embedded not only in institutional constraints but also in the internal dynamics of individual lives (Kohli, 1986, 2007). A second key question, therefore, is whether – and how – outcomes in this life stage are shaped by experiences and resources acquired at earlier stages of the biography, such as incomplete families in childhood (Grundmann, 1992), prior job shifts (Mayer et al, 1999), long episodes of precarious employment or unemployment (Pienta et al, 1994), educational careers (Henz, 1996), or family processes and events such as separation/divorce or absence of union and family formation.

The third key question is whether the gendering of transitions to later life occurs in both work and family life and to what extent there is a dynamic interplay between work and family trajectories during this life stage. Lifecourse literature on earlier life stages suggests strong linkages between women's family and work trajectories. However, the gendered lifecourse in early and middle adulthood seems to emerge more clearly in employment and career-building than in the pacing and structure of family life. However, there is a clear imbalance in male and female life expectancy in contemporary Western societies, which impacts on the numbers of older men and women and thereby on individuals' chances of finding a partner, living in conjugality or simply remarrying after divorce or widowhood. One might therefore expect a gendering of family as well as of work trajectories in later life.

This chapter uses data from a recent national survey on the lifecourse in Portuguese society to explore the midcourse life trajectories of men and women born between 1935 and 1940. A southern European setting poses additional challenges for research. While all European Union (EU) member countries today provide social insurance and while retirement has become a common transition, the development of social protection over time may vary considerably. Gender equality in paid and unpaid work and evolving family forms and policies may produce different patterns of work–family balance within and across national contexts (Aboim, 2010). Attention will therefore be given to the embeddedness of these individuals' life paths in a specific social, economic and political environment.

The chapter begins by describing social and political developments over the last few decades in Portugal, before examining data and methods. It then presents a gendered view of family and work trajectories, and examines the impact of social factors such as education, employment and earlier life events. Finally it discusses the main findings and their relevance for understanding the gendered lifecourse in ageing societies.

Background to the research: the pre-baby boom generation in historical and social context

Portugal is a southern European country with a population of approximately 10 million, predominantly Catholic, ethnically homogeneous (only 4% are foreigners) and has been a member of the EU since 1986. It is a highly developed country, ranked 41 among United Nations countries, but with a gross domestic product per capita below the EU average and among the lowest in the 17 countries of the Eurozone. As in other southern European countries, demographic ageing of the population has increased dramatically over the last few decades, in a context of falling birth rates and higher average life expectancy (Almeida et al, 1998). Between 1960 and 2011 the ageing index increased from 27 to 128. For every 100 young persons below age 15 there are 128 individuals over age 65, and estimates point to an increase of 30% by 2044, which will drive the index up to 231 older persons for every 100 persons under 15. The difference in male and female life expectancy at birth (76 years for men and 82 years for women in 2011, up from 49 years for men and 54 years for women in 1940) has also led to a significant gender imbalance in older age groups: women represent 52% of the total population, but as much as 62% of the total population over age 75.

Portugal has followed a specific historical pathway over the last century. After the fall of the monarchy in 1910 and the short period of the first Republic (1910-28), it had a right-wing dictatorship which lasted nearly fifty years and which the April Revolution brought to an end in 1974. The transition to democracy was therefore late, in common with some other southern European countries, but the revolution made for more rapid change, in particular in the domain of work–family and gender equality policies.

The contrast in public policies and social protection before and after the revolution in 1974 is of particular importance. During the dictatorship, pro-traditional family policies promoted a male breadwinner model emphasising women's subordinate role and men's role as 'head of family' and provider (Wall, 2011). Gender inequality and female responsibility for homemaking were written into the Constitution, and the norm of female caregiving and large families, given the absence of family planning and high infant mortality rates, was promoted by the state, the Catholic Church and female organisations. Compulsory education was brought down to three years instead of five and there was no national health system. Social protection was also incipient. Family benefits (set up in 1942) were only available to legally married male providers employed in the industrial and services sectors, at a time when almost half the active population was working in a poverty-stricken rural society where celibacy rates were still high, with many births outside marriage and lone mother families. Other benefits, such as pensions, paid maternity leave or unemployment benefits, only began to be introduced in the late 1960s. Those born in the late 1930s and 1940s therefore grew up in a backward, highly gendered, endemically poor and politically repressive society: they went to school for a few years or not at all, in particular the girls, and began working early on as young children in order to contribute to family income; migration to the city and to European countries recovering from World War II emerged as the major opportunities during their early adulthood, but several years of military service and the colonial war, from the late 1950s onwards, also marked men's transition to adulthood.

Democratisation, decolonisation and the development of the welfare state were experienced by these individuals in middle adulthood. The transition to democracy opened up new possibilities in private and public life. Public policies rejected previous gender models and focused on the state's responsibility for assisting full-time working men and women, leading to a steady increase in parents' entitlements to paid leave and in publicly subsidised services promoting work–family balance. Female activity rates (with the majority of women working full-time) increased rapidly, from 18% in 1960 to 70% in 2010. The educational system, the national health service and universal social protection, both contributory and non-contributory, developed rapidly, as part of a trend towards convergence in relation to the EU average. However, the late expansion of the welfare state is strongly reflected in the retirement and socioeconomic status of older people today. Irregular and weak contribution records mean that the majority of pensioners have very low pensions, in particular in the non-contributory system, and that over-65s have the second-highest rate of poverty risk. Gender differences are also significant: in 2011 the average value of pensions for women represented only 59% of the average old age pension for men (299 Euros compared to 509 Euros for men). Survivor's pensions follow a different trend, with women's pensions having a higher average value (214 Euros) than men's (147 Euros). Age of retirement for this generation may vary considerably, depending on the sector and type of employment. In the public sector, a civil servant could retire at any age with 35 years of contributions and entitlement to a full pension, even if they could also decide to work to age 70. In the private sector, retirement was only allowed at age 65, regardless of the number of years of contributions, and workers could carry on working indefinitely. Since 2008, the two sectors have been brought into line: civil servants must have 37 years of contributions and cannot retire before age 65.

Data and methods

Data stem from a Portuguese survey conducted in 2010, which collected retrospective data on education, family and occupational status from birth to age 75. From this survey, this chapter analyses data on 500 Portuguese men and women born between 1935 and 1940.[2] These people represent a generation born before World War II and were raised in the heyday of the Salazar regime. They witnessed major social transformations and different lifecourse regimes. Drawing on Mayer's (2004) classification, they experienced a family economy model characterised by weak regulation of the chronological organisation of life in their infancy and youth. In the 1940s and 1950s, Portuguese society was not yet regulated by the industrial lifecourse regime usually associated with the first half of the 20th century. The industrial and Fordist models,[3] representing the peak of lifecourse standardisation in most European societies, developed when the generation under scrutiny had already reached adulthood. Conversely, their transition to later life occurred in the context of yet another important transformation, akin to what Mayer calls the post-Fordist lifecourse model, in which processes of de-standardisation of individual lifecourses gained relevance. However, more individualised lifecourses are not incompatible with a movement towards public regulation of age, which, as Kohli (1986) argues, implies an intensification of normative and legally based stages of life, particularly in earlier (infancy and youth) and later (old age) periods of life. In contrast with adulthood, later life would therefore be more standardised than in the past, due to the public regulation of ageing and the development of welfare policies targeted at older people.

The analysis is based on the idea that individuals' biographies are simultaneously defined by external constraints and opportunities available in a given historical context and by the ways in which they are able to act on them. So the lifecourse approach allows for considering both macro and micro variables in individuals' family and work trajectories (Elder et al, 2003). In accordance with recent developments in lifecourse analysis (Abbott, 2001; Sapin et al, 2007), the authors adopted an inductive methodological strategy that allows for monitoring the sequence of events in each individual's biography. However, historical processes still play a key role in so far as macro-social changes define the constraints on each generation of individuals. By mapping events in men's and women's lives between ages 55 and 75, the authors sought to examine how diversity and de-standardisation or standardisation affect the private and public spheres. This involved three methodological procedures. First, given the conceptual aims and criteria used for sample construction, data analysis was always carried out through a gender comparison.

Second, the diversity of individual trajectories was explored through hierarchical cluster analysis, which is a method that identifies similar cases and groups them together (Kaufman and Rousseeuw, 2005). This approach allows us to identify a wide range of individual biographies, even those applying to only a minority of individuals. In line with the criticisms of Levine (2000) and Wu (2000), we considered that optimal matching relies on certain aprioristic assumptions that may detract from sociological meaningfulness, are often based on random mathematical criteria for creating sequence distance and tend towards an average view of life trajectories, which does not render minority patterns (Levy and Widmer, 2013). In the authors' assessment, the characterisation of the lifecourse in the transition to later life would be misleading if the small numbers were ignored in favour of the trajectories of the majority. This procedure rendered clusters of two different trajectories. Family trajectories were reconstituted through the analysis of household composition by examining each individual's changes in living arrangements from ages 55 to 75, the conventional stage of transition to retirement and old age, which is statutorily set at age 65. By covering life events over a period ranging from ten years before and ten years after age 65, the authors anticipated to observe events associated with the transition to retirement and senior citizen status. Work trajectories from ages 55 to 75 were also analysed through a cluster analysis of the age of retirement as well as employment status and type of work contract observed in each year of individuals' biographies. To determine the number of types of trajectories, we computed several hierarchical clusters.[4] After examining solutions from four to eight clusters, we found the group solutions presented in the following section to be the best suited in terms of balance between within-cluster homogeneity, parsimony and clarity.

Third, alongside gender differentiation, the analytical approach to ageing processes also explored the impact of other variables. It examined the influence of education and the effect of earlier stages of the lifecourse on later life trajectories. These additional procedures allow for confirming the key hypothesis – the gender effect – and for identifying other factors that help to predict the likelihood of having a particular type of family or work trajectory in mid and later life.

The lifecourse in the transition to later life: gender and diversity

Family trajectories

The hierarchical cluster analysis carried out to identify the different family trajectories of men and women between ages 55 and 75 isolated seven types of trajectories (Table 5.1). For analytical purposes, the number of years that each individual has lived in a specific household arrangement, and the transitions from one living arrangement to another, were considered of major importance for reconstructing family trajectories (Table 5.2).

Findings show considerable biographical diversity and indicate that the late fifties and early sixties often entail key turning points in family life. Despite the

Table 5.1: Family trajectories between ages 55 and 75 by gender (%)

	Men	Women	Total
From couple with children to couple without children	44.3	35.7	39.2
Couple with children	32.8	18.3	24.2
Living alone from the late 50s	8.7	25.5	18.6
Kinship oriented	5.5	8.0	7.0
Couple with children with others	3.8	4.9	4.5
From couple to couple with others	4.4	3.0	3.6
Single parent	0.5	4.6	2.9
Total	100.0	100.0	100.0

Note: Cramer's V = 0.29; $p < 0.000$

Table 5.2: Family trajectories by average number of years spent in each living arrangement between ages 55 and 75

	Alone	Single parent	Couple without children	Couple with children	With kin	Single parent with others	Couple with children with others	Couple without children with others
From couple with children to couple without children	1.1	0.0	15.9	2.4	0.0	0.0	0.0	0.0
Couple with children	0.1	0.5	1.5	16.7	0.0	0.1	0.3	0.0
Living alone from the late 50s	13.9	1.6	2.2	1.5	0.0	0.0	0.0	0.0
Kinship oriented	0.2	1.0	0.1	0.5	4.9	4.2	0.2	0.1
Couple with children with others	0.0	0.0	0.2	1.8	0.0	0.0	16.0	1.3
From couple to couple with others	0.1	0.0	6.5	0.2	0.0	1.3	3.3	6.8
Single parent	0.2	18.3	0.0	0.9	0.0	0.0	0.0	0.0
Total	2.9	0.9	7.6	5.5	0.3	0.3	1.0	0.3
Eta^2 (p=0.000)	0.79	0.75	0.84	0.80	0.27	0.24	0.87	0.35

Note: Hierarchical clusters (Ward method) by the average number of years that individuals spent in each living arrangement. For example, in the single parent trajectory, respondents spent on average 18.3 years in this type of living arrangement.

conjugalisation of family arrangements, the reality of family trajectories in the midcourse stage of life is more complex than that imagined by traditional lifecycle conceptualisations positing an almost linear transition to an 'empty nest' family (Hill and Rogers, 1964). The seven patterns uncovered through cluster analysis show the diversity and, most importantly, the paramount importance of gender differentiation.

Four of the seven types portray conjugal forms of family, meaning that the couple (married or cohabiting, with or without children) is always the structuring unit of the household. However, the overall percentage of these conjugal types is quite different for men and women. While 85% of men lived in conjugal families between ages 55 and 75, the figure is only 62% for women. In two types of conjugal family trajectories, men are clearly predominant, even if there are significant differences between the four conjugal types of trajectory. The first pattern – 'from couple with children to couple without children' – corresponds to the typical empty nest type and describes couples who have been living alone (without children or other people at home) for nearly 16 years. This pattern represents the majority of the cases, covering almost half the men and over one third of women included in this type. The second largest pattern – 'couple with children' – covers nearly 33% of the men and less than 20% of the women. Depicting an even stronger gender difference, this type identifies situations in which individuals live with their partner and their children (on average 17 years). The two remaining conjugal types – 'couple with children with others' and 'from couple to couple with others' – represent a minority of cases and show less gender differentiation. Both types have in common the presence of other people in the household and are, for the most part, related to the formation of complex family arrangements in which close relatives are brought into the household. A good example of this transition is when a couple with children starts to live with others (kin or non-kin) at a certain point of the mid and later lifecourse. This trajectory is overrepresented among women and amounts to 5% of cases.

In sharp contrast with the stronger conjugalisation of male lifecourses, female family trajectories in mid and later life are quite often experienced alone, at least from the late fifties onwards, or as a single parent. While a quarter of women experience living alone for a long period in this life stage (14 years on average), the same family trajectory applies to only 9% of men. For women, this is in fact the second most common type of family trajectory, a finding that, although not unexpected, is nonetheless quite striking in terms of the gendered dynamics that it entails. With regard to single parenthood, this is almost exclusively a life path of women (5%). Lastly, the 'kinship oriented' pattern is also more common among women (8% as against 6% among men), thus revealing another non-conjugal family trajectory characterised by the transition between living with kin (without children at home) for a number of years and living as a single parent in a household shared with others for some periods of time.

In sum, family trajectories in the midcourse of life are, above all, marked by the influence of well-established gender regimes. As shown for other societies (for example Arber and Ginn, 1995; Levy and Widmer, 2013), family lifecourses are so strongly gendered that education and other structural variables have no significant effect on what appears to be a phenomenon that cuts across different social groups.

Instead, the midcourse of family life is affected by the earlier stages of family and conjugal life. Rather than education, class inequality or other structural constraints, the internal dynamics of the whole of the lifecourse are paramount. These findings can be interpreted in accordance with the central tenets of lifecourse theory. From this perspective, lifespan development is characterised by the view that new situations and life stages (such as the transition to later life) are shaped by earlier experiences, their meanings and consequences (Elder et al, 2003). A greater emphasis has been placed on the impact of childhood or youth on adult life. However, the results show the impact of the earlier stages of the lifecourse on the trajectories of mid and later life. As Elder states, the lifecourse is shaped not only by abrupt transitions but also by durable processes, and, in effect, the experiences of young adulthood (from ages 18 to 35) set out the conditions in which the transition to later life is experienced by men and women. The effect of earlier transitions and processes is key in so far as the family transitions of early adulthood have a clear impact on later family trajectories (Table 5.3).

The impact of early adulthood is strongly associated with non-conjugal family trajectories in mid and later life. From the variables chosen to analyse, relational and conjugal transitions are of great importance. Not having any durable relationships or not having entered conjugal life in early adulthood are experiences that are overrepresented among those who, in the midcourse of life, have family trajectories centred on kinship relations or who live alone. The impact is nonetheless gendered. The early experience of separation or divorce is much stronger for women. Among women who live as single parents, nearly 60% suffered conjugal breakdown or lived as a single parent before age 36. For men, the correlation is weaker, though the impact of having lived alone for a period of time between ages 18 and 35 is stronger than for women. Due to migration or other typical male experiences in this generation (Wall et al, 2013), men lived alone much more often than women. Almost half of the men who live alone in mid and later life experienced living alone in youth and early adulthood. Finally, childlessness is also a relevant biographical element in shaping later family trajectories. Independently of past conjugal experiences (marriage or cohabitation), individuals who never had children are more often found living alone or with kin (siblings or even more distant kin) in later life. Lifecourse effects are cumulative and, as the findings reveal, the non-conjugal trajectories of the midcourse of life are particularly associated with the experiences of early adulthood, thereby reproducing similar and correlated patterns over the lifespan of both men and women.

Work trajectories

The second key domain of the lifecourse is work. Between ages 55 and 75, individuals are expected to make the transition to retirement and leave the labour market, which is a vital marker signalling the passage to old age. On average, the sample of individuals aged between 70 and 75 today retired at age 62, with men

Table 5.3: Family trajectories between ages 55 to 75 and early life course family and household transitions, by gender (% of cases)

	Individuals without relationships (ages 18-35)		Individuals without conjugal life (ages 18-35)		Lived alone (ages 18-35)		Lived as single parent (ages 18-35)		Divorced/ separated (ages 18-35)		Childless individuals	
	M	F	M	F	M	F	M	F	M	F	M	F
From couple with children to couple without children			2.5	6.4	16.0	1.1	1.2	5.3	6.2	6.4		
Couple with children	1.7	4.2	6.7	6.3	11.7	2.1	1.7	6.3	5.0	6.3		
Living alone from the late 50s	6.3	7.5	12.5	19.4	43.8	4.5	12.5	10.4	6.3	10.4	25.0	18.2
Kinship oriented	10.0	23.8	30.0	28.6	20.0	9.5	10.0	9.5	10.0	9.5	25.5	27.6
Couple with children with others					57.1		14.3		14.3			
From couple to couple with others			37.5		37.5			12.5	37.5	12.5	14.5	14.5
Single parent				8.3		8.3		58.3		58.3		
Total	1.6	4.6	8.2	11.0	19.7	3.0	3.3	9.5	7.7	9.9	7.2	9.7
Cramer's V	*n.s.*	0.22**	0.28***	0.27***	0.31**	*n.s.*	*n.s.*	0.38***	0.25*	0.37***	0.29**	0.25**

Note: Statistical significance: $^{*}p < 0.05$; $^{**}p < 0.01$; $^{***}p < 0.001$

being in paid work for two more years (until age 63) than women, who left the labour market at age 62. Though statistically significant, the difference between men and women is not very pronounced. Gender differences are best captured through a more thorough examination of the work trajectories of individuals across the 20-year period under analysis. Hierarchical cluster procedures on three sets of variables (age of retirement, employment status and type of work contract) identified five relevant patterns (Tables 5.4 and 5.5), which show the diversity of life paths towards retirement.

Early retirement, a pattern in which individuals leave paid work before age 65, is quite significant, both for men and for women. Around 30% of all individuals retire before reaching 65. Precarious retirement is also common, with a few more men falling into this type (25 of men as against 21% of women). Although people retire around age 65, the key feature in this pattern is that they were precarious workers during the final years (11, on average) of their occupational trajectory, thereby increasing the likelihood of receiving low pensions. In Portugal, 88% of retirees

Table 5.4: Work trajectories between ages 55 to 75, by gender (%)

	Men	Women	Total
Early retirement	30.1	28.9	29.4
Precarious retirement	25.1	20.9	22.6
Standardised retirement	30.6	13.3	20.4
Housework/housewife	1.1	25.9	15.7
Prolonged work/postponed retirement	13.1	11.0	11.9
Total	100.0	100.0	100.0

Note: Cramer's V = 0.37; $p < 0.000$

Table 5.5: Age of retirement, employment status and type of contract between ages 55 and 75

	Age of retirement (average)	Unemployed	Worker	Unpaid worker/ housewife	Retired	On sick leave	Permanent contract	Precarious contract
Early retirement	**58.13**	0.66	3.18	0.03	13.34	1.55	1.56	1.05
Precarious retirement	65.68	0.04	10.97	0.19	8.07	0.25	0.07	10.38
Standardised retirement	65.37	0.02	11.10	0.00	7.99	0.03	11.09	0.08
Housework/housewife	–	0.00	0.13	17.39	1.84	0.00	0.06	0.07
Prolonged work/ postponed retirement	–	0.00	18.74	0.04	0.21	0.00	0.00	18.74
Total	62.84	0.21	7.93	2.78	7.69	0.52	2.75	4.91
Eta^2 (p=0.000)	0.460	0.045	0.854	0.930	0.570	0.056	0.840	0.931

Note: Hierarchical clusters (Ward method) by the average number of years that individuals spent in each work situation

(2.79 million in total) receive a pension of less than 600 Euros per month, and those without permanent contracts are frequently below this. The impoverished circumstances of many pensioners are thus often associated with precarious work situations in the midcourse of life. And, strikingly enough, precarious retirement is the second largest pattern drawn from the analysis. Moreover, the instability of retirement and the low income of older people can also be inferred from the high numbers of those who remain in the labour market after age 65 (12%). In this type of prolonged work trajectory, individuals, and again both men and women, never made the transition to retirement, as the status of post-retired worker was only found in five cases. In their vast majority, men and women in this group continue in the labour market, thus postponing their retirement and the potential access to a retirement pension. These trajectories of prolonged work are always (that is, in 100% of the cases) of precarious work without any stable contract. Since age 55, individuals have worked under precarious contracts, which can hinder their real possibilities of retirement and predict a future of impoverishment in later years. Finally, in these three patterns, gender differences are not very marked. Most importantly, it is relevant to underline how men and women of this generation share the same circumstances of job instability and precarious work trajectories in their transition to later life.

On the other hand, in contrast with the more precarious patterns previously described, significant gender differences come into view when comparing standardised retirement with the housewife trajectory. While the latter is exclusively (or almost exclusively) female and covers a quarter of women, standardised retirement is clearly overrepresented among men (31% of men as against 13% of women). In the standardised retirement pattern, individuals leave the labour market around age 65. Contrary to the previous cases, the work contract was permanent. This is perhaps the gender imbalance that best reflects the prevalence of a male breadwinner model among certain groups of the generation under investigation. However, one should note that the housewife model applies to only 25% of women, a figure that shows the relevance of female paid work in Portugal, even among older women. Although in their youth the normative gender regime encouraged the male breadwinner norm, difficult circumstances as a result of poverty, male migration or job instability often pushed women into paid work, in order to ensure financial survival. Indeed, the gendered figure of the housewife contrasts with the large numbers of women who were – or are still – in the labour market and very often in precarious circumstances.

The diversity of biographical journeys under changing historical conditions may account for some of the variations observed. However, the variety of work trajectories is not random. As in family trajectories, the effect of past events is extremely important. Once again, ageing processes, when seen through the lens of lifecourse theory, can be seen as processes affected by the cumulative effects of life experiences rather than as abrupt radical transitions. The impact of earlier work trajectories (between ages 18 and 35) on later work trajectories is clear (Table 5.6). Type of contract, employment status, several years spent in military

Table 5.6: Work trajectories between ages 55 and 75 and early lifecourse occupational situation, by gender (% of cases)

	Precarious contract (age 18–35)		Housewife (age 18–35)		Military service (age 18–35)		Non-dependent work (age 18–35)		Total number of years in paid work (average)	
	M	F	M	F	M	F	M	F	M	F
Standardised retirement	21.6	31.4	–	0.0	30.6	–	4.0	5.6	50.0	48.7
Prolonged work/postponed retirement	87.5	100.0	–	0.0	20.8	–	30.4	23.8	58.5	55.6
Early retirement	49.0	53.6	–	22.1	46.2	–	5.8	7.4	36.6	32.1
Precarious retirement	81.4	92.7	–	19.5	31.0	–	41.9	19.5	50.2	49.4
Housework/housewife	33.3	88.4	–	77.5	0.0	–	0.0	4.8	11.0	10.3
Total	54.1	69.4	–	26.6	33.7	–	17.6	10.6	46.7	34.9
Cramer's V	0.35***	0.31***	–	0.43***	0.20*	–	0.32***	0.13*	Eta^2 0.51***	Eta^2 0.65***

Note: Statistical significance: *p <0.05; **p < 0.01; ***p < 0.001

service (in the case of men) or as housewives (in the case of women) in early adulthood mark work trajectories significantly. The age of starting work and the total number of years spent in paid work are also of key importance for later work trajectories and, more specifically, the timing of retirement.

In Portugal, for this generation, the average age at which both men and women joined the labour market was around 14/15. In this respect there are no significant gender differences: 60% of boys and girls started working rather early in life, before age 15. As a result, a large number of men and women spent many years in paid work: around 50 years in the standardised retirement pattern and even longer in the prolonged worker type. Early retirement meant no less than 37 years of work for men and 32 for women. In sum, apart from housewives (who still worked for an average period of 10 years over the course of their lives), the vast majority of men and also women were paid workers for many years.

Most importantly, precarious work trajectories in the transition to later life are related to precarious and non-dependent work between ages 18 and 35. Among those who postponed their retirement and are still workers, even if already above age 70, 87.5% of men and 100.0% of women had temporary work contracts in their younger years. Similar percentages are applicable to all individuals who have had a precarious transition to retirement. Non-dependent work, which was very common among individuals from this Portuguese generation who often survived through small (or even very small) businesses and unstable self-employment, appears overrepresented in the precarious retirement and prolonged work types, especially among men. Also of importance to men from this generation is the impact of military service, which could last for several years, most of it spent fighting in Africa during the period of the colonial war (1961-74). Among men who retired early, over 40% spent some years in military service between ages 18 and 35. Among women, the housewife pattern is also replicated: for women who have mid and later life trajectories as housewives, 77% were at home in early adulthood. In sum, the impact of early life work trajectories is also the key to explaining the diversity found in the midcourse of life.

Unlike family trajectories, occupational situations and transitions in later life are affected by educational resources (Table 5.7), which are very low among individuals aged 70 to 75. Illiteracy and the incidence of only a few years' schooling were extremely high: 61% of women and 37% of men have less than four years' schooling; only 48% of men and 23% of women completed primary education (4 years' schooling); and the number of those who have more than just primary education is even lower, representing no more than 19% of men and 16% of women. In the latter group, those men and women who reached university level are a very small group: 13 men and 6 women. Against this background, primary education represented an important barrier. Those who failed to complete 4 years of schooling are clearly associated with prolonged work and precarious retirement. Conversely, individuals, both men and women, who have a work trajectory of standardised retirement are above average among those who went beyond primary education.

Table 5.7: Work trajectories 55-75 by education and gender (%)

	Illiterate or primary incomplete		Primary (4 years)		4+ years (secondary and university)		Total	
	M	F	M	F	M	F	M	F
Standardised retirement	26.1	9.5	31.1	14.9	34.7	21.9	30.8	13.3
Prolonged work/ postponed retirement	15.2	12.9	11.1	8.8	15.2	12.5	13.2	11.1
Early retirement	21.7	26.7	31.1	27.2	37.0	40.6	30.2	28.6
Precarious retirement	34.8	25.0	26.7	21.9	10.9	3.1	24.7	21.0
Housework/housewife	2.2	25.9	–	27.2	2.2	21.9	1.1	26.0
Total	100.0	100.0	100.0	100.0	100.0	100.0	100.0	100.0

Notes: Men-Cramer's V=0.20; $p<0.01$; Women-Cramer's V=0.19; $p<0.01$

Conclusions

The aim of this chapter was to explore the gendering of the lifecourse and how it shapes work and family trajectories in the midcourse of life, between ages 55 and 75. This issue was examined in the context of other relevant factors, such as historical and social coordinates and differences in earlier life transitions. Four main conclusions can be inferred from the data.

First, gender was found to be a consistent and strong predictor of the mid and later lifecourse. Whether one analyses family or work trajectories in the transition to later life, gender differences are of great importance and show that women are required to be more flexible and suffered greater uncertainty than men in this life stage. However, family trajectories emerge as more embedded in gender inequalities than occupational trajectories. Men are mostly associated with conjugal trajectories, while a large number of women live in non-conjugal arrangements (for example living alone, with kin and non-kin, or as a single parent). In the sphere of work, the main contrast is between the standardised male retirement trajectory and the female housewife trajectory. However, both men and women are to be found, and in similar numbers, in the more precarious work trajectories associated with job instability, poverty and difficulty in retiring. In this generation, many people experienced the midcourse stage of life carrying the cumulative weight of de-standardised work trajectories. Only a minority reproduced the normative pattern of their time.

Second, there is, in this generation – which lived in-between and across a variety of lifecourse regimes and joined the labour market before there was strong public regulation of work and age – a plurality of trajectories. In the domain of paid work, despite the increase in the standardisation of labour regimes, there is a fair diversity of transitions in mid and later life towards retirement. Historical context is crucial in explaining this diversity. Indeed, the pre-baby boom generation in Portugal was tightly constrained by harsh circumstances, low levels of education, and an incipient welfare state. As a result, the lower variation that some would expect to see in the transition to later life, which has been the object of increased public regulation as argued by Kohli (1986), does not apply to older generations, nor does it account for the diversity of work and family trajectories in Portuguese society in the transition to later life.

Third, alongside the impact of historical contexts and gender differences on later life trajectories, earlier stages of the lifecourse are also key to explaining the range of diversity found in the midcourse of life, both in work and family. In contrast, education is only significant for work trajectories, showing the paramount impact of social inequalities in this sphere of life. Family trajectories are more independent of structural variables and, instead, reflect the greater cumulative impact of earlier life experiences. In this age group, as well as in the two younger generations in the survey, family life emerges as a more autonomous and complex social process. This does not mean that social inequalities are not a shaping factor of family life. However, the dynamics of the lifecourse and individual agency seem to override a linear connection between structural variables and the social construction of families over time.

Finally, against the authors' initial expectations, there is no significant connection between family and work trajectories. Interestingly, family and work lifecourse regimes seem to be independent of each other. Rather than a feature of the transition to later life, similar conclusions apply to earlier stages of the lifecourse (for example young adulthood). The independent dynamics of work and family trajectories are not only a characteristic of the older pre-baby boom generation but, surprisingly, identical results are replicated in the analysis of the younger generations in the original sample. In spite of the way in which work and family are interrelated in people's lives, they seem to pertain to independent lifecourse regimes, with their own particular dynamics and forms of regulation. In the transition to later life, this separation is neat, which suggests that processes of ageing should be approached from various perspectives and through the analysis of different domains of life.

Notes

[1] Gender regime is a concept used to describe the key dimensions (employment, unpaid work, gender policies or culture) of gender relations or arrangements, which predominate in a specific society (for example Pfau-Effinger, 2004).

[2] The sample corresponds to a stratified probability sample of Portuguese men and women residing in the country (response rate equals 60% and overall sampling error corresponds to ±2.5%; $\alpha = 0.05$). Foreigners and individuals with mental or physical disabilities were defined as not eligible. Interviews were conducted by a group of trained interviewers in the respondents' household and following the PAPI method (Paper And Pencil Interviewing).

[3] According to Kohli (2007: 258), 'In life course terms, the model consisted in a "normal work biography" of continuous full-time employment and long job tenure for most of the male population – with most women gravitating around a male breadwinner with

various forms of limited engagement in paid work or none at all – and in a "normal family biography" set in motion by early and almost universal marriage and childbearing.'

[4] The cluster analysis was carried out in two stages: we first conducted a hierarchical analysis (using the Ward method; Batagelj, 1988) and then used the 'quick cluster' to optimise the classification obtained earlier. This statistical analysis is in line with the research methodology, which does not limit at the outset the number of types, allowing room for new combinations of types of answer.

References

Abbott, A. (2001) *Time matters: On theory and method*, Chicago: University of Chicago Press.

Aboim, S. (2010) 'Gender cultures and the division of labour in contemporary Europe: A cross-national perspective', *The Sociological Review*, 58, 2, 171-96.

Almeida, A.N., Guerreiro, M.D., Lobo, C., Torres, A. and Wall, K. (1998) 'Relações familiares: Mudança e diversidade' ['Family relations: Change and diversity'], in J.M.L. Viegas and A.F. da Costa (eds) *Portugal, que modernidade?* [*Portugal, which modernity?*], Oeiras: Celta, 45-78.

Arber, S. and Ginn, J. (eds) (1995) *Connecting gender and ageing: A sociological approach*, Buckingham: Open University Press.

Batagelj, V. (1988) 'Generalized Ward and related clustering problems', in H.H. Bock (ed) *Classification and Related Methods of Data Analysis*. Amsterdam: North-Holland, 67–74.

Billari, F.C. (2001) 'The analysis of early life courses: Complex description of the transition to adulthood', *Journal of Population Research*, 18, 119-42.

Elder, G.H., Johnson, M.K and Crosnoe, R. (2003) 'The emergence and development of the life course', in J.T. Mortimer and M.J. Shanahan (eds) *Handbook of the life course*, New York: Kluwer, 3-18.

Elzinga, C.H. and Liefbroer, A.C. (2007) 'De-standardization of family-life trajectories of young adults: A cross-national comparison using sequence analysis', *European Journal of Population*, 23, 225-50.

Grundmann, M. (1992) *Family structure and life course. Historical and social conditions of individual development*, Frankfurt am Main/New York: Campus Verlag.

Grunow, D. (2006) *Convergence, persistence and diversity in male and female careers – Does context matter in an era of globalization? A comparison of gendered employment mobility patterns in West Germany and Denmark*, Opladen: Barbara Budrich Publishers.

Hareven, T. (1982) *Family time and industrial time*. Cambridge: Cambridge University Press.

Henz, U. (1996). *Intergenerationale Mobilität. Methodische und empirische Untersuchungen* [*Intergenerational mobility. Methodological and empirical analyses*], Berlin: Max-Planck-Institut für Bildungsforschung.

Hill, R. and Rogers, R. (1964) 'The developmental approach', in H.T. Christensen (ed) *Handbook of marriage and the family*, Chicago: Rand McNally, 171-211.

Hochschild, A. and Machung, A. (1989) *The second shift: Working parents and the revolution at home*, New York: Viking Penguin.

Kaufman, L. and Rousseeuw, P.J. (2005) *Findings groups in data: An introduction to cluster analysis*, Hoboken: Wiley.

Kohli, M. (1986) 'Social organization and subjective construction of the life course', in A.B. Sorensen, F.E. Weinert and L.R. Sherrod (eds) *Human development and the life course: Multidisciplinary perspectives*, Hillsdale: Erlbaum, 271-92.

Kohli, M. (2007) 'The institutionalization of the life course: Looking back to look ahead', *Research in Human Development*, 4, 3-4, 253-71.

Krüger, H. and Lévy, R. (2001) 'Linking life courses, work and the family: Theorizing a not so visible nexus between women and men', *Canadian Journal of Sociology*, 26, 2, 145-66.

Levine, J. H. (2000) 'But what have you done for us lately? Commentary on Abbott and Tsay', *Sociological Methods and Research*, 29, 1, 34-40.

Levy, R. and Widmer, E.D. (eds) (2013) *Gendered life courses*, Berlin: LIT Verlag.

Mayer, K.U. (2004) 'Whose lives? How history, societies, and institutions define and shape life courses', *Research in Human Development*, 1, 3, 161-87.

Mayer, K.U., Diewald, M. and Solga, H. (1999) 'Transitions to post-communism in East Germany: Worklife mobility of women and men between 1989 and 1993', *Acta Sociologica*, 42, 1, 35-53.

Moen, P. (2001) 'The gendered life course', in L. George and R.H. Binstock (eds) *Handbook of aging and the social sciences*, San Diego, CA: Academic Press, 179-96.

Moen, P. (2004) 'Midcourse: Navigating retirement and a new life stage', in J.T. Mortimer and M.J. Shanahan (eds) *Handbook of the life course*, New York: Plenum Press, 267-91.

Pfau-Effinger, B. (2004) *Development of culture, welfare states and women's employment in Europe*, Ashgate: Aldershot.

Pienta, A.M., Burr, J.A. and Mutchler, J.E. (1994) 'Women's labor-force participation in later life: The effects of early work and family experiences', *Journals of Gerontology*, 49, 5, 231-9.

Rossi, A.S. (ed) (1985) *Gender and the life course*. New York: Aldine.

Sapin, M., Spinie, D. and Widmer, E. (2007) *Les parcours de vie. De l'adolescence au grand âge* [*The life-courses. From youth to old age*], Lausanne: Presses Polytechniques et Universitaires Romandes.

Shanahan, M.J. (2000) 'Pathways to adulthood in changing societies: Variability and mechanisms in life course perspective', *Annual Review of Sociology*, 26, 667-92.

Wall, K. (2011) 'A intervenção do Estado: Políticas públicas de família' ['On state intervention: Public family policies'], in A.N. Almeida (eds) *História da vida privada em Portugal: os nossos dias* [*The history of private life in Portugal: Our days*], Lisboa: Círculo de Leitores, 340-74.

Wall, K., Aboim, S., Ramos, V. and Nunes, C. (2013) 'Geographical mobility and family life: Comparing generations from a life course perspective', *Comparative Population Studies – Zeitschrift für Bevölkerungswissenschaft*, 38, 2, 341-70.

Widmer, E. and Ritschard, G. (2009) 'The de-standardization of the life course: Are men and women unequal?', *Advances in Life Course Research*, 14, 1-2, 29-39.

Wu, L.L. (2000) 'Some comments on Sequence analysis and optimal matching methods in sociology: review and prospect', *Sociological Methods and Research*, 29, 1, 41-64.

SIX

Socioeconomic status in ageing Poland: a question of cumulative advantages and disadvantages

Konrad Turek, Jolanta Perek-Białas and Justyna Stypińska

Introduction

In this chapter, we focus on the development of intra-cohort and inter-cohort socioeconomic inequalities in an ageing society in a period of deep social change. Based on the Polish experience, we trace lifecourse patterns in times of system transition that change individuals' aspirations, opportunities and behaviours, with an attempt to recognise the mechanisms that drive the 'within' and 'between' cohort inequalities observed today. The main goal is to analyse whether the mechanism of cumulative advantages and disadvantages (CAD) is an important factor in shaping diversity in societies of post-transitional countries, as it is in the more stable western countries.

In modern societies, diversity and socioeconomic inequalities are very often found to be greater in older cohorts than in younger cohorts (Morgan and Kunkel, 2007; Lynch and Brown, 2011). According to the theory of CAD, this situation results from the differentiation of lifecourses as people age (Dannefer, 1987; O'Rand, 1996; Ferraro et al, 2009). An initial socioeconomic advantage of an individual, expressed in possession or access to certain resources and capitals, is cumulative throughout the lifecourse and results in higher advantages in their later life. On the other hand, the disadvantaged position in the early stages of life will eventually result in a lower socioeconomic status, usually measured by education, income and occupation. Consequently, according to CAD, the intra-cohort inequalities should increase with time, as the cohort grows older. Regarding the ageing population, such an assumption has significant meaning as the life expectancy and the share of older age groups increase, as well as their impact and role in society. However, CAD assumes a stability of the mechanism which work for advantage or disadvantage of individuals over the lifecourse, which may not necessarily be the case during significant changes in societies.

The between-cohort inequalities are best explained by the lifecourse approach, as a combination of the effects of ageing, life stage and historical time (Elder, 1994). An individual's ageing entails biological and mental changes, while different life stages are associated with different opportunities and social expectations.

Historical time, in which specific cohorts proceed through their particular life stages, sets similar conditions and experiences for a majority of individuals. People construct their lifecourses through choices and actions within the opportunities and constraints of history and social circumstances (Grenier, 2012). The changing context is a major reason why cohorts age differentially and may result in inequalities between them (Dannefer and Kelly-Moore, 2009).

System transition in all post-socialist countries caused deep and rapid changes of social structures and social relations (Domański, 1996, 2000; Słomczyński, 2002; Titma and Tuma, 2005). The economy evolved from state-owned to free market, changing the characteristics of the labour market. The macro-level system transition also reshaped individual lifecourses, aspirations, barriers and opportunities. Hitherto, advantages and disadvantages gained or lost their meaning as the rules of the game changed. The transitions caused a growth of social diversity and an increase of inequalities within and between cohorts (Svejnar, 1999; Pollert, 2003; Heyns, 2005; Słomczyński and Janicka, 2008; Plessz, 2009). The greatest declines in income and quality of life have been observed in older groups, who lost most of the support previously offered by the state, and who were unable to compete effectively with younger cohorts in the new economic reality (for example Titma and Tuma, 2005, for the states of the former Soviet Union; Svejnar, 1999, and Plessz, 2009, for Central and Eastern European countries; Diewald et al, 2006, for East Germany). Thus, the main advantage of young adults was simply their fortunate historical timing, as they were at a favourable stage of life to seize new opportunities.

The transition from socialism in Central and Eastern European (CEE) countries had meaningful consequences in population ageing (Gavrilova and Gavrilov, 2009; Hoff, 2011). In Poland, the fertility rate has dropped dramatically since the 1990s: from about 2.0 in 1990, to 1.4 in 2010 (Eurostat, 2012). This is mainly the result of changes in lifestyles and family models (Frątczak, 2011) and the increase of time spent in education, especially among women. At the same time, life expectancy in Poland increased: in 1990 it equalled 66 years for men and 75 for women; in 2010 it was 72 years and 81 years respectively (Eurostat, 2011). The integration of Poland into the European Union (EU) facilitated emigration, which became a mass phenomenon among younger cohorts after 2004. All of these processes resulted in rapid population ageing, turning Poland, as well as other post-socialist countries, into the fastest-ageing societies of Europe.

The primary research questions of this chapter are: (a) how did the lifecourse patterns change during system transition and what were the consequences for inequalities between cohorts; (b) what was the impact of system transition on the mechanism of CAD and how did it influence the inequalities within ageing cohorts?

Theoretical perspective

Lifecourse outcomes at population level

The lifecourse perspective focuses primarily on continuity and change across the lifespan of individuals, analysing stages of development and social roles with linkage to historical time and social structures (Grenier, 2012). This extensive theoretical framework offers two general explanations of lifecourse outcomes: a personological one and a sociological one (Dannefer and Uhlenberg, 1999; Dannefer and Setterson, 2010). The former approach focuses on explaining lifecourse outcomes based on individual characteristics, age-related changes, earlier lifecourse experiences and agency or choice (George, 1993; Elder et al, 2003). The latter approach assumes that trajectories do not develop in a vacuum, but are socially and institutionally generated (Kohli, 2007; Ferraro et al, 2009). The life of individuals is embedded in, and shaped by, historical time and experiences (Elder, 1994; Grenier, 2012).

The following analysis fits into the approach of sociological explanation of population outcomes of lifecourses (Dannefer and Kelly-Moore, 2009). The causes of socioeconomic inequalities will be sought in the change of social structures and relations during the transition from socialism. A useful tool for tracing changing lifecourses is the concept of *lifecourse regimes* (LCRs) (DiPrete, 2002; Leisering, 2003; Mayer, 2005; Hofacker, 2010). LCRs describe the typical patterns of sequences and the character and timing of various life phases, particularly referring to patterns of education and training, labour force entry, career progression, mobility and retirement. In other words, LCRs refer to the collective patterning of individual lifecourse structures in a population and sketches the paths of transitions.

Socioeconomic inequalities within and between cohorts

O'Rand (2006) states that stratification remains at the heart of lifecourse studies, which focus on the interplay of ageing, life stages and historical circumstances. The advanced parts of the lifecycle are characterised by an increased heterogeneity, including biological, psychological, social and economic characteristics (Lynch and Brown, 2011).

We can distinguish four general concepts explaining the trajectories of economic status across the life of individuals (Crystal and Waehrer, 1996). The first is the hypothesis of levelling, which focuses on the shift of principal income sources from employment to pensions (Fuchs, 1984); it assumes that the change is particularly beneficial to lower-income individuals and leads to an equalisation of income distribution. The second concept of divergence and convergence predicts similar changes: inequalities grow within the lifecourse, but only to a certain point in time, when they decrease again (Ross and Wu, 1996; Prus, 2007). The third model of status maintenance assumes that the effect of retirement on socioeconomic status is limited and that individuals maintain their relative positions (Henretta and Campbell, 1976). However, some more sophisticated longitudinal analysis has shown that individual economic status is not necessarily maintained throughout the lifespans of individuals, because significant changes in relative position occur relatively often (Crystal and Waehrer, 1996). The fourth approach is the concept of CAD, and its modification in a form of cumulative inequalities.

The theory of cumulative advantages and disadvantages (CAD)

The main idea of CAD is relatively simple and can be illustrated by colloquial sayings: 'success breeds success' and 'the rich get richer; the poor get poorer' (DiPrete and Eirich, 2006). It predicts an increase in the overall level of economic inequality within a cohort as it ages, because of different pathways of relative advantage or disadvantage. On the one hand, early advantages reduce the risk of exposure to adverse transitions and increase the access to beneficial opportunity structures. Early disadvantages, on the other hand, may increase the likelihood of persistent disadvantage (Crystal and Shea, 1990). For instance, low socioeconomic position in childhood is more likely to commence a chain of adverse transitions and risks, such as poor educational attainment, lower occupational position and income, and poorer health (Hayward and Gorman, 2004).

According to Dannefer (2003), CAD is not a characteristic of individuals, but of populations or collectives, resulting in a 'tendency for inter-individual divergence in a given characteristic (for example money, health, or status) with the passage of time'. He proposes to put emphasis on general stratification mechanisms, which differentiate the situation of individuals within a certain cohort, in contrast to what had so far been articulated by most demographic researches, to measure inter-cohort differences, and thus contributing to a false assumption of the homogeneity of the inter-cohort experiences and outcomes (Dannefer, 1987). Vast evidence of the mechanism of CAD exists in research on inequalities in later life, for example in health (Prus, 2007; Willson et al, 2007), cognitive functioning (O'Rand, 2006) and income (Crystal and Waehrer, 1996; Ferraro et al, 2009).

An important modification to CAD theory was offered by Ferraro et al. (2009). Their theory of cumulative inequality connects macro- and micro-sociological levels of analyses. It states that the basic assumption of path-dependent CAD is too simplistic, because a disadvantage does not simply produce another disadvantage – it only increases exposure to risks. The outcome, however, still depends on the resource mobilisation and human agency (Ferraro et al, 2009). Additionally, people may simultaneously hold positions of advantage and disadvantage across different domains.

Lifecourse, CAD and social change

Works by Dannefer and colleagues (Dannefer and Kelly-Moore, 2009; Dannefer and Setterson, 2010) consider the impact of social structures on patterns of ageing and the mechanisms of CAD. These mechanisms depend on the stability of social structures, institutions, social relations and social norms. In this chapter, we claim that one of the problematic features of the idea of CAD is the assumed stability of mechanism of differentiation shaping lifecourses. The socioeconomic changes, which occurred in Eastern Europe, often led to dramatic modification of individuals' trajectories: new conditions may encourage or force an individual to take a different path, whereas previous life opportunities and barriers may no longer exist. Therefore, not only do the patterns of CAD have to be taken into account, but also the nature of advantages and disadvantages themselves, since some of them can lose impact and some may gain impact in the new social reality. It is also possible that the nature of particular assets may fully reverse from being advantageous to becoming disadvantageous.

Socioeconomic differences in today's Poland

The most conspicuous dimension of 'between' inequalities in Poland is the education level (Figure 6.1). Along with subsequent age groups, the size of the population with higher education decreases, while the share with lower education grows.

The Gini coefficient amounted in 2010 to 0.34 and was higher than the EU average. However, for the households of pensioners it was much lower and equalled only 0.25 (Panek, 2011; Główny Urząd Statystyczny, 2012). Significant differences in income level were due to gender and education levels (Figure 6.2).

Figure 6.1: Level of education in 2011 in Poland, by age

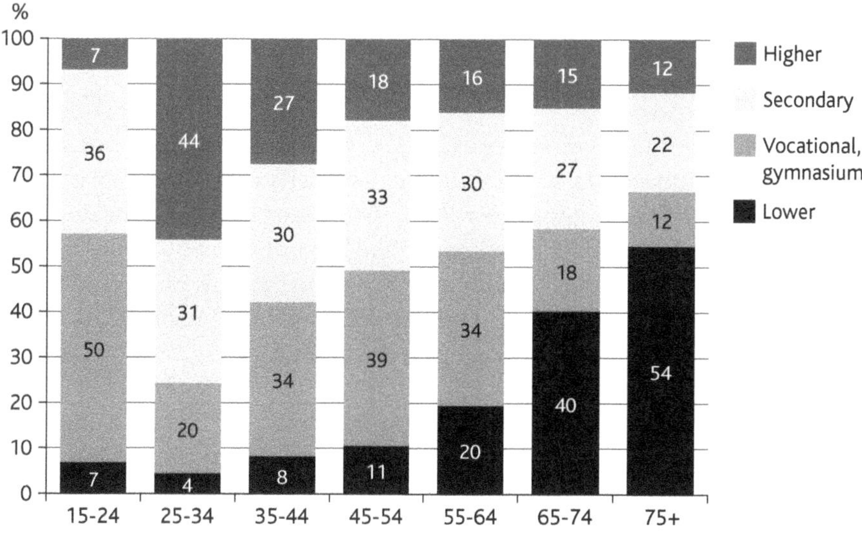

Source: Social Diagnosis, 2011

Figure 6.2: Earnings, by gender and educational level around 2011 in Poland

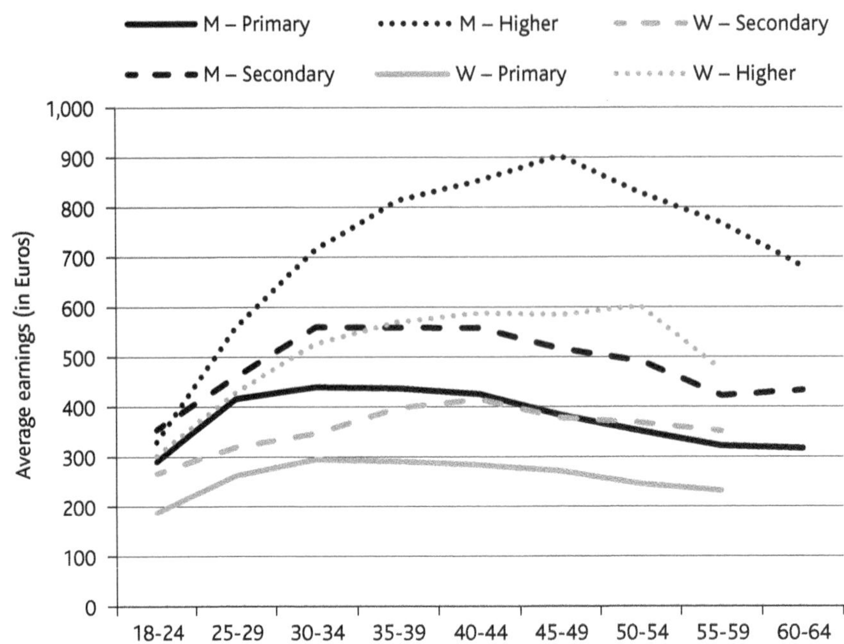

Notes: 'm' = 'men', 'w' = 'women'
Levels of education: primary – ISCED level 0–2; secondary – ISCED 3–4; higher – ISCED 5–6
Exchange rate: 1 Euro = 4.15 PLN

Source: Bilans Kapitału Ludzkiego, 2010-12

One aim of this chapter is to try to understand what kind of mechanisms drove the inequalities between cohorts in Poland, as well as those within cohorts. We will focus on the interaction of two mechanisms: system transition and CAD.

Transition of lifecourse regimes in Poland

The year 1989 was the beginning of a deep transformation in Poland, as well as in other CEE countries. Democracy and the free market economy replaced the socialist political and economic system. The 1990s was a period of turbulence and profound changes in the political, economic and labour market situation. Among the most urgent problems of transition were system reforms and privatisation of public enterprises, galloping inflation, growing unemployment (the socialist regime had no official unemployment), pauperisation of some groups and growth of social inequalities (Gilejko, 2005). Becoming a member of the EU in 2004 was a symbolic end of transition and a start of the development of modern democracy. The labour market improved, unemployment began to decrease and economic growth occurred (Figure 6.3).

Historical turbulence in Poland profoundly influenced the frameworks of people's lives. Opportunities, barriers and aspirations of people changed,

Figure 6.3: Unemployment rate and enrolment rate in higher education in Poland, 1990-2013

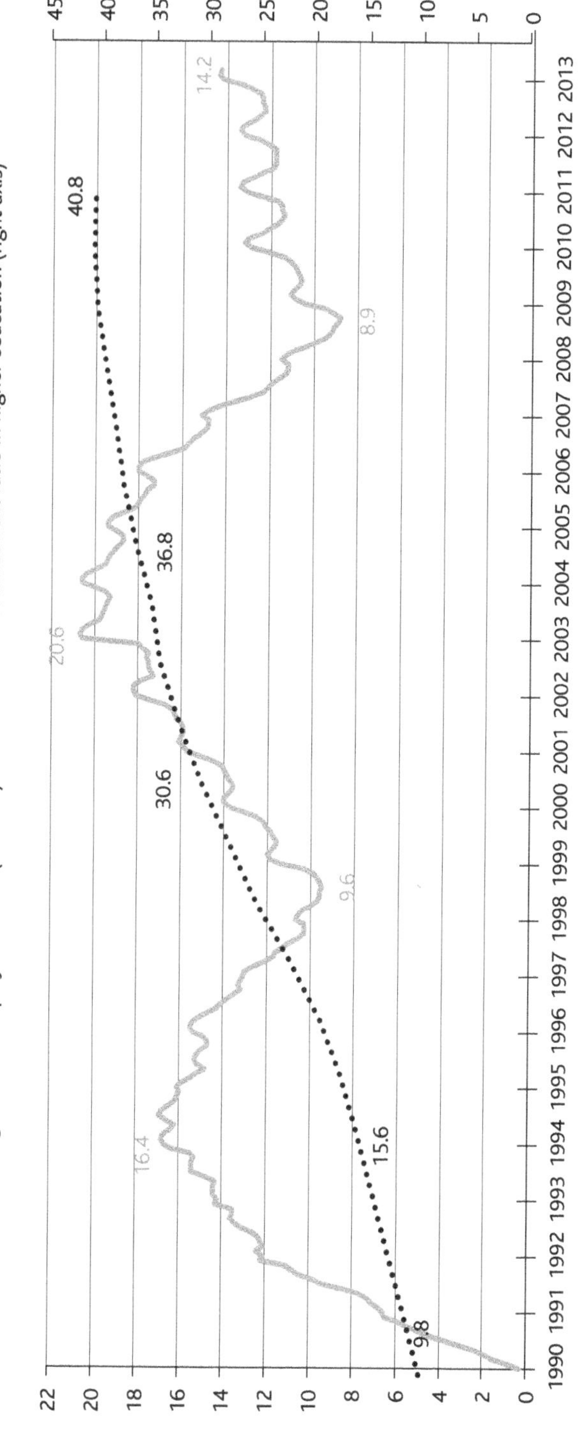

Note: Percentage of population aged 18–24 enrolled in higher education

Source: Główny Urząd Statystyczny, 2012

modifying the standard lifecourses – the typical sequences, as well as the character and timing of life phases. When aggregated, they composed into different LCRs. In order to trace the changes of life trajectories that accompanied the system transition, three separate LCRs can be specified:

- *state socialism regime* – characterised by state-controlled political and economic system, low competition in the labour market, no official unemployment, limited personal freedom and human rights, low standards of living and low inequalities;
- *system transition regime* – characterised by vast and rapid reforms towards free market economy and democracy, high unemployment and high competition in the labour market, growing inequalities;
- *post-transition regime* – the last period, which symbolically started with the accession of Poland to the EU, is relatively short and additionally coincides with the current economic crisis.

Table 6.1 summarises the main characteristics of the three LCRs in the framework of the classical tripartite model of life stages: early-life education, adulthood and work, old age and retirement (Kohli, 1986).

Early-life education

People who attended schools in the 1960s, 1970s or 1980s had quite different possibilities and aspirations than the youth of the 1990s and 2000s. The older cohorts did not have such an easy access to higher education, and socialism did not necessarily favour this type of education. On the contrary, more accessible and with greater prospects was vocational education, which became marginalised in the 1990s. Observable changes in education levels began during the transition period. While there were about 0.4 million university students in 1990, the number reached 2 million at the beginning of the 21st century (Główny Urząd Statystyczny, 2012). In late transition and early post-transition years, education was considered to be a 'passport' to better-paid jobs and a way of securing one's chances in later life (Niezgoda, 2011). Recently, not just a higher education but also the quality of that education is considered to increase one's chances in later life.

Adulthood and work

During socialism, entering the labour market was supported and secured by the state and the working career was predictable until retirement. People had stable jobs and often worked in the same company for their whole life. Employment rates were high, as officially unemployment did not exist. Education strongly correlated with occupation, but not necessarily with income (Domański et al, 2007). Since the introduction of the market economy, career paths have been less predictable and unemployment has become part of the lifecourse of many people,

Table 6.1: Characteristics of life course regimes in Poland before and after the system transition

Lifecourse sequences	State socialism regime (before 1989)	System transition regime (1989-2004)	Post-transition regime (after 2004)
Early-life education			
Education	Lower access to universities; the labour market did not necessarily prefer higher education; vocational and technical training offered greater prospects	Educational boom of the 1990s; increased importance of tertiary education	Increase of the importance of the quality of education, skills and competences
Adulthood and work			
Transition from education to work	Earlier labour market entry, supported by the state	Difficulties in getting first job; high competition in employment – increasing number of young and well educated; delaying labour market entry	Difficulties in getting first job; high unemployment of the youth; internationalization of career patterns – popular work migrations of the youth
Work situation stability	Stable work situation, low risk of unemployment – work secured by the state	Increased risk of unemployment; problem of long- term unemployment (e.g. older generations); high competition at the labour market	As in system transition regime
Career paths	Predictable and stable work careers; long work status; low mobility between companies and occupations	Mobility increased in terms of changes of jobs and firms, however changes of occupations relatively rare	Increasing mobility; more flexible work approach; education does not have to be matched with job, labour migrations
Earnings life-trajectories	Wages increasing over the life, due to seniority rule (public sector);	Earning dependent on occupation and job position; seniority still rules in public sector;	As in system transition regime
Family patterns	Traditional models of family prevailing, early marriage; relatively high fertility; early parenting; stronger family relations, rare divorces	Fertility decline, weakening of family ties, increasing mobility of young people	Delayed marriage; delayed parenting , fewer children, migrations, weaker family ties, alternative models of families, increasing number of divorces

(continued)

Table 6.1: Characteristics of lifecourse regimes in Poland before and after the system transition (continued)

Lifecourse sequences	State socialism regime (before 1989)	System transition regime (1989-2004)	Post-transition regime (after 2004)
Old-age and retirement			
Transition from employment to retirement	Early retirements options for many occupational groups; state-guaranteed pension benefits, based on earnings from the last 10 years of work; relatively high replacement rate	Early retirement options; policy of pushing older workers out to retirement	Since 2013 eligible retirement age gradually increased up to 67 for both men and women; limited early retirement options
Life on retirement	Shorter lifespan; more homogeneity between pensioners, low differences in pensions benefits; rather passive life style	Increasing longevity, but the life on retirement is inactive and not financially independent; health problems quite common; increasing income inequalities in old age	Continuous increasing in longevity and a slight improvement in health situation; emergence of active ageing programs – more active life style
Organisation of elder care	Within family, the small role of state	Family is the main supplier, the role of state has even decreased and others actors are lacking	Families have to deal with reconciliation of work and care
Cross-sequential dimensions			
Gender relations	Gender-related lifecourse; relatively high women employment rate; sufficient child care facilities, easy return to work after maternity leave; patriarchal family structures, possibilities for early retirement for many women; higher gender gap in earnings	The women's employment rates plummeted, problems with continuation of work after maternity, rising educational aspirations, increase in female entrepreneurship; movement towards more equality in public and private spheres; decrease of gender gap in earnings	Employment rates increasing, gender equality higher on political agenda, increasing role of fathers in childcare, more females with university degrees than males; decrease of gender gap in earnings
Human agency in choice making	Limited personal freedom of choice; authoritarian political and ideological control	Democratic standards of personal freedom	Democratic standards of personal freedom
Lifespan	Longer working lives; less time on retirement; shorter lifespan	Shorter working lives; longer retirement; increasing longevity	For current cohorts shorter working lives, for future longer working lives, longer retirement due to longevity

despite their education level. Long-term unemployment became an important problem, especially for older age groups (Szatur-Jaworska, 2000).

After joining the EU, the situation in the labour market improved, but graduates had difficulties in acquiring their first jobs. The result was high emigration rates among young people, as even a university degree did not guarantee employment. Longer education and difficulties in finding jobs among the youth caused an increase in the average age of entry to the labour market – up to 23 years old in 2009 (Kancelaria Prezesa Rady Ministrów, 2010). Labour market mobility increased in terms of changes to jobs and firms, however changes in occupations were – and still are – relatively rare.

During socialism, earnings had been increasing over the lifespan, mainly as an effect of the seniority rule existing in the public sector. After transition, income trajectories differentiated. Instead of tenure, occupation and position in the job became much more important (Słomczyński and Janicka, 2008).

During the time of socialism, Polish families were of a more traditional character, in terms of earlier marriages, higher levels of fertility and fewer divorces. After transition, family patterns changed considerably, and the traditional model gave way to cohabitation, patchwork, fragmented or same-sex families, while increased mobility weakened family ties (Slany, 2002; Frątczak, 2011). One of the indicators showing this change is the increasing rate of divorces among Poles – from 0.5 in the 1960s to 1.7 in 2011 (Eurostat, 2012).

Old age and retirement

During socialism, the transition from employment to retirement was smooth and predictable. Early retirement options existed for many occupational groups. Due to seniority rules, the replacement rate was relatively high. The group of pensioners was rather homogeneous in terms of income and standards of living. The lifestyle was also similar, passive and mostly limited to family life and their household.

In the first years of transformation, the policy of pushing older people out of the labour market was treated by policy makers as a remedy for high unemployment, especially among young people (Ruzik-Sierdzińska et al, 2013). As a result, at the end of the 1990s, the employment rate of older workers and the labour market exit age were among the lowest in Europe. Since then, the government has slowly introduced reforms to stop this trend: the pension reform in 1999, limitation of early retirement options in 2008-09, and a gradual increase of the eligible retirement age up to 67 for men and women. Consequently, pensioners are becoming more active, although an adverse health and financial situation is still a significant barrier (Ostrowska, 2008).

A cross-sequential dimension: gender

In state socialism, the situation of women was mostly described as being equal to men due to the egalitarian principles of the communist ideology (Mishtal, 2009). This was expressed primarily in equal education and employment chances (although high feminisation of certain sectors occurred), but also in sufficient childcare services allowing women to combine work and care. Nevertheless, the gender gap in earnings was relatively high, and it only started to decrease in the 1990s (Domański et al, 2007). After the transformation, radical cuts in public social services were introduced and resulted in an acute decrease of childcare services (Szelewa, 2012). Together with mass reductions in employment due to privatisation, this has been one of the reasons for relatively low employment rates for women in the first decade after transformation. Since joining the EU, the situation of women has improved in terms of increasing employment rates, participation in higher education and a decreasing wage gap.

Result of lifecourse regimes transition: three coexisting generations

As a result of the system and of LCR transitions, we can currently distinguish three generations coexisting in the labour market in Poland, differing significantly in the aspect of their early-life conditions and lifecourses. The oldest one was raised, educated and lived most of their professional careers under socialism. Their skills did not always match the expectations of the labour market after transition. The second generation lived their youth in socialism but began their professional careers in the transition period, quickly adapting to the new work situation. The third generation does not remember socialism. It was raised and attended school in times of EU membership, open borders, mass higher education and the internet revolution. These three distinct generations, with their specific life histories, sets of skills, experiences and perspectives, interact differently within the current reality.

Discussion

Impact of system transition on CAD

The continuous development of societies influences generational differences and inequalities. Due to life timing, younger cohorts can be in a more advantageous position in many fields; for example the progress in medicine extends their life expectancy, or in new abilities that are more easily acquired in younger age, such as new technology skills. However, sometimes history offers up revolutionary events that reshape the structures and relations in societies relatively quickly, and which also affect lifecourses.

As we have shown, transition from a socialist state in Poland was followed by transition of LCRs: change of individuals' aspirations, future outlooks and behaviours resulting in new life patterns. As a result, people who started their lives in different LCR, ruled by different mechanisms of advantages and disadvantages, coexist in the same post-socialist reality. The question is: what is the impact of the past experiences on inequalities between and within age groups observed today? Literature provides numerous analyses of the socioeconomic structure before and after the transition, changes in individuals' position, as well as the increase of inequalities in former socialist countries after 1989 (Svejnar, 1999; Domański, 2000; Słomczyński, 2002; Heyns, 2005; Krzemiński and Raciborski, 2007; Słomczyński and Janicka, 2008; Plessz, 2009). However, the theory of CAD did not gain popularity in analysis of the changing lifecourse pathways during transition. Thus, the final question remains: what was the impact of system transition on the mechanism of CAD, and how did it influence the inequalities within ageing cohorts? This does not refer to Polish experiences only. It is a more general question about the theory of CAD, the interaction of its mechanism with other structural forces and – finally – about the validity of the theory in times of sudden social change.

According to the theory of CAD, life events, position and assets determine much of the late-life situation. The theory predicts an increase of inequalities within cohorts as they age. This increase is, however, not confirmed in Poland. Currently, inequalities among older generations are higher than under socialism, but still much lower compared to the rest of society (Panek, 2011; Główny Urząd Statystyczny, 2012). Although there are models that provide alternatives to CAD (levelling and divergence/convergence, assume decrease of inequalities in older cohorts), the situation in Poland does not follow these patterns either. The explanation is found in an issue that is usually omitted in academic deliberations (Dannefer and Kelly-Moore, 2009), namely the implicitly assumed stable nature of CAD and lifecourses. According to CAD, what elevates an individual to the top of the socioeconomic structure in early life should also help them in seizing opportunities and maintaining the status in later life. On the other hand, barriers and deficiencies, which place someone in an unfavourable position from the start, should contribute to adverse transitions and risks later on.

Such a mechanism of CAD does not necessarily have to function in the same way in times of rapid social change. Other factors seem to have a much more powerful influence for structuration than lifecourse did hitherto. The assumed stability of mechanism of differentiation that shapes the lifecourses has no application in the transitional reality of CEE. The standard CAD approach, developed in the US and in Western Europe, requires a profound reconsideration, following the reflections of Dannefer and Kelly-Moore (2009) and Dannefer and Setterson (2010) about the impact of social structural factors on cohort patterns of ageing and the mechanism of CAD. Evidence does not come only from CEE countries: for example, Chen, Yang and Liu (2010) conclude their China-based study by suggesting relatively weaker support for CAD theory than is found in US studies, due to the importance of other factors, such as rapid social change and a powerful state government. To sum up, our conclusion supports Mayer's general opinion that the idea of CAD still requires more consideration to become 'something more than just a metaphor' (Mayer, 2009), especially in application to non-Western societies or where rapid social change occurred.

Certainly, the transition in Poland, as in other post-socialist countries, increased inequalities between cohorts, favouring primarily younger cohorts that were able to redirect their lifecourses more easily towards the expectations of the new reality. However, it also modified the strength and nature of some advantages and disadvantages. Assets that worked positively or negatively in socialism did not have to continue as such in a democratic, free-market reality. New LCRs set a new structure of advantages and disadvantages. The transition produced 'big winners' and 'big losers' (Krzemiński and Raciborski, 2007). This can be observed most clearly when analysing the changing value of educational level for socioeconomic position.

The level of formal education is one of the fundamental determinants of future labour market chances, and in CEE it has a strong impact on social position (Titma and Tuma, 2005). Today's workers aged 50+ received their education under a socialist regime, and their skills and knowledge are often inconsistent with the requirements of a free market. On the other hand, technical and vocational education was much more available and prospective, but was marginalised after transition. In the Soviet Union, at the end of the regime, education was a strong predictor of the position in occupational position, but not a strong predictor of income (Titma and Tuma, 2005). Similar conclusions apply to Poland. Before 1989, the correlation of income and educational level was weak (Domański, 2000). Additionally, in situations of strong employment protection, motivation for studying was definitely lower.

During system transition years, the educational level gained importance (Domański et al, 2007). Because the labour market changed substantially after 1989, the educational boom was driven mainly by the intention of improving advantages in a highly competitive labour market. Access to higher education became much easier; the role of competencies and education increased; the free market was no longer controlled by the state; unemployment emerged and started to increase rapidly; and social protection decreased. University diplomas, which were not necessarily an advantage for economic position, became a valuable feature after 1989. On the other hand, lower education, which did not necessarily indicate low socioeconomic status in the socialist workers' society, significantly limited the labour market position and outcomes after the transition. Today, income inequalities between educational groups are quite high. Not much is changed by adult learning – participation of Poles in lifelong learning has always been low, but in older cohorts it even decreases. In 2012, about 17% of the population aged 25-44 years participated in informal training, while in the age group 50-64 years it was only 9%. About one third of the people aged 50-64 never attained any training or schooling in their lives (Turek, 2013). Generally, low and outdated competencies of the older people limited their position and chances in the labour market during and after transition (Perek-Białas and Ruzik, 2004; Turek and Perek-Białas, 2013).

System transition changed the mechanism of income distribution and brought about a higher rate of return on education, as the free market forces started to reward human capital, causing a greater diversity in levels of wages than in the centrally planned economy of socialism (Svejnar, 1999). Since 1989, earnings depend primarily on occupation, education and whether employment was in the public or private sector (Svejnar, 1999; Domański et al, 2007).

Certainly, not all disadvantages and advantages modified their effects for socioeconomic status after system transition. Titma and Tuma (2005) suggest the existence of stable cumulative advantages in states of the former Soviet Union, and that human and social capital provided opportunities for individual initiative and self-realisation prior to the collapse of the communist system, as well as under post-transition economic and political conditions. Also in Poland, the top-income groups of socialism (managers, specialists) maintained or even increased their income and gained more prestige after the transition (Domański et al, 2007; Słomczyński and Janicka, 2008). In contrast, those occupational groups who were below the average income level remained unchanged (Domański, 2000). Important exceptions are two groups of 'big losers' from the first years of transition: manual labourers and farmers. They experienced a significant worsening of their labour market position, a drop in income, an increase in unemployment (also long-term), and a decrease in social prestige and privileges (Gilejko, 2005). However, after Poland joined the EU, the situation of farmers improved due to structural funds.

What is specific for authoritarian regimes is also the importance of political attitudes for the socioeconomic situation. In the times of socialism, being a member of the only political party (Polish United Party of Workers) gave huge advantages in everyday life, while manifestation of anti-socialist opinions resulted in a limitation of life opportunities (such as work dismissal or school expulsion), or more harmful consequences (for example prison). In the democratic reality, the sides reversed – former communists lost their status and prestige, while opposition activists gained social approval, although this was not straightforwardly transmitted into socioeconomic status (Wasilewski, 2001).

All in all, the system transition not only increased, but also generated new dimensions of inequalities, both between and within cohorts. However, we claim that the mechanism of CAD may not be easily applied to explain late-life socioeconomic status when rapid and vast social change occurs. If the transition modifies what is advantageous or disadvantageous for life progress, then the middle-aged or old-aged cohorts can experience unpredicted changes to their life situation and socioeconomic position. Under socialism, different rules shaped the social hierarchy than in the period of democracy. Transition modified the importance of various resources, and as a result changed the effect of advantages and disadvantages from the early-life stages; therefore, it is no longer relevant to speak of their accumulation throughout life. Instead, one should consider the continuous interplay of the current framework, sketched by social system requirements and opportunities, with people's assets and capital worked out in life. Whether the advantages or disadvantages from a previous LCR will continue to function depends on the character and strength of social change. The main forces driving inter-cohort inequalities are found in the timing of age and certain life stage with social change.

Socioeconomic inequalities in ageing societies

Finally, the question of the role of population ageing for inter- and intra-cohort inequalities arises. Undoubtedly, the increasing average life expectancy, as well as the expected postponement of retirement age, will result in the growth of age diversity in society. More generations will coexist next to each other, also in the labour market. Additionally, the increasing speed of civilisation changes can result in a deepening of generational differences and inequalities based, among other things, on new technology skills or knowledge requiring continuous updating. From this perspective, population ageing can influence social inequalities, however, can be mitigated by adequate policies and measures. The panacea for such a process lies primarily in the system of lifelong learning and the ability to maintain, update and develop the human capital of an ageing population.

A reversed perspective on the relation of socioeconomic hierarchy and population ageing also reveals an important mechanism: people of different socioeconomic status drive population ageing to different extents. Socioeconomic structures differentiate lifestyles, family models, standards of living and risk behaviours. People with a high socioeconomic status have, on average, fewer children and live longer, contributing to population ageing (Balicki et al, 2007). As mentioned in the introduction, a significant change of education structure in Poland in the 1990s contributed to a rapid decrease in fertility rates (Frątczak, 2011). Similar processes were observed in other CEE transition countries, affecting population ageing (Hoff, 2011).

A look into the future inclines to think about the expected stability of lifecourses. If a flexibility of life patterns became a rule, it might no longer be reasonable to speak of LCRs (compare Mayer, 2005; Kohli, 2007). Already, there are no single trajectories, such as education – work – retirement, as they can exist simultaneously. Will the forthcoming cohorts experience a stable structure of LCR and mechanisms of CAD from early life stages? More arguments speak against such a thesis. The experience of ageing in tomorrow's society can be dominated by change and constant progress. In such a reality, as in a period of system transition, the mechanism of cumulative late-life effects of early-life advantages/disadvantages can lose power or even disappear.

These worries, as well as the underestimated evidence from transitional societies, make a claim for further revision of CAD theory, which so far has been dominated by Western European and particularly American perspectives. This chapter has attempted to examine the complex relation of socioeconomic inequalities, system transition, population ageing, lifecourses and CAD. As each of these concepts deserves much attention, we were only able to present a brief overview of how inequalities arose in post-transition ageing societies and how the theory of CAD is consistent with these experiences.

References

Balicki, J., Frątczak E. and Nam, C.B. (2007) *Przemiany ludnościowe. Fakty-Interpretacje-Opinie* [*Population changes. Facts-Interpretations-Opinions*], Warszawa: Wyd.Uniwersytetu Stefana Wyszyńskiego.

Bilans Kapitału Ludzkiego (2010-12) Bilans Kapitału Ludzkiego [Human Capital Balance]. http://bkl.parp.gov.pl/

Chen, F., Yang, Y. and Liu, G. (2010) 'Social change and socioeconomic disparities in health over the life course in China: A cohort analysis', *American Sociological Review*, 75, 1, 126-50.

Crystal, S. and Shea, D. (1990) 'Cumulative advantage, cumulative disadvantage, and inequality among elderly people', *The Gerontologist*, 30, 437-43.

Crystal, S. and Waehrer, K. (1996) 'Later-life economic inequality in longitudinal perspective', *Journal of Gerontology*, 51B, 6, 307-18.

Dannefer, D. (1987) 'Aging as intracohort differentiation – Accentuation, the Matthew effect, and the life course', *Sociological Forum*, 2, 2, 211-36.

Dannefer, D. (2003) 'Cumulative advantage, and the life course: Cross-fertilizing age and social science knowledge', *Journal of Gerontology*, 58B, 6, 327-37.

Dannefer, D. and Kelly-Moore, A. (2009) 'Theorizing the life course: New twists in the paths', in V.L. Bengtson, M. Silverstein, D. Putney and D. Gans (eds) *Handbook of Theories of Aging*, New York: Springer, 389-412.

Dannefer, D. and Setterson, R. (2010) 'The study of the life course: Implications for social gerontology', in D. Dannefer and C. Phillipson (eds) *Sage handbook of social gerontology*, London: Sage, 3-19.

Dannefer, D. and Uhlenberg, P. (1999) 'Paths of the life course: A typology', in V.L. Bengtson and K.W. Schaie (eds) *Handbook of theories of aging*, New York: Springer, 306-26.

Diewald, M., Goedicke, A. and Mayer, K.U. (eds) (2006) *After the fall of the wall. Life courses in the transformation of East Germany*, Stanford: Stanford University Press.

DiPrete, T. (2002) 'Life course risks, mobility regimes, and mobility consequences: A comparison of Sweden, Germany, and the U.S.', *American Journal of Sociology*, 108, 2, 267-309.

DiPrete, T. and Eirich, G.M. (2006) 'Cumulative advantage as a mechanism for inequality: A review of theory and evidence', *Annual Review of Sociology*, 32, 271-97.

Domański, H. (1996) *Na progu konwergencji: stratyfikacja społeczna w krajach Europy Środkowo-Wschodniej* [*On the threshold of convergence: social stratification in Central and Eastern Europe*], Warszawa: IFiS PAN.

Domański, H. (2000) *Hierarchie i bariery społeczne w latach dziewięćdziesiątych* [*Social hierarchies and barriers in 1990s*], Warszawa: Instytut Spraw Publicznych.

Domański, H., Sawiński, Z. and Słomczyński, K. (2007) *Nowa klasyfikacja i skale zawodów. Socjologiczne wskaźniki pozycji społecznej w Polsce* [*A new classification and scales of occupations. Sociological indicators of social position in Poland*], Warszawa: Wydawnictwo IFiS PAN.

Elder, G.H. (1994) 'Time, human agency, and social change: Perspectives on the life course', *Social Psychology Quarterly*, 57, 1, 4-15.

Elder, G.H., Johnson, K. and Crosnoe, R. (2003) 'The emergence and development of life course theory', in J.T. Mortimer and M.J. Shanahan (eds) *Handbook of the life course*, New York: Kluwer Academic Publishers, 3-22.

Eurostat (2011) *Healthy life years and life expectancy at age 65, by gender.* http://epp.eurostat.ec.europa.eu/tgm/download.do?tab=table&plugin=0&language=en&pcode=tsdph220

Eurostat (2012) *Total fertility rate.* http://epp.eurostat.ec.europa.eu/tgm/table.do?tab=table&init=1&language=en&pcode=tsdde220&plugin=0

Ferraro, K.P., Schippee, T.P. and Schafer, M.H. (2009) 'Cumulative inequality theory for research on aging and the life course', in V.L. Bengtson, M. Silverstein, D. Putney and D. Gans (eds) *Handbook of theories of aging*, New York: Springer, 413-34.

Frątczak, E. (2011) 'Population ageing in Poland', in A. Hoff (ed) *Population ageing in Central and Eastern Europe. Societal and policy implications*, Aldershot: Ashgate, 11-31.

Fuchs, V.R. (1984) ' "Though much is taken": Reflections on aging, health, and medical care', *Health and Society*, 62, 143-66.

Gavrilova, N.S. and Gavrilov, L.A. (2009) 'Rapidly aging populations: Russia/ Eastern Europe', in P. Uhlenberg (ed) *International handbooks of population*, New York: Springer, 113-32.

George, L.K. (1993) 'Sociological perspectives on life transitions', *Annual Review of Sociology*, 19, 353-73.

Gilejko, L. (2005) 'Robotnicy w transformacji: ocenaichpołożeniaiszans [The workers in transition: assessment of their position and chances]', in M. Jarosz (ed) *Wygrani i przegrani polskiej transformacji* [*The winners and losers of Polish transition*], Warszawa: OficynaNaukowa, 183-208.

Grenier, A. (2012) *Transitions and the lifecourse: Challenging the constructions of 'growing old'*, Bristol: Policy Press.

Główny Urząd Statystyczny (2012) *Ubóstwo w Polsce w 2011 [Poverty in Poland 2011]*, Warszawa: Główny Urząd Statystyczny.

Hayward, M.D. and Gorman, B.K. (2004) 'The long arm of childhood: The influence of early-life social conditions on men's mortality', *Demography*, 41, 1, 87-107.

Henretta, J.C. and Campbell, R.T. (1976) 'Status attainment and status maintenance: A study of stratification in old age', *American Sociological Review*, 41, 981-92.

Heyns, B. (2005) 'Emerging inequalities in Central and Eastern Europe', *Annual Review of Sociology*, 31, 163–97.

Hofacker, D. (2010) *Older workers in a globalizing world: An international comparison of retirement and late-career patterns in Western industrialized countries*, Cheltenham: Edward Elgar.

Hoff, A. (2011) 'The drivers of population ageing in Central and Eastern Europe – Fertility, mortality and migration', in A. Hoff (ed) *Population ageing in Central and Eastern Europe. Societal and policy implications*, Aldershot: Ashgate, 5-10.

Kancelaria Prezesa Rady Ministrów (2010) *Wejście młodych na rynek pracy* [*Labour market entry of the youth*], Warszawa: Kancelaria Prezesa Rady Ministrów.

Kohli, M. (1986) 'The world we forgot: A historical review of the life course', in V.W. Marshall (ed) *Later life: The social psychology of ageing*, Beverly Hills, CA: Sage, 271-303.

Kohli, M. (2007) 'The institutionalization of the life course: Looking back to look ahead', *Research in Human Development*, 4, 3-4, 253-71.

Krzemiński, I. and Raciborski, J. (eds) (2007) *Oswajanie wielkiej zmiany* [*Adapting to the big change*], Warszawa: Wydawnictwo IFiS PAN.

Leisering, L. (2003) 'Government and the life course', in J.T. Mortimer and M.J. Shanahan (eds) *Handbook of the life course*, New York: Kluwer Academic/Plenum, 205-25.

Lynch, S. and Brown, J. (2011) 'Stratification and inequality over the life course', in R. Binstock and L. George (eds) *Handbook of ageing and the social sciences*, San Diego, CA: Elsevier, 105-20.

Mayer, K.U. (2005) 'Life courses and life chances in a comparative perspective', in S. Svallfors (ed) *Analyzing inequality: Life chances and social mobility in comparative perspective*, Palo Alto, CA: Stanford University Press, 17-55.

Mayer, K.U. (2009) 'New directions in life course research', *Annual Review of Sociology*, 35, 413-33.

Mishtal, J.Z. (2009) 'Understanding low fertility in Poland', *Demographic Research*, 21, 599-626.

Morgan, L.A. and Kunkel, S. (2007) *Aging, society, and the life course*, New York: Springer Publishing.

Niezgoda, M. (ed) (2011) *Społeczne skutki zmiany oświatowej w Polsce* [*Social results of education change in Poland*], Kraków: Wydawnictwo Uniwersytetu Jagiellońskiego.

O'Rand, A.M. (1996) 'The precious and the precocious: Understanding cumulative disadvantage and cumulative advantage over the life course', *The Gerontologist*, 36, 2, 230-38.

O'Rand, A.M. (2006) 'Stratification and the life course: Life course capital, life course risks and social inequality', in R.H. Binstock and L.K. George (eds) *Handbook of aging and the social sciences*, New York: Academic Press, 145-62.

Ostrowska, A. (2008) 'Nierówności społeczne a zdrowie [Social inequalities and health]', in H. Domański (ed) *Zmiany stratyfikacji społecznej w Polsce* [*Changes of social stratification in Poland*], Warszawa: Wydawnicwto IFiS PAN, 181-210.

Panek, T. (2011) *Ubóstwo, wykluczenie społeczne i nierówności. [Poverty, social exclusion and inequalities*], Warszawa: Oficyna Wydawnicza SGH.

Perek-Białas, J. and Ruzik, A. (2004) 'Aktywizacja starszych ludzi na rynku pracy [Increasing economic activity of older people]', in J.T. Kowaleski and P. Szukalski (eds) *Nasze starzejące się społeczeństwo* [*Our ageing society*], Łódź: Wydawnictwo Uniwersytetu Łódzkiego, 431-9.

Plessz, M. (2009), 'Life stages and transformations of the labor market. The case of Central Europe (Poland, the Czech Republic, Hungary)', *European Societies*, 11, 1, 103-36.

Pollert A. (2003) 'Women, work and equal opportunities in post-communist transition', *Work, employment and society*, 17, 2, 331-57.

Prus, S. (2007) 'Age, SES, and health: A population level analysis of health inequalities over the life course', *Sociology of Health & Illness*, 29, 2, 275-96.

Ross, C.E. and Wu, C.L. (1996) 'Education, age, and the cumulative advantage in health', *Journal of Health and Social Behavior*, 37, 1, 104-20.

Ruzik-Sierdzińska, A., Perek-Białas, J. and Turek, K. (2013) 'Did transition to market economy and the EU membership have an impact on active ageing policy in Poland?', in R. Ervik and T. Linden (eds) *The making of aging policy: Theory and practice in Europe*, Cheltenham: Edward Elgar, 124-47.

Slany, K. (2002) *Alternatywne formy życia małżeńsko-rodzinnego w ponowoczesnym świecie* [*Alternative forms of marriage and family lives in postmodern world*], Kraków: Nomos.

Słomczyński, K. (ed) (2002) *Social structure: Changes and linkages: The advanced phase of the Post-Communist transition in Poland*, Warsaw: IFiS Publishers.

Słomczyński, K. and Janicka, K. (2008) 'Polarized social-class structure: On the Matthew Effect and increasing inequality', *Polish Sociological Review*, 164, 341-57.

Social Diagnosis (2011) *Level of education*. www.diagnoza.com

Svejnar, J. (1999) 'Labor markets in the transitional Central and East European economies', in O. Ashenfelter and D. Card (eds) *Handbook of Labor Economics*, Amsterdam: Elsevier, 2809-57.

Szatur-Jaworska, B. (2000) *Ludzie starzy i starość w polityce społecznej* [*Older people and older age in social policy*], Warszawa: Aspra-JR.

Szelewa, D. (2012) Childcare policies and gender relations in Eastern Europe: Hungary and Poland compared, *Harriet Taylor Mill-Institut für* Ökonomie und Geschlechterforschung Discussion Paper 17, 03/2012.

Titma, M. and Tuma, N.B. (2005) 'Human agency in the transition from Communism: perspectives on the life course and aging', in W. Schaie and G. Elder (eds) *Historical influences on lives and aging*, New York: Springer, 108-43.

Turek, K. (2013) 'Starzenie się ludności jako wyzwanie dla gospodarki, rynku pracy, polityki i obywateli [Population ageing as a challenge for economy, labour market, policy and citizens]', in J. Górniak (ed) *Młodość czy doświadczenie? Kapitałludzki w Polsce* [*Youth or experience? Human capital in Poland*]. Warszawa: PARP, 74-105.

Turek, K. and J. Perek-Białas (2013) 'The role of employers' opinions about skills and productivity of older workers: Example of Poland', *Employee Relations*, 35, 6, 648-64.

Wasilewski, J. (2001) 'Three elites of the Central-East European democratization', in R. Markowski and E. Wnuk-Lipiński (eds) *Transformative paths in Central and Eastern Europe*. Warsaw: Ebert Foundation & Institute of Political Studies, 133-42.

Willson, A.E., Shuey, K.M. and Elder, G.H. (2007) 'Cumulative advantage processes as mechanisms of inequality in life course health', *American Journal of Sociology*, 112, 1886-924.

SEVEN

Ethnicity in ageing America: a tale of cultures and lifecourse

Takashi Yamashita, Timothy S. Melnyk, Jennifer R. Keene, Shannon M. Monnat and Anna C. Smedley

Introduction: race and ethnicity and population ageing

The race and ethnic composition of the older population in the United States (US) is expected to change in the coming decades. The older population is becoming more racially and ethnically diverse as the overall race and minority ethnic population grows (Administration on Aging, 2010). Furthermore, minority populations aged 65 and older are expected to increase from 8.0 million in 2010 (20.1% of the older population) to 12.9 million in 2020 (23.6%) (Administration on Aging, 2010). These trends have important implications for the racial/ethnic composition of America's ageing population and for how we think about inequality over the lifecourse. The goal of this chapter is to trace the significance of race/ethnicity for the population ageing. Specifically, using the available demographic data, we focus on the diversity of the older population itself as well as on the diversity of younger cohorts in view of future workforce and implications for health/long-term care in the ageing American society.

This chapter describes the significance of race and ethnicity – mainly by focusing on non-Hispanic white, non-Hispanic black and Hispanic peoples in the US – for population ageing in the US (that is, an increase in the numbers or proportions of older people at the societal level), which results from a combination of three main demographic factors: fertility, mortality and migration[1] (Weeks, 2008). In this chapter, we trace the pathways that link race and ethnicity to population ageing, with an emphasis on social inequality and health in American society (Link and Phelan, 1995; Kawachi and Kennedy, 1997). We adopt a relatively narrow definition of 'inequality', focusing on socioeconomic status and health, although inequality could also be considered the general differences between racial/ethnic groups in other contexts. We also highlight the complex relationship between race and ethnicity, and social inequality, which may directly and indirectly impact on population ageing through various processes and outcomes related to health (Williams and Wilson, 2001).

This chapter consists of four sections. The first section explains race and ethnicity in the American historical context. In the second section, we discuss the theoretical relationships between race and ethnicity, social inequality and population ageing. The third section summarises recent sociodemographic and socioeconomic trends, and their relationship to health and population ageing vis-á-vis race and ethnicity. We discuss these socioeconomic trends in the context of three typical stages of the lifecourse: (1) preparation for employment (that is, education); (2) participation in the labour force; and (3) retirement (Henretta, 2003). In the last section, we summarise the main points from the chapter and identify key areas for future research.

The concepts of race and ethnicity in the American context

From a lay perspective, race typically refers to a group's shared physical attributes, while ethnicity relates to a shared cultural heritage drawn from nationalistic, religious or historical origins. For over 200 years, race has been a standard item in the decennial US Censuses. Earlier, enumerators assigned individuals to racial categories, but in 1960, the Census moved to self-enumeration. Beginning in 1970, the Census included a distinct 'Hispanic identity' question. Individuals were identified by both a race and an ethnicity (for example, Non-Hispanic white and Hispanic white). Starting in 1980, individuals who identify as Hispanic select from a subgroup of Hispanic nativity categories, including Mexican, Puerto Rican, Cuban, and Other. Perhaps the most major change – the addition of the 'multiple races' category – to Census racial classifications occurred in 2000 (US Census Bureau, 2012). Despite the changing nature of racial and ethnic categories, they remain valid constructs for social and political demarcation in the US. The Census definitions have been an important driver of how race and ethnic categories are used in social life and by the state to identify categories of people.

From a sociological perspective, however, race does not merely specify static biological categories, but is instead understood as a social construct. In the American historical context, the meaning of race has been transformed over time through political struggle (Omi and Winant, 1994). The model of distinct racial categories is a modern concept that emerged out of the European exploration and colonisation of the Western world. The 'discovery' of the indigenous population, aesthetically different from the European colonisers, fuelled the 18th- and 19th-century scholarly practice of identifying and ranking separate human categories (Omi and Winant, 1994).

Prior to the 1980s, the most salient racial divide in the US was the black/white distinction (Bonilla-Silva, 1997; Lee and Bean, 2004). This biracial social order consisted largely of descendants of white European immigrants and black descendants of the African slave trade. According to DuBois (1899), black people experienced inequality at a more extreme level than other unassimilated groups, such as Jewish and Italian immigrants. More recently, Bonilla-Silva (2004) suggested that the contemporary American racial landscape is a tri-racial system, comprising 'whites', 'honorary whites' and the 'collective black'. Over time, increased immigration from Asia and Latin America in the 20th century has been the impetus for change from a biracial to a multiracial and multiethnic society (Lee and Bean, 2004).

Sociological definitions of race and ethnicity take into account recent patterns of immigration and interracial marriage. According to Lee and Bean (2004), some 85% of immigrants to the US since the 1980s originated from Asia, Latin America or the Caribbean, and the rates of intermarriage between the white and Asian or Latino communities has increased substantially; one in 40 Americans currently describe themselves as multiracial, and it is estimated that by 2050, this proportion could reach one in five.

Theoretical perspectives on race and ethnicity, social inequality and population ageing

Social inequality is a major topic of discussion among US scholars, media and politicians. American society is stratified by demographic and/or social statuses, such as age, gender, race/ethnicity and socioeconomic status – education, income and occupation typically represent socioeconomic status in the US. This system of stratification results in differing opportunities and resources over the lifecourse (Alwin and Wray, 2005). Race and ethnicity have consistently been an important focus of social scientists studying social inequality (Williams and Wilson, 2001). This section first describes the theoretical pathways connecting race and ethnicity with social inequality in the US. We then turn to the ways in which social inequality relates to population ageing via health disparities over the lifecourse.

Race and ethnicity and social inequality

Racial and ethnic minority groups in the US systematically receive, and have access to, fewer resources and opportunities than white people do over the lifecourse (Healey, 2012). Although race and ethnicity are often misunderstood and misrepresented as biological characteristics, social scientists have demonstrated that they are, in fact, socially constructed categories that are influenced by historical, social and political processes (Omi and Winant, 1994). The power of these social categories has contributed to – and has been used to justify – systematic discrimination against racial/ethnic minorities over time.

Before addressing the pathways linking race and ethnicity to social inequality, it is important to distinguish first between prejudice, racism and discrimination, since their definitions have implications for how race relations in society are viewed. 'Prejudice is a hostile attitude toward a person who is presumed to have negative characteristics associated with a group to which he or she belongs' (Andersen and Collins, 2013: 67). Prejudice is specifically about individual attitudes. Racism, however, is a system of power and privilege, and although it can manifest in individuals' behaviours through their treatment of others (discrimination), it has an additional component that is rooted in the social structure of society (Andersen and Collins, 2013). Sociologists have several definitions of racism, but one of the most useful comes from Joe Feagin (2000), who describes racism as 'a complex array of anti-black practices, the unjustly gained political-economic power of whites, the continuing economic and other resource inequalities along racial lines, and white racial ideologies and attitudes created to maintain and rationalize white privilege and power' (Feagin, 2000: 5). Although the definition is centered on racism against blacks, it can be applied to the unequal treatment of any racial/minority ethnic group. In the US, non-Hispanic blacks have been the numerical and power minorities since the early 1600s (the colonial era) (Healey, 2012). The roots of racism stem from between-group conflict that results in one or more groups being considered inferior to others (Bonilla-Silva, 1997). Discrimination is the result of both prejudice and racism, and is the act of treating certain groups differently, based on their characteristics rather than their actual merit.

Williams and Wilson (2001) argue that race is the key determinant of socioeconomic status in contemporary American society; race still significantly regulates access to education, income and occupations. From a lifecourse perspective, historical forces perpetuating structural and individual-level racism, discrimination and/or prejudice have ensured that advantages/disadvantages granted to specific racial/ethnic groups are passed on through the generations. As an example of the power of race-based ideologies, recent data show that more than half of the US population holds negative views of race/minority ethnic groups (for example, being lazy, being violent) (Smith et al, 1972-2010). Additionally, Pager (2003) found that non-Hispanic black people with no criminal record (14%) had lower chances of getting a callback from potential employers than non-Hispanic white people with a criminal record (17%).

We use the case of racial residential segregation to illustrate the intertwined relationship between race/ethnicity and socioeconomic status in the US (Farley, 1987; Williams, 1999). Massey and Denton (1993: 9) describe racial residential segregation as 'the key structural factor responsible for the perpetuation of black poverty in the US. Residential segregation is the principal organizational feature of American society that is responsible for the creation of the urban underclass.'

In the early 20th century, property owners, realtors and banks were legally allowed to discriminate against potential homebuyers based on race (for example via racially restrictive covenants, and higher interest rates for racial/ethnic minorities) (Boustan, 2011). Such racially restrictive policies resulted in the physical separation of racial and ethnic minority groups from residential areas with non-Hispanic white communities (Massey and Denton, 1993; Williams, 1999). Despite several policy changes, including the federal Fair Housing Act 1968 and the Equal Credit Opportunity Act 1974, racial residential segregation remains a key feature of American neighbourhoods. While black communities continue to be the most highly segregated racial/minority ethnic group, many subgroups of Hispanics, including the Mexicans and Puerto Rican communities, also experience high rates of segregation.

Residential segregation is not a neutral fact; it systematically undermines the social and economic wellbeing of racial minorities in the US. The long-term effects of residential segregation perpetuate and amplify social inequality. For example, lack of job opportunities in segregated communities and distant job locations are associated with greater unemployment rates of race and ethnic minorities (Farley, 1987). Access to quality education is often limited in minority neighbourhoods (Williams, 1999). Furthermore, lifetime wealth is influenced by residential segregation due to lower property values in disadvantaged communities. Thus, the lifecourse consequences of these structural arrangements result in persistent race and ethnic wealth inequality in old age, which is linked to wellbeing and health outcomes. Here, the complex relationship between racial residential segregation, access to quality education, and unemployment from generation to generation can be considered another vicious cycle.

Social inequality and populating ageing

Social inequality is linked to population ageing through multiple pathways, including health, life expectancy and demographic forces (that is, fertility, mortality and migration). In addition, race and ethnicity are among the most powerful determinants of socioeconomic status and social inequality, which indirectly influence population ageing in the US. Such social inequality becomes more salient over the lifecourse due to the cumulative exposure to disadvantage (Adler et al, 1994). This section uses cumulative disadvantage theory as a framework to describe how racial/ethnic-based social inequality relates to population ageing (Dannefer, 2003).

Socioeconomic status and health

Health is arguably one of the most important predictors of three population-ageing-related demographic factors – fertility, mortality and migration. A long history of social science and public health research exists on the relationship between socioeconomic status and health (Oakes and Rossi, 2003). Although there are not yet concrete conclusions about the specific pathways linking socioeconomic status and health, socioeconomic status is considered a fundamental cause of health inequality, because it influences access to health-promoting resources (Link and Phelan, 1995). We discuss later three major pathways through which socioeconomic status acts as a fundamental cause of health disparities that influence population ageing: access to health-related resources; stress; and health behaviours.

First, socioeconomic status is appreciably linked to access to health resources. The US remains the only developed nation without universal health coverage to all residents. As such, in the US, economic status often determines individuals' accessibility to health care services; lower socioeconomic status is associated with the lower utilisation of health care services (De Boer et al, 1997). Additionally, underutilisation of preventative health care services, including regular check-ups, prenatal care, immunisations and health screening tests (for cancer, for example), is common in the US (Cockerham, 2012). Underutilisation of health care services influences premature mortality[2] and poorer health with age, since early detection and intervention are positively associated with lower morbidity and mortality.

Mirowsky and Ross (2003) suggest that education is a salient factor that provides knowledge, skills and resources that enable individuals to make better choices about health care. When information about health promotion is available, those with more resources are best able to take advantage of protective opportunities, such as cancer screenings and annual examinations. In addition, socioeconomic status also determines one's ability to live in neighbourhoods that facilitate healthy behaviour choices and that provide health care resources. In general, poor neighbourhoods and communities are more likely to have health risk factors, including hazardous waste, polluted air, residential crowding, noise and higher crime rates compared to wealthier areas (Evans and Kantrowitz, 2002). Furthermore, low-income residential areas have significantly less access to healthy foods (for example, fresh produce) yet greater access to unhealthy foods (for example, fast food) (Cummins and Macintyre, 2006). Exposure to environmental health risks accumulate over time and manifest as health disparities over the lifecourse and in later life (Taylor, 2008). In short, socioeconomic status determines the availability/affordability of protective factors as well as exposures to health risk factors.

Second, lower socioeconomic status is associated with greater exposure to stress. Individuals with lower socioeconomic status are more likely to experience stressful life events and living conditions and are less likely to effectively manage stress and preserve health compared to those with higher socioeconomic status. Lower socioeconomic status leads to less satisfactory, more physically demanding, and riskier job conditions, all of which cause chronic distress (Tausig and Fenwick, 1999). In addition, lower socioeconomic status is associated with a greater chance of involuntary job loss/unemployment (Bureau of Labor Statistics, 2013). Lower socioeconomic status is associated with financial distress that is known to have both short-term and long-term negative effects on health (Kahn and Pearlin, 2006). From a lifecourse perspective, repeated or constant physiological reactions to acute and chronic distress increase risk of morbidity and mortality over time (Lantz et al, 2005). Individuals with lower socioeconomic status often have poorer knowledge and fewer resources to properly manage stress than their counterparts (Adler et al, 1994).

Low socioeconomic status is also associated with health-detracting behaviours, including increased likelihood of smoking, excessive drinking, drug use, unhealthy eating and a sedentary lifestyle (Lantz et al, 1998). This relationship between low socioeconomic status and poor health behaviours is attributed to lack of knowledge about healthy lifestyles and interactions with unhealthy social networks (Fuchs, 1979; Mirowsky and Ross, 2003). Stressful life events, such as accidental injury, job loss and family emergency are associated with greater likelihood of engaging in unhealthy behaviours, including smoking, drinking, drug use and overeating among racial and ethnic minorities (Jackson et al, 2010). Unhealthy behaviours often manifest themselves during childhood and become habitual and harmful over time, particularly in mid to later life.

Race and ethnicity above and beyond socioeconomic status

Race and ethnicity, socioeconomic status and health outcomes are independently and jointly linked to population ageing. Although socioeconomic status is one important determinant of population ageing via various health indicators (for example, life expectancy), race and ethnicity seem to have effects above and beyond socioeconomic status. In several studies, older adults from minority ethnic communities were less likely to utilise health care services and more likely to have health problems (for example, cardiovascular diseases) than non-Hispanic whites even after adjusting for socioeconomic status (Dunlop et al, 2002; Rooks et al, 2002). Cultural minorities' attitudes toward the health care system and bias against minorities among health care professionals also explain their underutilisation of health care services (Ford and Cooper, 1995).

Being from a minority is itself also associated with greater distress related to existing racism (Hatch and Dohrenwend, 2007) and also amplifies the impact of socioeconomic status on wellbeing. Racial minorities with lower socioeconomic status have significantly greater incarceration rates, which deteriorates their subsequent employment opportunities and their subsequent socioeconomic status and health outcomes (London and Myers, 2006). Moreover, being a minority intensifies the effects of socioeconomic status on health. Indeed, minorities with lower socioeconomic status had significantly poorer health than non-Hispanic white people with lower socioeconomic status (Shuey and Willson, 2008). We may speculate that an individual's race and ethnicity is related to their socioeconomic status disadvantages and lower social mobility. At the same time, despite disadvantageous economic positions, the Hispanic population generally has better health outcomes and longer life expectancy than non-Hispanic whites communities and other racial/ethnic groups (known as 'the Hispanic paradox') (Markides and Eschbach, 2005). In summary, race and ethnicity relate to population ageing through the processes of cumulative advantages/disadvantages that include direct effects, socioeconomic status, health resource access, distress and health behaviours.

Sociodemographic and socioeconomic trends by race and ethnicity

Data

To illustrate the relationships between socioeconomic status and race and ethnicity we draw on various data sources and provide empirical examples. The purpose of this section is to provide current empirical data that can be used for further discussions on race and ethnicity in the context of population ageing. The data were selected to help illustrate the relationships between race and ethnicity and inequality in socioeconomic status, described in the earlier sections.

Data on population demographics were retrieved from American FactFinder,[3] the official website of the United States Census Bureau.[4] In addition, American FactFinder presents data from a supplementary study, the American Community Survey,[5] which samples approximately 3.5 million households annually and collects detailed information on socioeconomic status. Wealth data were computed using the Health and Retirement Study.[6] Data on health, mortality and life expectancy come from the Center for Disease Control and Prevention DC,[7] a component of the United States Department of Health and Human Services. Also, the Center for Disease Control and Prevention has a series of other regular health-related data collection/management programmes, for example the Behavioral Risk Factor Surveillance System.[8]

Sociodemographic trends by race and ethnicity

According to the most recent Census data, in 2010 the American population was 308.7 million. The country has experienced 9%-12% population growth per decade in the 20th century, with the exception of the baby boom that occurred in the 1950s, which led to a 19% increase in the overall population. As the population has expanded, the age composition of the US has experienced a dramatic transformation. Similar to other advanced industrial nations, the US has undergone significant improvements in sanitation, health services, food production, work safety and life-prolonging technologies, which have cumulatively decreased mortality rates while raising life expectancy (Omran, 1971). These factors, coupled with the post-World War II baby boom, have resulted in the largest proportion of citizens over the age of 65 in the nation's history at the beginning of the 21st century.

Figure 7.1 shows the changes in the age composition of the American population since 1900. As the population pyramids shift from triangular to more rectangular forms, we can see evidence of population ageing as the proportion of older groups relative to the total population increases. Importantly, race and ethnicity as well as immigration are important aspects of this trend. The data show that 62% of Hispanics in 2011 were under the age of 35 compared to only 44% of white communities and 53% of black communities (US Census Bureau, 2011). This is partially explained by the recent influx of immigrants from Latin America, and Mexico especially, who are primarily young families entering the country in search of employment. These trends in the racial/ethnic composition of the population as well as in immigration have important implications for population ageing in the US. Specifically, the young Hispanic population's lower educational attainments relative to the non-Hispanic white group and their increasing share in current/future workforce are of immediate concern. From a lifecourse perspective, cohorts of young Hispanics may face conflicts between social disadvantages due to lack of formal education (for example, lower credentials and skills) and high

Figure 7.1: Age composition of the United States, 1900-2000

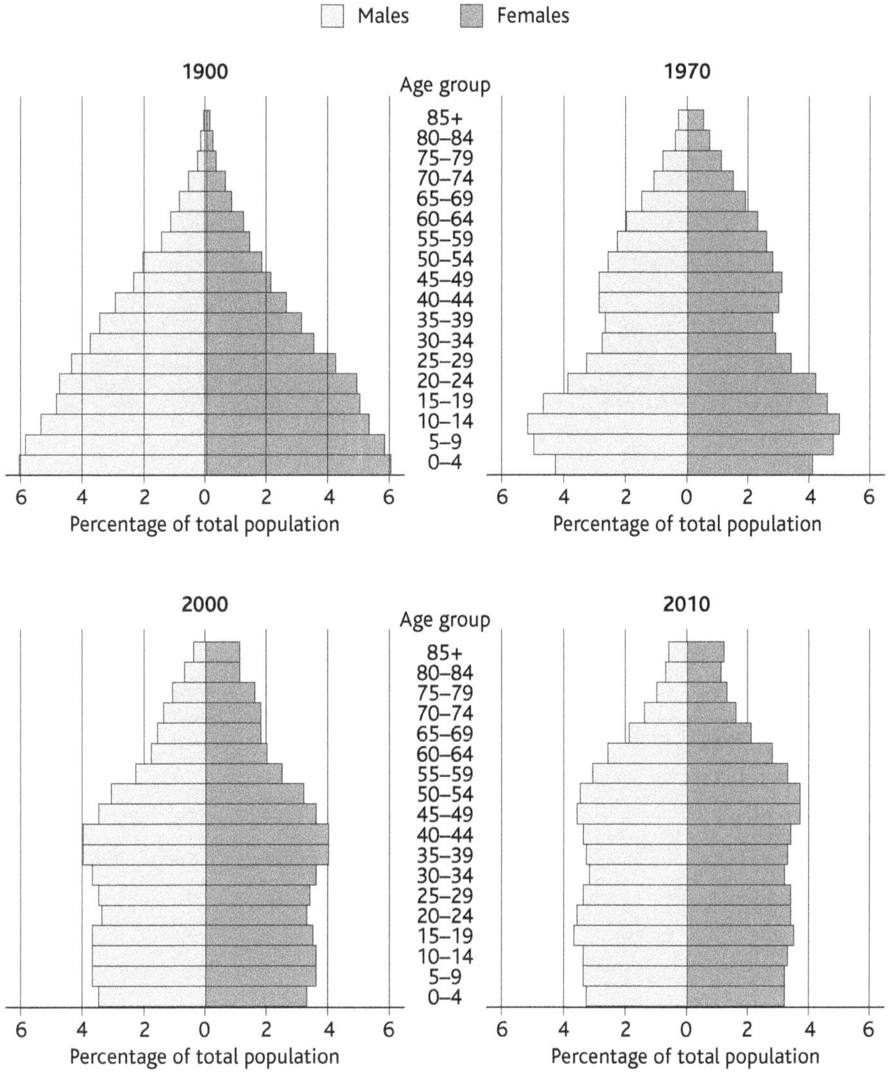

Males Females

1900 | 1970 | 2000 | 2010

Age group: 85+, 80–84, 75–79, 70–74, 65–69, 60–64, 55–59, 50–54, 45–49, 40–44, 35–39, 30–34, 25–29, 20–24, 15–19, 10–14, 5–9, 0–4

6 4 2 0 2 4 6
Percentage of total population

Data sources:
Hobbs, Frank & Stoops (2002). Demographic trends in the 20th century, US Census Bureau (http://www.census.gov/prod/2002pubs/censr-4.pdf).
US Census Bureau (2012). Statistical Abstract of the United States. Resident population by sex and age: 1980 to 2010 (http://www.census.gov/compendia/statab/2012/tables/12s0007.pdf).

expectations as a main workforce due to the increasing proportion of older adults (that is, possible lack of workforce).

The overall racial composition of America remained relatively constant for much of the 20th century, with a roughly 90:10 split between the white and black ethnic groups, with other races comprising a negligible proportion of the population (see Figure 7.2). By the late 1970s, due to increasing immigration

Figure 7.2: Race distribution in the United States, 1900–2010

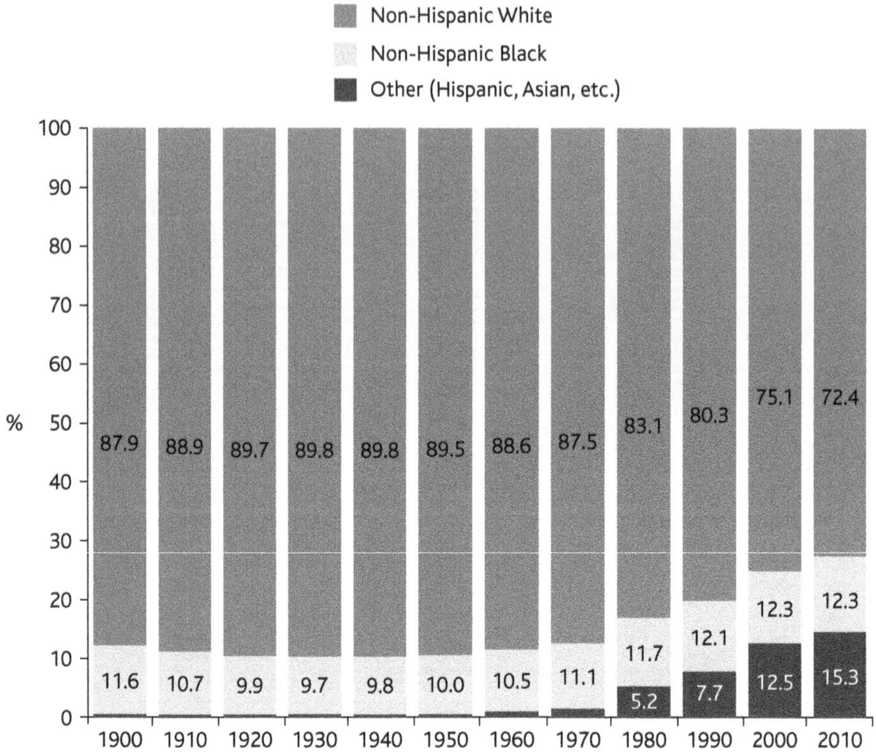

Data sources:
1. US Census Bureau, Population Estimates, National Estimates by Age, Sex, Race: 1990–1979 (http://www.census.gov/popest/data/national/asrh/pre-1980/PE-11.html)
2. US Census Bureau 'Overview of Race and Hispanic Origin: 2010', p. 4 (http://www.census.gov/prod/2002pubs/censr-4.pdf)

from Asia and Latin America, especially Mexico, races other than white or black came to represent a growing percentage of the American populace. In 1980, just over 5% of Americans reported being a race other than white or black, and by 2000 this statistic had increased to 12.5%.

Socioeconomic trends by race and ethnicity

Education

In 2011, a sizable education gap existed between non-Hispanic white population and other racial and ethnic groups in the US (see Figure 7.3). Again, education is one of the fundamental determinants of subsequent socioeconomic status, and greater educational disparities suggest increasing inequality in the future. About 30% of the non-Hispanic white population has completed at least a Bachelor's degree compared to slightly less than 20% of black people and 12% of Hispanics.

Figure 7.3: Highest educational attainment by race and sex, 2011 in the United States

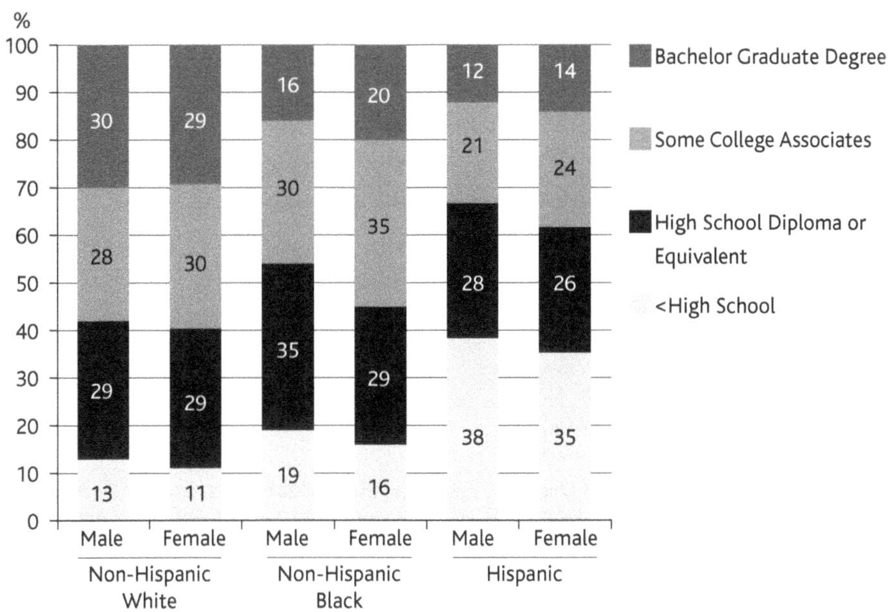

Data source: US Census Bureau, 2010 American Community Survey (Table B15002: Sex by Educational Attainment for the Population 25 and Over). Data retrieved at http://factfinder2.census.gov/faces/nav/jsf/pages/index.xhtml. Steps to find data: (1) 'Advanced Search', enter 'B1502', (2) 'Race and Ethnic Groups', select '002 – White Alone', '004 – Black or African American Alone', '400 – Hispanic or Latino', (3) Select file 'Sex by Educational Attainment for the Population 25 and Over'.

Moreover, only 11% of white people have less than a high school education compared with 18% of the black and over one third of the Hispanic populations. It is likely that Hispanics will play more important roles in the future workforce in the US due to a rapidly increasing Hispanic population. In this regard, Hispanics' lower educational attainment may significantly impact on their economic contributions to the upcoming ageing society. For example, population ageing or increasing life expectancy means that more people will live into older ages and will likely need a variety of medical and health care resources and services. Young Hispanics may help to meet such future demand for the health care and caregiving workforce, but greater educational backgrounds would be necessary for providing higher-quality services in the expanding health care industry in the ageing society.

Employment and income

Examining the population of employed adults in the US, certain race patterns emerge in employment type. Figure 7.4 shows a substantial gap in unemployment rates between the white and Asian ethnic groups as compared to other racial groups. The unemployment rate among the black population (17.7%) is roughly

Figure 7.4: Unemployment rates by race, 2011 in the United States

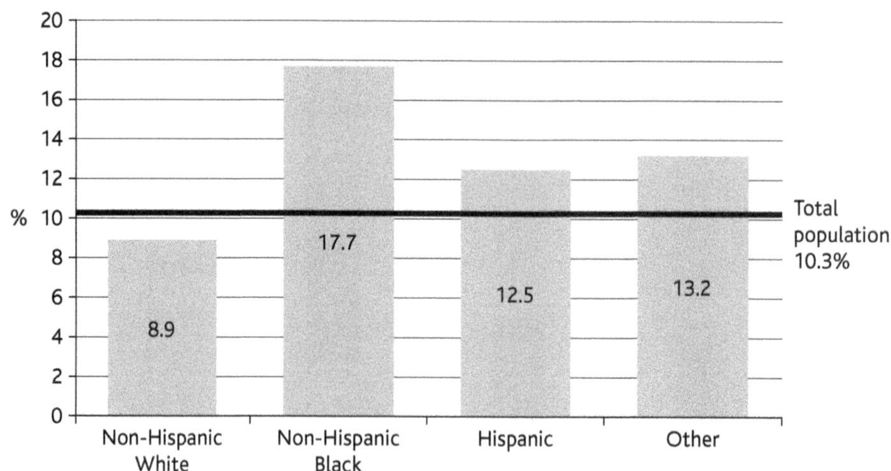

Data source: US Census Bureau, 2011 American Community Survey (S0201: Selected Population Profile in the United States). Data retrieved at http://factfinder2.census.gov/faces/nav/jsf/pages/index.xhtml. Steps to find data: (1) 'Advanced Search', enter 'S0201', (2) 'Race and Ethnic Groups', select '002 – White Alone', '004 – Black or African American Alone', '400 – Hispanic or Latino', (3) Select file 'Population Profile in the United States'.

Note: Includes only US citizens 16 years of age and older.

double that of the white (8.9%) and Asian (7.9%) populations. Hispanics and all other races have unemployment rates that fall at about the midpoint between the white and black ethnic groups.

Non-Hispanic white people are more likely to be employed in the most prestigious jobs – management positions, business, sciences, arts and engineering – than either non-Hispanic black people or Hispanics. In addition, non-Hispanic black people and Hispanics are more likely to work in unskilled service positions, or blue collar occupations such as manufacturing or transportation.

The result of higher unemployment rates and lower-prestige occupations is shown in Table 7.1. Black households in America earn $33,223 in terms of median yearly income, compared to Hispanic households who earn $39,589 and white

Table 7.1: Selected occupations as a percentage of the employed population, 2011

	Non-Hispanic White (%)	Non-Hispanic Black (%)	Hispanic (%)
Management, business, science, arts	**37.9**	27.7	19.8
Computer, engineering, science	5.0	3.2	2.2
Production, transportation occupations	11.1	15.8	15.8
Service occupations	16.7	**25.7**	**27.4**

Note: Not all occupational categories listed, columns will sum to less than 100%.

Data source: US Census Bureau, 2011 American Community Survey (S0201: Selected Population Profile in the United States). http://factfinder2.census.gov/faces/nav/jsf/pages/index.xhtml. Steps to find data: (1) 'Advanced Search', enter 'S0201', (2) 'Race and Ethnic Groups', select '002 – White Alone', '004 – Black or African American Alone', '400 – Hispanic or Latino', (3) Select file 'Population Profile in the United States'.

Figure 7.5: Household median income by race, 2011 in the United States

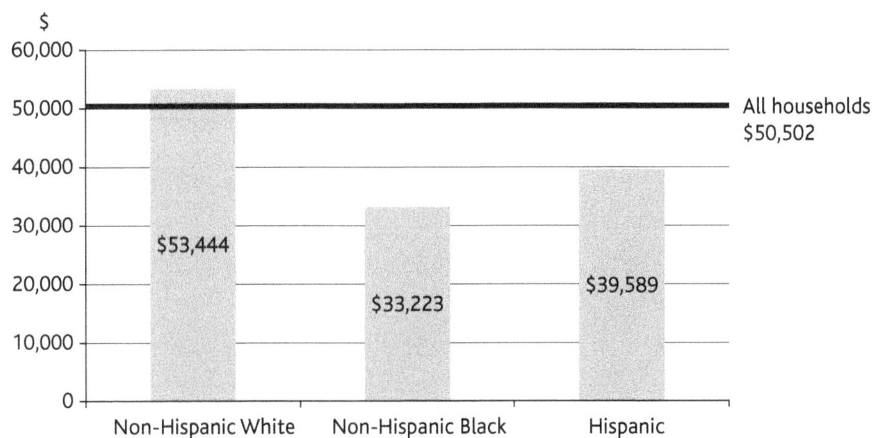

Data source: US Census Bureau, 2011 American Community Survey (S0201: Selected Population Profile in the United States). Data retrieved at http://factfinder2.census.gov/faces/nav/jsf/pages/index.xhtml. Steps to find data: (1) 'Advanced Search', enter 'S0201', (2) 'Race and Ethnic Groups', select '002 – White Alone', '004 – Black or African American Alone', '400 – Hispanic or Latino', (3) Select file 'Population Profile in the United States'.

households at $53,444 (see Figure 7.5). Figures 7.1, 7.2 and 7.3 show a clear pattern of race-based inequality in the US regarding access to employment, and this directly impacts overall individuals' lifetime incomes. Unemployment among racial/ethnic minorities has particularly troubling implications for economic resources in old age. As previously discussed, race and ethnic minorities are less likely to accumulate the same wealth and income over their lifetimes as their white counterparts, resulting in greater socioeconomic inequality in old age. Prolonged unemployment exacerbates existing inequality, and helps to ensure that racial/ethnic minorities have lower lifetime earnings and less wealth in their later lives.

Retirement

As shown in Figure 7.6, racial disparities in wealth that are generally accumulated throughout the working age among older populations are even more salient than education and income. This is another example of cumulative disadvantages over the lifecourse. Possible explanations include complex interactions between disparities in educational attainment, income, residential segregation, housing values and health status (for example, individual health care costs). Since wealth in later life is an outcome of earlier life experiences, wealth differences by race and ethnicity in older populations inhibit disadvantaged groups' economic wellbeing for the rest of their lives. This is of particular concern, because the vast majority of older adults do not experience an increase in income in later years. Unequal wealth distributions across racial groups are realistically irreversible in later life despite social welfare programmes like Social Security and Medicare, which are not designed to be redistributive. Consequently, family members of

Figure 7.6: Household median wealth at age 65+ by race, 2010 in the United States

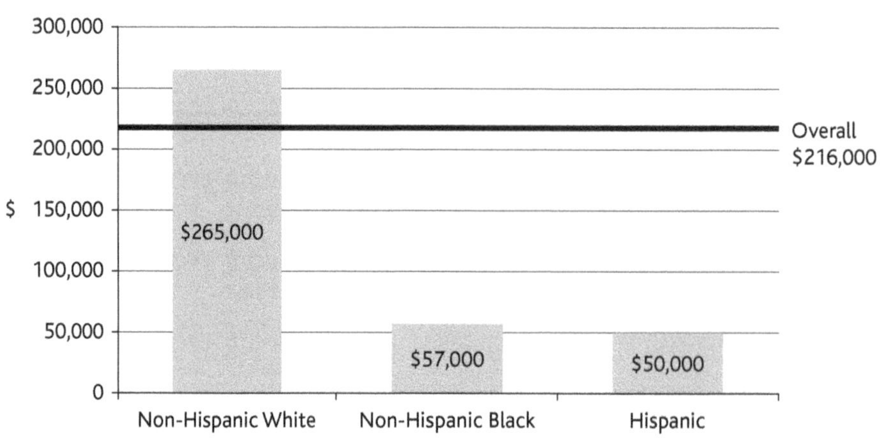

Data source: 2010 Health and Retirement Study (http://hrsonline.isr.umich.edu/); weighted median household wealth computed by Dawn C. Carr, PhD at the Stanford Center on Longevity.

older disadvantaged racial and ethnic minorities may experience added economic struggles as they provide support to older parents/relatives.

Fertility, migration and mortality by race and ethnicity

Fertility rates

In 2011, the total fertility rate in the US was about 1.9 births per woman (see Figure 7.7). This rate has remained fairly consistent for the past 40 years, although it is up slightly from the 1970s when fertility dipped to 1.7. At its 20th-century peak, fertility rates hit 3.6 in the decade following World War II (Mather, 2012). The post-war era was a time of economic prosperity and optimism in the US. Conversely, periods of economic decline and uncertainty tend to correspond with lower rates of birth, such as during the Great Depression of the 1930s, the Energy Crisis of the 1970s, and the so-called Great Recession beginning in 2007.

American birth rates declined between 1990 and 2010, although there are notable differences between racial groups (see Figure 7.8). For the past two decades, the non-Hispanic white group had fewer than two births per woman, on average. In comparison, non-Hispanic black women have had higher fertility rates at 2.5 in 1990 and 2.0 in 2010, while Hispanic women have the highest fertility rates with 3.0 births on average in 1990 and 2.4 births according to the most recent statistics. Again, fertility is one of the most important driving forces of demographic changes. Cohorts with more babies in one or more specific racial/ethnic groups will certainly change the racial/ethnic composition in the American population at every stage of the lifecourse (for example, school, work, retirement).

Figure 7.7: US fertility rate (number of children per woman), 1970-2010

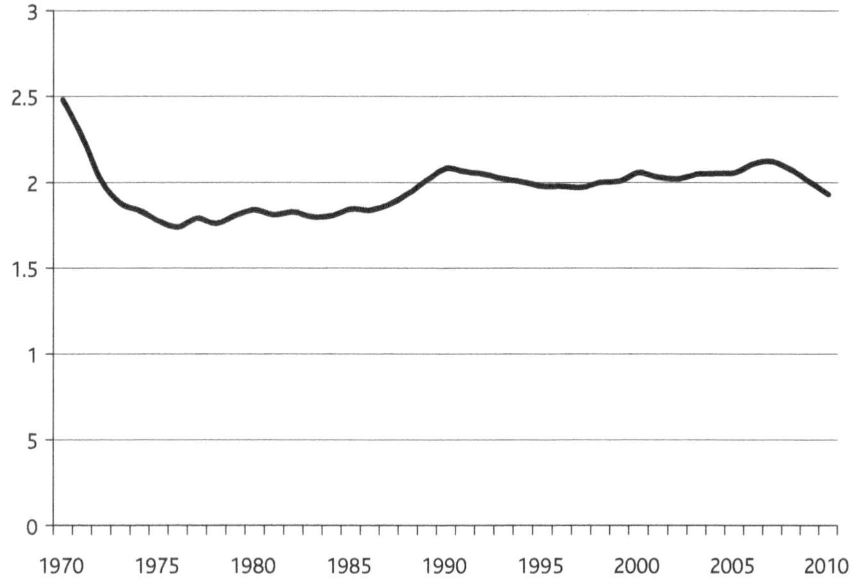

Data source: Center for Disease Control (www.cdc.gov) 'National Vital Statistics Reports, 61(1)', Table 4 (http://www.cdc.gov/nchs/data/nvsr/nvsr61/nvsr61_01.pdf).

Figure 7.8: US fertility rate (number of children per woman) by race, 1990-2010

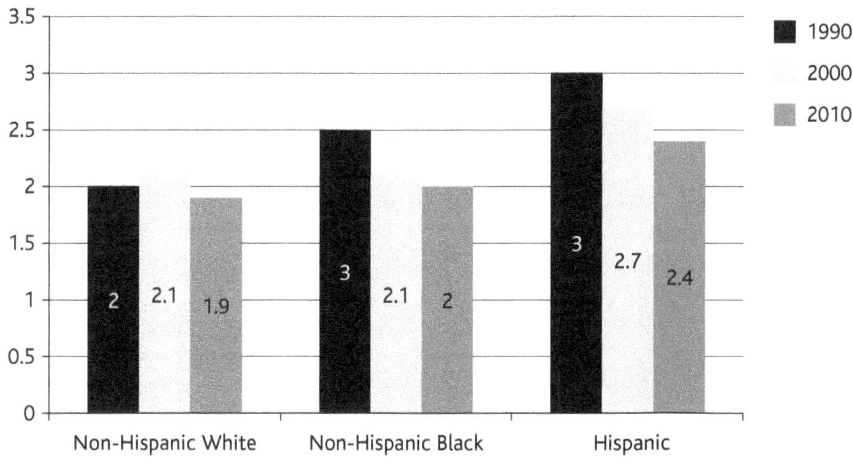

Data source: Center for Disease Control (www.cdc.gov) 'National Vital Statistics Reports, 61(1)', Table 4 & 8 (http://www.cdc.gov/nchs/data/nvsr/nvsr61/nvsr61_01.pdf).

Immigration

For the past 20 years, the US has received approximately 1 million immigrants per year as permanent legal residents. This period represents the highest immigration rates in the nation's history, and is remarkable for having been sustained for over two decades. Official records maintained by the Department of Homeland Security[9] indicate the country of origin for new arrivals, but do not distinguish by race. Nonetheless, the pattern of immigration by region has changed dramatically over the course of the 20th century. From 1900 to 1919, some 86% of immigrants hailed from Europe, with large populations entering the US from Italy, Russia, the United Kingdom and Austria-Hungary. From 2000 to 2009, only 13% of immigrants originated in Europe, while 35% came from all across Asia and 44% moved from other North American countries. In total, 1.7 million or 17% of new immigrants arrived from Mexico during this time, the largest proportion of whom settled within the border states of Texas and California in the American south and south-west.

Life expectancy

In 2008, the life expectancy of an American newborn was approximately 78 years, although this figure varies by race and sex. Females of all races are expected to live on average about five years longer than their male counterparts. By race, white people have a life expectancy of 78.5 years compared to 74.0 years for black people and 81.0 for Hispanics (see Figure 7.9).

It is paradoxical that Hispanic people have a longer life expectancy than non-Hispanic white people, considering their relatively disadvantageous social statuses in terms of education, income and employment. However, this apparent discrepancy is referred to as the 'Hispanic paradox' and can be explained by a combination of selective migration and culture (Markides and Eschbach, 2005). That is, only selected healthy working-age Hispanic immigrants come to the

Figure 7.9: Life expectancy at birth and age 65 by race, 2008 in the United States

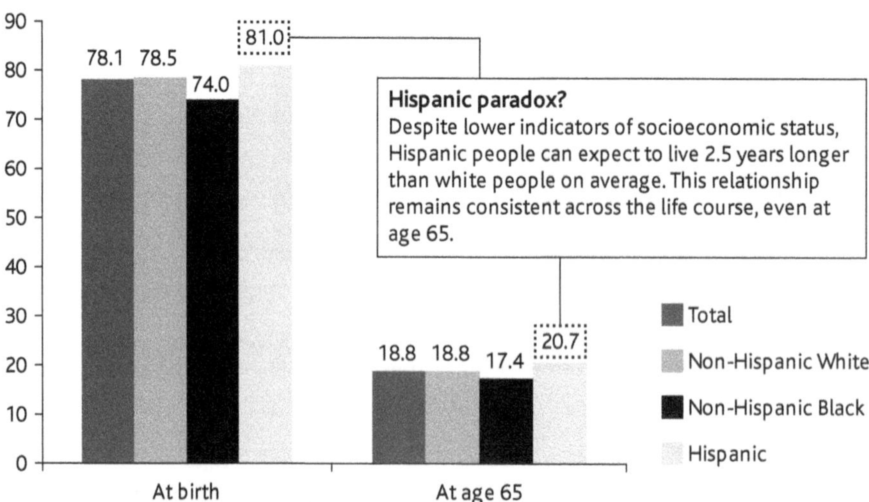

Data source: Center for Disease Control and Prevention, 'National Vital Statistics Report', 61(3), p 3 (www.cdc.gov/nchs/data/nvsr/nvsr61/nvsr61_03.pdf)

US and they typically go back to their home countries when they get sick. Also, cultural preferences in health behaviours (for example, diet) and reciprocal social support within families may contribute to Hispanics' health advantages (Gallo et al, 2009). However, as the second largest racial and ethnic group in the US, Hispanics are tremendously heterogeneous. Recent research shows that health advantages are not the feature of the entire Hispanic population but only certain sub-populations enjoy longer life expectancy (for example, Cubans consistently face poorer health compared with other Hispanics) (Pinheiro et al, 2009). Further inquiry regarding the Hispanic subgroups (for example, Mexicans) in each life stage and comparison to other racial/ethnic minorities are needed to better understand possible implications for the ongoing and future population ageing.

Over the past 40 years, life expectancy of all racial cohorts has increased substantially. The nation's life expectancy transitions are well represented and easily interpretable in the interactive data graphics developed by Hans Rosling (2007).[10] Non-Hispanic black males have shown the largest increase, gaining some 10 years of increased life expectancy between 1970 and 2008, although they continue to fare worse than non-Hispanic white males, and non-Hispanic black or white females. However, the data suggest that the racial gap in life expectancy has somewhat narrowed since the turn of the 21st century.

Concluding remarks

The goal of this chapter was to explain the relevance of race and ethnicity to population ageing in the US in view of the persistent social class-based inequality over the lifecourse. Based on the data presented, we see race and ethnic diversity in socioeconomic status and we have considered how these differences may be entrenched and exacerbated in old age. As the race and ethnic composition of the US is increasingly diverse, and also facing the baby boomers' retirement, population ageing is an increasingly critical topic of concern. But the baby boomers themselves are racially and ethnically diverse, as are the younger cohorts who will replace them in the workforce and will provide social, economic and medical support for them as they age.

As we have discussed, race and ethnicity are particularly important since, in trying to anticipate the needs of retiring large cohorts, we also need to take into account their diverse race and ethnic identities, communities, cultures and, in many cases, languages. While age cohorts are often considered as monolithic groups, their individual experiences of ageing are broadly diverse and linked to advantages and disadvantages (for example, socioeconomic status) over the lifecourse. Immigration to the US also plays a role in explaining how race and ethnicity relate to various outcomes (for example, socioeconomic status, health) among older adults. Specifically, Hispanic immigrants are important contributors to an ageing American society as potential future labour force participants working with/for older populations. Indeed, the socioeconomic and racial/ethnic diversity of new immigrants to the US in recent decades makes understanding the ageing process and preparations to meet the needs of an ageing society even more difficult.

Cumulative disadvantage is arguably the most powerful theoretical explanation for racial/ethnic variation in economic resources, health and wellbeing in old age and, in turn, population ageing. However, the possible consequences of racial and ethnic disparities in socioeconomic status and health, for example, are yet to be rigorously investigated. On one hand, as one of the most racially and ethnically diverse societies, the US faces population-ageing related challenges. On the other hand, the case of the US is an opportunity to understand the role of race and ethnicity in the context of population ageing, and perhaps to inform other racially/ethnically diverse developed nations. At the same time, it is important to recognise that the US is relatively young compared to other developed nations. As such, research and experience in population ageing in other nations provide indispensable insights for the future of an ageing American society. On a related note, some of the theoretical discussions of race, racism, social inequality and population ageing may not be applicable to other contexts (for example, nations), as this chapter focuses specifically on the racial/ethnic composition of US society.

Given the theoretical perspectives and recent data presented in this chapter, several important areas for future research are identified. First, from a lifecourse perspective, identifying possible starting points of future racial and ethnic disparities in socioeconomic status is critical, because timely interventions could be implemented. Despite a relatively long history of the vicious cycle of racial discrimination in the US, appropriate timing of intervention may alleviate race- and ethnicity-based cumulative disadvantages in socioeconomic status. Particularly, more attention should be paid to residential segregation and its impact on socioeconomic status (for example, educational attainment, types of occupation) in subsequent life stages. Second, the role of young minorities as a future workforce as caregivers for older populations needs to be better understood. Specifically, the observed disadvantages (for example, lower educational attainment) of rapidly increasing young Hispanic populations should receive growing attention. Third, extensive discussion regarding the racial and ethnic disparities in wealth is warranted, both in terms of managing existing disadvantaged older populations and preventing future populations with scarce wealth in later life. Fourth, more detailed comparisons between racial/ethnic minority groups rather than non-Hispanic white and black people over the lifecourse are needed to better understand the impacts of race/ethnicity on population ageing in the US. On a related note, additional systematic data collection from racial/ethnic minorities is highly desirable, as currently available nationally representative data are not sufficient for rigorous analysis of other minorities. Finally, specific occurrence mechanisms of race- and ethnicity-based socioeconomic status disadvantages – and their theoretical influence on population ageing – need further exploration in future research.

Notes

[1] Fertility is the total number of births divided by the total number of women in the childbearing age (generally age 15 to 44) during a specific time period. Mortality is the number of new deaths in the population during a specific time period. Migration is the number of individuals/families permanently changing residence from one geographic location to another during a specific time period. This includes both in-migration (immigration) and out-migration (emigration).

[2] Premature mortality is the numbers of new deaths before a set age (generally age 65 years) in the population during a specific time period.

[3] American FactFinder: http://factfinder2.census.gov/faces/nav/jsf/pages/index.xhtml

[4] United States Census Bureau: www.census.gov

[5] American Community Survey: www.census.gov/acs/www/

[6] Health and Retirement Study: http://hrsonline.isr.umich.edu/

[7] Center for Disease Control and Prevention: www.cdc.gov/

[8] Behavioral Risk Factor Surveillance System: www.cdc.gov/brfss/

[9] Department of Homeland Security: www.dhs.gov/

[10] See www.gapminder.org/ for the interactive graphics.

References

Adler, N.E., Boyce, T., Chesney, M.A., Cohen, S., Folkman, S., Kahn, R.L. and Syme, S.L. (1994) 'Socioeconomic status and health: The challenge of the gradient', *American Psychologist*, 49, 15-24.

Administration on Aging (2010) *Profile of Older Americans: 2010*, Washington, DC: US Department of Health and Human Services.

Alwin, D.F. and Wray, L.A. (2005) 'A life-span developmental perspective on social status and health', *The Journals of Gerontology Series B: Psychological Sciences and Social Sciences*, 60(Special Issue 2), S7-S14. doi: 10.1093/geronb/60.Special_Issue_2.S7

Andersen, M.L. and Collins, P.H. (2013) *Race, Class & Gender: An Anthology*, Belmont, CA: Wadsworth Cengage.

Bonilla-Silva, E. (1997) 'Rethinking racism: Toward a structural interpretation', *American Sociological Review*, 62(3), 465-80.

Bonilla-Silva, E. (2004) 'From bi-racial to tri-racial: Towards a new system of racial stratification in the USA', *Ethnic and Racial Studies*, 27(6), 931-50. doi: 10.1080/0141987042000268530

Boustan, L.P. (2011) 'Racial residential segregation in American cities', in N. Brooks, K. Donaghy & G.-J. Kanaap (eds) *The Oxford Handbook of Urban Economics and Planning*, Oxford, UK: Oxford University Press.

Bureau of Labor Statistics (2013) 'Employment status of the civilian population 25 years and over by educational attainment', *Economic News Release*. Retrieved 28 February 2013, from www.bls.gov/news.release/empsit.t04.htm

Cockerham, W.C. (2012) *Medical Sociology*, Upper Saddle River, NJ: Pearson Education, Inc.

Cummins, S. and Macintyre, S. (2006) 'Food environments and obesity – neighbourhood or nation?', *International Journal of Epidemiology*, 35, 100-4.

Dannefer, D. (2003) 'Cumulative advantage/disadvantage and the life course: Cross-fertilizing age and social science theory', *The Journals of Gerontology Series B: Psychological Sciences and Social Sciences*, 58, S327-37.

De Boer, A.G.E.M., Wijker, W. and De Haes, J.C.J.M. (1997) 'Predictors of health care utilization in the chronically ill: A review of the literature', *Health Policy*, 42, 101-15.

Du Bois, W.E.B. and Eaton, I. (1899) *The Philadelphia negro: A social study*, Published for the University of Pennsylvania Press.

Dunlop, D.D., Manheim, L.M., Song, J. and Chang, R.W. (2002) 'Gender and ethnic/racial disparities in health care utilization among older adults', *The Journals of Gerontology Series B: Psychological Sciences and Social Sciences*, 57, S221-33.

Evans, G.W. and Kantrowitz, E. (2002) 'Socioeconomic status and health: The potential role of environmental risk exposure', *Annual Review of Public Health*, 23, 303-31.

Farley, J.E. (1987) 'Disproportionate Black and Hispanic unemployment in US metropolitan areas: The roles of racial inequality, segregation and discrimination in male joblessness', *American Journal of Economics and Sociology*, 46, 129-50.

Feagin, J.R. (2000) *Racist America: Roots, current realities, & future reparations*, New York: Routledge.

Ford, E.S. and Cooper, R.S. (1995) 'Racial/ethnic differences in health care utilization of cardiovascular procedures: A review of the evidence', *Health Service Research*, 30, 237-52.

Fuchs, V.R. (1979) 'Economics, health, and post-industrial society', *The Milbank Memorial Fund Quarterly. Health and Society*, 153-82.

Gallo, L.C., Penedo, F.J., Espinosa De Los Monteros, K. and Arguelles, W. (2009) 'Resiliency in the face of disadvantage: Do Hispanic cultural characteristics protect health outcomes?', *Journal of Personality*, 77, 1707-46.

Hatch, S. and Dohrenwend, B. (2007) 'Distribution of traumatic and other stressful life events by race/ethnicity, gender, SES and age: A review of the research', *American Journal of Community Psychology*, 40, 313-32.

Healey, J.F. (2012) *Diversity and society: Race, ethnicity, and gender*, Thousand Oaks, CA: Sage.

Henretta, J.C. (2003) 'The life-course perspective on work and retirement', in R.A. Settersten (ed) *Invitation to the life course: Toward new understandings of later life*, Amityville, NY: Baywood Publishing Company, Inc.

Jackson, J.S., Knight, K.M. and Rafferty, J.A. (2010) 'Race and unhealthy behaviors: Chronic stress, the HPA axis, and physical and mental health disparities over the life course', *American Journal of Public Health*, 100, 933-9.

Kahn, J.R. and Pearlin, L.I. (2006) 'Financial strain over the life course and health among older adults', *Journal of Health and Social Behavior*, 47, 17-31.

Kawachi, I. and Kennedy, B.P. (1997) 'Socioeconomic determinants of health: Health and social cohesion: Why care about income inequality?', *BMJ*, 314, 1037.

Lantz, P.M., House, J.S., Mero, R.P. and Williams, D.R. (2005) 'Stress, life events, and socioeconomic disparities in health: Results from the Americans' Changing Lives Study', *Journal of Health and Social Behavior*, 46, 274-88.

Lantz, P.M., House, J.S., Lepkowski, J.M., Williams, D.R., Mero, R.P. and Chen, J. (1998) 'Socioeconomic factors, health behaviors, and mortality: Results from a nationally representative prospective study of US adults', *JAMA*, 279, 1703-8.

Lee, J. and Bean, F.D. (2004) 'America's changing color lines: Immigration, race/ethnicity, and multiracial identification', *Annual Review of Sociology*,30, 221-42.

Link, B.G. and Phelan, J. (1995) 'Social conditions as fundamental causes of disease', *Journal of Health and Social Behavior*, 35, 80-94.

London, A.S. and Myers, N.A. (2006) 'Race, incarceration, and health: A life-course approach', *Research on Aging*, 28, 409-22.

Markides, K.S. and Eschbach, K. (2005) 'Aging, migration, and mortality: Current status of research on the Hispanic paradox', *The Journals of Gerontology Series B: Psychological Sciences and Social Sciences*, 60, S68-75.

Massey, D.S. and Denton, N.A. (1993) *American Apartheid: segregation and the making of the underclass*, Cambridge, MA: Harvard University Press.

Mather, M. (2012) 'Fact sheet: The decline in US fertility', *World population data sheet 2012*, Population Reference Bureau.

Mirowsky, J. and Ross, C.E. (2003) *Education, social status and health*, New York: Walter De Gruyter, Inc.

Oakes, J.M. and Rossi, P.H. (2003) 'The measurement of SES in health research: Current practice and steps toward a new approach', *Social Science & Medicine*, 56, 769-84.

Omi, M. and Winant, H. (1994) *Racial formation in the United States*, New York: Routledge.

Omran, A.R. (1971) 'The epidemiologic transition: A theory of the epidemiology of population change', *The Milbank Memorial Fund Quarterly*, 49, 509-38.

Pager, D. (2003) 'The mark of a criminal record', *American Journal of Sociology*, 108(5), 937-75. doi: 10.1086/374403

Pinheiro, P.S., Sherman, R.L., Trapido, E.J., Fleming, L.E., Huang, Y., Gomez-Marin, O. and Lee, D. (2009) 'Cancer incidence in first generation US Hispanics: Cubans, Mexicans, Puerto Ricans, and New Latinos', *Cancer Epidemiology Biomarkers & Prevention*, 18, 2162-9.

Rooks, R.N., Simonsick, E.M., Miles, T., Newman, A., Kritchevsky, S.B., Schulz, R. and Harris, T. (2002) 'The association of race and socioeconomic status with cardiovascular disease indicators among older adults in the health, aging, and body composition study', *The Journals of Gerontology Series B: Psychological Sciences and Social Sciences*, 57, S247-56.

Rosling, H. (2007) 'Visual technology unveils the beauty of statistics and swaps policy from dissemination to access', *Journal of the International Association for Official Statistics*, 24, 103-4.

Shuey, K.M. and Willson, A.E. (2008) 'Cumulative disadvantage and black-white disparities in life-course health trajectories', *Research on Aging*, 30, 200-25.

Smith, T.W., Marsden, P.V., Hout, M. and Kim, J. (1972-2010) *General social surveys*, Chicago: Center NOR.

Tausig, M. and Fenwick, R. (1999) 'Recession and well-being', *Journal of Health and Social Behavior*, 40, 1-16.

Taylor, M.G. (2008) 'Timing, accumulation, and the black/white disability gap in later life: a test of weathering', *Research on Aging*, 30, 226-50.

US Census Bureau (2011) 'Selected population profile in the United States', *American Community Survey*, American FactFinder.

US Census Bureau (2012) *The Two or More Races Population: 2010*. Retrieved from www.census.gov/prod/cen2010/briefs/c2010br-13.pdf

Weeks, J.R. (2008) *Population: An introduction to concepts and issues*, Belmont, CA: Thomson Higher Education.

Williams, D.R. (1999) 'Race, socioeconomic status, and health. The added effects of racism and discrimination', *Annals of the New York Academy of Sciences*, 896, 173-88.

Williams, D.R. and Wilson, C.M. (2001) 'Race, ethnicity, and aging', in R.H. Binstock and L.K. George (eds) *Handbook of aging and the social sciences* (5th edn), San Diego, CA: Academic Press.

EIGHT

The urban–rural split in ageing Australia: diverging lifecourses, diverging experiences

Rachel Winterton and Jeni Warbuton

Introduction

This chapter explores the diverse experiences of older people and the places in which they live. Given its geographical land mass, Australia is a country of contrasts and divergent spaces, and one of the major divides is between urban and rural areas. Most of Australia's population resides in urban settings, and historically research in ageing has focused on the experiences of older people in metropolitan environments. It is only recently that, across the world, there has been a surge in interest in the lives of older people living in rural areas. Authors such as Keating (2008b) have highlighted the challenges associated with rural ageing, by questioning whether rural locations are good places to grow old, prompted by concerns in relation to the increased proportions of people ageing in rural areas internationally (United Nations, 2009). This includes Australia, where population ageing is more pronounced in rural than urban settings (Davis and Bartlett, 2008).

Thus, this chapter aims to contribute to understandings of the urban–rural split in an ageing Australia. By considering some of the socioeconomic and demographic differences that are experienced in these settings across the lifecourse, we are contributing to a richer appreciation of ageing in the contemporary context. In response to rural population ageing, attention has been directed towards how rural environments, and the demographic shifts that occur within them, influence the ageing process (Wahl and Weisman, 2003), particularly in considering factors associated with rurality that impact on individuals across the lifecourse. However, while lifecourse studies have become fundamental within social gerontology (Bengtson et al, 2012), there has been limited exploration of how the diverse trajectories of older people shape their experience of ageing in a rural environment. Deconstructing this is important, as older rural residents and communities are diverse, and their lifecourse interactions with rurality will differ (Keating and Phillips, 2008). Thus, we draw on environmental gerontology and lifecourse theory to explore how older Australians' relationships with their rural environments are influenced by lifecourse interactions.

Understanding the demography of rural ageing

In identifying the lifecourse impact of rurality, defining the 'rural lens' is critical. **Locality-based** definitions (Halfacree, 1993; Woods, 2005) reflect measurable characteristics, such as population size, density and distance from urban centres (Halfacree, 1993; Keating and Phillips, 2008). In the Australian context, these definitions prevail, with the Australian Bureau of Statistics (ABS) remoteness structure typically used to define the rural in relation to service provision and policy development (Australian Bureau of Statistics, 2011b). Based on road distances to service centres, this measure groups Australia into regions that share characteristics of remoteness (major cities, inner and outer regional, remote, very remote), with classifications outside major cities generally categorised as rural (ABS, 2011b).

However, the ABS Main Structure (ABS, 2011a) is also used, where areas are classified as urban or rural in relation to population density. 'Rural' localities are categorised at four levels relating to social, demographic and economic characteristics. Statistical Area (SA) 1 locations generally have less than 800 residents, with rural SA1 locations containing less than 200 persons per km^2. These aggregate to form SA2 regions, which represent socially and economically functioning communities with approximately 3,000-25,000 persons. SA2 regions group to form SA3 locations, which have populations of 30,000-130,000 persons and often reflect functional areas of regional towns. These aggregate to create SA4 regions, which are related to industry and labour markets and have populations of over 100,000 persons. Locality-based definitions prevail internationally, with the UK employing a rural definition of less than 10,000 inhabitants (Office for National Statistics, 2004). Canada has also adopted a series of classifications incorporating population size, density and distance from urban centres, with census definitions indicating that rural areas encompass all areas outside population centres with at least 1,000 residents and a density of 400 persons or more per km^2 (Statistics Canada, 2013).

If this definition is employed in relation to population ageing, Australian rural places typically have higher proportions of people aged 65 years and above, and higher old age dependency ratios when compared with urban regions (ABS, 2009). While 69% of Australians live in major urban areas, only 65% of older Australians reside in these regions, and almost a quarter of older people live in smaller cities and towns (ABS, 2013). This trend has been observed in other developed regions (United Nations, 2009), and is linked to rural youth out-migration, the tendency of rural older people to age in place, and the migration of retirees into rural areas for lifestyle change, known as 'retirement migration' (McKenzie and Frencken, 2001; Costello, 2007).

However, rural and urban settings differ demographically, and ageing in a rural area presents alternate challenges and opportunities. While Australia is geographically large, with a relatively small population of approximately 23 million, it is highly urbanised: 76% of Australians reside on 0.33% of the land mass, with a density of 100 persons or more per km^2, while 0.8% of the population inhabit 70.5% at a density of 0.1 persons or less per km^2 (Hugo, 2012). As such, two thirds of the population reside in capital cities (Black, 2005), and the low population density in rural areas has health and socioeconomic implications. Rural places comprise a large proportion of Australia's most disadvantaged areas (Alston, 2007), due to limited educational opportunities, increased at-risk health behaviours, limited access to health services due to small, dispersed populations, and higher proportions of Indigenous populations, who often have poorer health. Thus, older rural Australians have poorer health, lower life expectancy and higher mortality rates than urban populations (Australian Institute of Health and Welfare, 2007). Further, while urban centres are experiencing population growth, numerous inland rural communities are experiencing population decline, also impacting on service availability (Australian Bureau of Statistics, 2010). When coupled with population ageing, this heightens demand on health services, which is compounded by a lack of working-age populations to deliver these (Davis and Bartlett, 2008).

However, the rural demographic disadvantage is but one piece of the puzzle relating to the ability to age well rurally, and criticisms of locality-based approaches relate to their inability to consider diversity, and tendencies to describe, rather than define 'rural' (Halfacree, 1993; Woods, 2005). Thus, rural is often considered as a **social representation**, which describes how specific places, practices and people reflect rurality, the impact of these constructions across the lifecourse, and how people view relationships between themselves and their rural environments (Woods, 2005; Keating and Phillips, 2008). Environmental gerontology highlights the importance of older people's relationships with social and physical environments in framing wellbeing (Wahl and Weisman, 2003), which are propagated across the lifespan and influenced by both macro and micro factors (Bronfenbrenner, 1977). The rural–urban divide has been highlighted as a significant macro issue, due to the different contexts that rural areas present (Wahl and Weisman, 2003; Keating and Phillips, 2008).

In relation to the social construction of place, urban and rural locations exhibit differences. However, these constructions are unique to individuals and cultural groups, and framed by social and historical interactions with particular places. For example, research has determined that for some, rural communities represent peaceful picturesque environments, with urban places seen as impersonal and busy (Winterton and Warburton, 2012). Conversely, urban places can be viewed as exciting and dynamic by others, with rural places regarded as dull and stagnating (Twigger-Ross and Uzzell, 1996). Rural communities are not homogeneous (Keating and Phillips, 2008), and in Australia rural places can encompass farming areas, mining and retirement communities, agricultural towns, wilderness areas and major regional centres (Black, 2005). However, when compared with urban places, rural environments generally exhibit higher levels of social capital, cohesion and civic engagement (Ziersch et al, 2009). Rural people are also seen as more resilient and self-determining in response to the demographic challenges associated with rural living (Davis and Bartlett, 2008). These constructions provide a set of guiding beliefs across the lifecourse, and a basis for belonging and attachment (Gray and Phillips, 2001).

Thus, individuals' relationships with rural environments across the lifecourse can influence capacity for healthy ageing, and this is linked to the ability of rural places to foster place attachment and identity. **Place attachment** reflects the emotional relationship between an individual and a place (Bonnes and Secchiaroli, 1995), with **place identity** reflecting the ability to regulate the self through attachment to place (Peace et al, 2006). Studies have noted the role of place relationships in facilitating wellbeing in older age, by promoting reminiscence, competence, independence and belonging, facilitating adjustments and maintaining self-esteem (Rowles, 1983; Rubinstein and Parmelee, 1992; Peace et al, 2006; Wiles et al, 2009), with rural characteristics being influential in shaping attachment and identity in ageing (Rowles, 1983; Walsh et al, 2012). While attachment and identity processes evolve as a result of rural interactions across the lifecourse, with long-term residency a key contributor (Rowles, 1983), retirement migrants also experience attachment to their rural locations (Burholt and Naylor, 2005). However, macro-level changes such as drought, development and demographic change can adversely impact on place relationships for older people (Winterton and Warburton, 2012).

Thus, while demographic factors may have lifecourse implications that will impact on the wellbeing of older rural residents, there has been little exploration of how older people's lifecourse interactions with rural places influence healthy ageing in this context. This is significant when considered against research that highlights the role of lifecourse factors in contributing to social exclusion for older rural residents (Scharf and Bartlam, 2008). This chapter explores the interactions of diverse older people with their rural communities across the lifespan, utilising the four lifecourse principles identified by Giele and Elder (Elder, 1998; Giele and Elder, 1998):

- **Location** refers to position in time and place, and the importance of social and historical contexts in influencing individuals.
- **Linked lives** denotes how individuals are connected through interactions with family and friends, which are temporally linked by changing times, places and institutions, and social and historical influences experienced and shared across social networks.
- **Human agency** reflects the impact of choices and actions within historical and social contexts, such as family settings, life stage, and structural arrangements.
- Finally, **timing** signifies the importance of the stages of life changes, in terms of their impact on later transitions (Elder, 1998; Giele and Elder, 1998; Bengtson et al, 2012).

The chapter draws on data from a small Australian study exploring the meaning of rural living to older people, which was undertaken within two rural communities located in the Hume region in Victoria. This rural region is ranked as an SA4 within the ABS Main Structure, and is situated on the border of Victoria and New South Wales, approximately 3 hours from Melbourne and 5 hours from Sydney (see Figure 8.1).

Both communities are classified as inner regional, but on the cusp of an outer regional classification. One community is classified as an SA2, with the other contained within a larger SA2 region that encompasses a number of SA1 communities. While farming communities predominate within the region, its proximity to the Murray River has resulted in increased tourism and retirement migration, with the closest regional centre within a 100 km radius of both communities. Community selection was based on similarities in terms of ageing profiles (approximately 30% of residents aged 65+) and smaller populations (less than 6,000), with data pooled rather than compared to increase sample diversity. While one community was experiencing population growth as a result of retirement migration, the other was experiencing population decline. Sixteen interviews were conducted across both communities with retired, community-dwelling adults aged between 64 years and 98 years, recruited through community stakeholders and snowball sampling. Selection was based on diverse residential histories, including long-term residents, and those who had moved into the local town from farms or from another rural area. Others had little experience of rural life and had in-migrated from a city in retirement, with time in the region ranging from 2 years to 98 years (see Table 8.1).

Approval was received from La Trobe University ethics committee, with informed consent obtained from all participants and pseudonyms utilised to protect identities. Rigour was ensured through use of a semi-structured interview tool and qualitative data analysis program to ensure consistency in data collection and analysis, and the use of direct quotes to represent key themes and to ensure that diverse views were presented (Guba and Lincoln, 1982). Data were collected in

Figure 8.1: Case study region

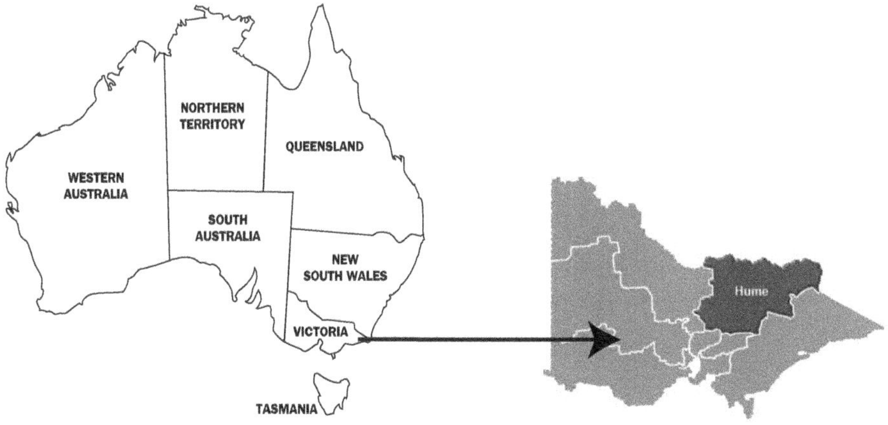

Source: Polyvore (2014) and Victorian Community Transport Association (2014)

Table 8.1: Participant characteristics

Name	Age (years)	Time in area (years)	Residential history
Al	69	69	Long term rural resident
Betty	73	14	Retirement migrant from city
Bob	73	13	Retirement migrant from city; previously lived in a regional area
Clarrie	98	98	Long-term rural resident; moved in from a farm
Donald	66	11	Retirement migrant from city
George	76	14	Retirement migrant from city
John	66	66	Long term rural resident
Joan	64	11	Retirement migrant from city
Ken	77	7	Retirement migrant from city
Mary	74	7	Retirement migrant from city
Molly	73	2	Retirement migrant from city; grew up in a rural area
Peggy	77	22	Retirement migrant from regional centre
Robert	66	40	Long-term rural resident; previously lived in a rural community
Tom	82	82	Long term rural resident; moved in from a farm
Val	67	11	Retirement migrant from city
William	68	11	Retirement migrant from city

order to explore how lifecourse rural interactions impacted on healthy ageing. Thus, the focus of interviews was on meanings and decisions associated with rural living, with all interviews being tape recorded, transcribed and analysed thematically. Data were analysed in a two-step process (Patton, 2002), where the data were evaluated using an interpretive approach to identify emergent themes. A higher order deductive analysis was then conducted using Elder's (1998) lifecourse principles as a framework. Findings explore how older residents' ability and desire to age rurally was shaped by lifecourse experiences of rurality with reference to location, linked lives, agency and timing.

Rurality and healthy ageing: a lifecourse perspective

The ability and desire of older rural residents to age in place was influenced by congruence between the individual and their community. This was discussed both in relation to the role of their rural community in enabling functionality, and in facilitating attachment and identity processes. However, this was guided by interactions within the demographic, social, physical and historical contexts associated with rurality, and the relationships they shared with people within these contexts across their lives. It also reflected choices and actions within rural contexts across the lifecourse, and the importance of life transitions in shaping their relationships with their rural places.

Location

As Elder (1998) has illustrated, older people's lives are embedded in the historical and social contexts they experience over the lifecourse. Thus, participants highlighted ways in which historical contexts and social change associated with rurality, and their experience of this over the lifecourse, had shaped their ability to age well in these locations. While some had always resided in their communities, and identified strongly with the historical context, those who had relocated in retirement had also experienced changing social and historical contexts. A number had holidayed in the area with young children, or even as children themselves, or had lived in other rural areas throughout their lives. These associations had led them to identify strongly with their rural setting, despite having previously resided in urban locations.

As a result of prolonged engagement with their rural communities, older residents were intimately familiar with their physical settings. They were also familiar with historical events and transitions that had occurred within the community, and had experienced these either actively or passively. For example, older residents within one community had experienced the relocation of their rural town as teenagers in the 1950s, and some had witnessed the rebuilding of their communities from the ground up:

> 'With the shift there was a lot of portable buildings and that of course, the workmen when they were building the town had a whole lot of little huts along Thomas St in the town, little one man huts, and they all lived there, and then gradually, all the wooden buildings that were worthwhile [were] shifted by truck down to here' (John, resident for 66 years).

Some recalled the difficulties and isolation associated with living in their community prior to cars, proper roads and air conditioning. Others discussed changes relating to local government and economic restructuring, business centralisation, housing development, declines in health and community services, and the influence of demographic and climate change on their communities. The impact of events such as the Great Depression and prolonged drought were also highlighted:

> 'We've had the 10 year drought and the lake was virtually drying up, it was down to about 2 or 3% or something like that volume at one

stage, we understand that because we'd seen dry weather before' (Bob, resident for 13 years).

This embeddedness in the historical milieu of their communities was significant in creating a sense of attachment for older residents. Through recollections of place across different stages of their lives, they felt 'part of' that community, and length of residence was a significant predictor of this for those ageing in place. Their experience of the community and the historical context over time created an 'embeddedness' that provided security and a status within the community as they aged, in that they felt they were a 'local'. While it was perceived that newcomers could not identify with this, this embeddedness was also described by those newer to the community:

> 'I've got good friends that are people that have only moved here recently, just they have that feeling they don't think that sort of, they're locals yet, maybe it's because of all the things we've done here they can't relate to any of the stories' (John, resident for 66 years).

> 'I think it's just that I know the place. That I've always known it since I was about, oh I suppose I would have been about 14 I suppose since I first came here' (Joan, resident for 11 years).

The impact of these historical events was also significant in creating community resilience and shaping place satisfaction. Where community improvements had occurred, older residents derived a sense of pride in watching these take place, or having contributed to them, particularly in relation to traditional community events or community infrastructure. The response of communities to adverse historical events such as bushfires and the loss of community structures promoted feelings of pride and belonging, as one participant indicated:

> 'Oh yeah, I'm proud of the place, yeah. And as I say I'm proud of the workforce that lays dormant and if something big came up exactly like [the local bushfires] we can rise to the occasion' (Al, resident for 69 years).

However, changes that had occurred within communities impacted on perceived person-environment fit, both functionally and in terms of attachment. These related to perceptions of what living in a rural area should be like based on historical experience, or comparative assessments with how rural communities used to be. Participants highlighted concerns such as not knowing their neighbours; increased tourism and development, and resultant vandalism and traffic; youth out-migration and the impact of local population ageing; and change in traditional community events. This impacted on community satisfaction and, for some, decreased their ability to negotiate their environments. Some then experienced a lack of fit with their environment, prompting isolation and disengagement, which was particularly pronounced among long-term residents.

Linked lives

While location in time and place related closely to the fit of older individuals with the physical and historical nature of rurality, the concept of 'linked lives' reflected the fit between older rural residents and their communities. This emphasised the importance of social connectivity in older age and specifically, the interconnections between friends and family across the lifecourse. For older residents, community relationships were critical from the perspective of maintaining historical links, fostering a sense of belonging and identity, and in maintaining autonomy. Most participants indicated that friendship was a key motivator for remaining in their communities, and for retirement migrants, connections with friends and family had shaped their initial motivations to reside in their rural community. Some had moved to be close to friends who had relocated, or to parents ageing in rural areas:

> 'So we said, we may as well come up there and build and live up there, because your mum and dad are getting older' (Donald, resident for 11 years).

For long-term rural residents, generational links with place further embedded them in the locale. As well as being historically entrenched, they were socially entrenched, with up to three generations residing in their regions. These links, both current and historical, were influential in dictating their desire to age in place. Living in their communities allowed them to draw on the support of their families, as was also discussed by retirement migrants who had family members relocate to their regions. A number of participants highlighted the importance of the region in linking them with prior generations, with one participant indicating that living in a community where he could fish connected him with memories of his childhood. Those who had moved in from farms also emphasised the significance of generational connections in relation to family farming. One participant indicated that her involvement in community activities across the lifecourse had been, and continued to be, influenced by her late husband:

> 'I was always Herb's backstop. That was- whatever he did, I was- because we were married just on 55 years. Whatever he's done, I've always just been there behind him sort of thing. But I find now that- well, I'll still keep on whatever he's done. Maybe take more of a role in it than what I did before' (Peggy, resident for 22 years).

As well as this, long-term relationships with local friends were critical in fostering attachment, in that they shared a common history that extended across the lifecourse:

> 'We've just got such a lot in common you know. We talk about the old town a lot, all that sort of thing and what's going on in the community' (Al, resident for 69 years).

In discussing linked lives, all participants highlighted the theme of 'community', and the importance of the collective experience of social and historical contexts, especially in relation to dealing with adversity. Participants described the manner in which small populations, coupled with high levels of community involvement, created linked lives, where they became familiar and involved with the lives of other local residents. This was achieved by involvement in community services and activities across the lifecourse, or through the long-term experience of events such as drought and flood:

> 'I think we tend to laugh and cry with the farmers. You never had that empathy with them when we were in Melbourne but now when we see them, they've got these beautiful crops of canola all ready to harvest and boom, down comes weeks of rain and the stuff's degraded horribly or wrecked altogether. That's been a change in your life … you understand what the poor man on the land is going through' (George, resident for 14 years).

Participants highlighted the interconnectedness of families in the regions, and the benefits of small communities in this regard. This provided an identity which was often created through family lineage or community connections and which fostered a sense of social belonging. The demographic ageing of rural communities was also significant in fostering integration in terms of common experiences of ageing:

> 'When you get neighbours in your own age group too, I think it makes a difference. Older ones shifting into young areas, sometimes they don't fit in because the young ones have got their children and their activities and things like that, you don't fit in as well' (Mary, resident for 7 years).

Shared social engagement resulted in enhanced social capital and security, which was integral in compensating for some of the disadvantages associated with rural living. Connections developed across the lifecourse also meant that older residents were familiar with service providers at both a personal and a professional level, resulting in enhanced personal agency. Conversely, some participants highlighted the difficulties associated with a lack of, or decline in, personal linkages at this stage of life. A number of retirement migrants intimated that pull factors relating to pressure from adult children who resided in cities, the desire to spend more time with grandchildren and the potential ill health or death of a spouse would influence their intention to age in place in their rural communities, despite these attachments. Further, as participants aged and close friends and family died or relocated due to ill health, this was detrimental to the attachment and functionality of other older residents.

Human agency

Within the social and historical context of rural living, participants had made choices across the lifecourse that impacted on their ability to age well rurally. All participants had made the decision to age in a rural community based on historical and social connections. For retirement migrants particularly, this was also based on a subjective assessment of the positive and negative aspects associated with rurality in comparison with urban environments. Participants noted positive dimensions of rural living, such as safety, cleaner air, quieter roads, high amenity, sociable communities and quality of care; and compared these elements positively to experiences of urban living. Thus, their lifecourse experiences in urban environments, in conjunction with previous interactions with rural locations, had shaped their desire to age in rural communities.

For long-term residents, agency in relation to rural residence was discussed primarily in terms of the factors that had led them to remain in rural communities. For some, rural living was not necessarily a choice, but something they were accustomed to. Other participants discussed agency across the lifecourse in relation to selecting to return to their rural communities, or in taking over family farms. While some participants had been forced to move into rural communities from farms due to loss of mobility, they often left these farms as late as possible, and maintained connections, often by passing the farm on within the family. However, while all felt that their decision to live rurally was theirs alone, a small number indicated that geographic isolation and financial constraints had limited their options to consider other environments across the lifecourse:

> 'I grew up and everything was going all right and the Great Depression smashed- well most of the farm were hard pressed. We didn't have money to run every here there and everywhere and of course then, well, desperate. I was more, would have like to have had a look around and well … money wasn't plentiful' (Clarrie, resident for 98 years).

Others suggested that they had had opportunities, but had not taken them up due to their attachment to their rural community:

> 'Well I was born here I suppose, I haven't known anything else, I've never been in a big town or city or something. Actually when I left school was applying for a job I put in for a technicians job with PMG or Telecom as it is now Telstra and I was accepted in there and all the rest and I had my board booked in Melbourne, and the day before I

> was to go I turned round and said "I don't think I could stand it in the city" and that was it I stopped home' (John, resident for 66 years).

Most participants noted that they had made a conscious effort to support their communities throughout life in order to ensure the survival of their communities and the availability of services and supports later in life. Some noted that they were now forced to take a backseat from active involvement, and others suggested that they would be forced to move from their rural communities, particularly where reduced health and mobility limited personal agency.

Timing and life transitions

Finally, participants discussed the impact of key life transitions on the ageing process in rural contexts. This was pronounced among retirement migrants, who noted how life changes such as retirement or family leaving home played a role in influencing their decision to relocate, in that relocating to a rural location was significant in heralding this life transition:

> 'We'd thought about it for a while, but anyway- yeah so one day we'd had enough of work and said oh well, the boys are off our hands' (Joan, resident for 11 years).

Retirement migrants emphasised the importance of deciding to relocate while they were in good health, so that they could experience the benefits that rurality had to offer, while being able to cope with the disadvantages. A number expressed regret that they had not been able to do it earlier due to difficulties in obtaining sufficient employment to support their families. However, their particular life stage had influenced their favourable perception of rural living, as one participant suggested:

> 'I wouldn't have liked to come here as a young person, a kid or something like that growing up in it because there is very little to do' (Robert, resident for 40 years).

Relocating while in 'active' retirement was critical in terms of having the resources for social participation, and to formulate the connections to facilitate attachment, community identity and to ensure social support as they aged. Timing was also significant in dictating why they would not relocate by choice in older age, even in the context of difficulties posed by rurality:

> 'Especially not at our age not ... because I think the older you get the harder it gets to make- your friends are not, they just become acquaintances and not- that's my thoughts, not real close friends like you make when you're younger' (Betty, resident for 14 years).

Long-term residents discussed the importance of timing of life decisions; and how past decisions that they had made in relation to employment or family had dictated that they would remain in their rural community. Significantly, a number mentioned the importance of key life transitions (such as marriage or the death of a parent) in dictating their residential or working histories within their rural communities, and thus their status in the community. Those who had lived on farms also highlighted the importance of retiring while their children had expressed an interest in taking it over, and while they were healthy enough to assist with the handover process to negate a sense of loss.

Discussion

Rural communities are often demographically, socially and aesthetically dissimilar to urban locations, and present specific challenges and advantages across the lifecourse. As Keating (2008a) has proposed, older people's ability to age well rurally is dependent on position in the lifecourse, community settings and the manner in which they construct their relationships with people and place. Building on this assertion, the intersections of different aspects of rurality across certain lifecourse principles are critical in shaping healthy ageing, through promoting functionality, resilience and agency, and fostering attachment and identity processes that reflect rurality. These findings closely mirror research undertaken by the authors using identity process theory, where successful ageing was contingent on the ability of rural communities to foster distinctiveness, continuity, self-esteem and self-efficacy (Winterton and Warburton, 2012). Significantly, in reference to ongoing structure/agency debates in rural ageing (Keating, 2008b), older people's lifecourse trajectories are impacting on the demographic and social characteristics of rural places. However, these demographic shifts simultaneously impact on older people across the lifecourse through altering or sustaining constructions of the rural, and influencing their capacity to foster place satisfaction, attachment and identity processes.

First, older people's historical and social links with rural locations across the lifecourse influenced their decisions either to age in place, or to relocate to rural communities in retirement. As noted earlier, the lifecourse trajectories of both retirement migrants and those ageing in place were instrumental in constructing rural spaces. Rural retirement migration in particular has been attributed to a shift towards second modernity, prompting increased individualisation and choice within consumer-driven lifestyles and the development of 'third age' identities (Higgs and Gilleard, 2006). These identities are altering the meanings associated with older age (Dannefer and Shura, 2009), which has contributed to the notion of rural places as spaces of consumption, and the creation of new rural spaces with altered meanings and practices (Perkins, 2006). For those ageing in place, their length of residence and efforts to be involved with their rural communities across the lifecourse were significant in constructing their locations as cohesive, supportive places. Similarly, the decisions of retirement migrants to relocate while they were able to participate in rural community life, and wanted to do so, were also advantageous. However, the differing lifecourse trajectories of these two groups can be a source of tension for long-term residents in terms of who is considered as 'rural', in relation to experience of historical time, place and linked lives in these locations (Brown et al, 2008). In the context of the redefinition of identities associated with late modernity (Higgs and Gilleard, 2006), and the importance of place-related identity to wellbeing in older age (Peace et al, 2006), management of this has significant implications.

However, changing demography of rural locations across the lifecourse also shapes the experience of rural ageing. For older people residing in communities that had experienced population decline, this was potentially beneficial in enabling the creation of a shared history with a small cohort of community members. This enhanced personal agency where support from family and relationships with service providers compensated for some of the service-related challenges. Rural population ageing was also beneficial in fostering linked lives, through allowing older residents to age within a similar cohort. However, retirement migration is prompting growth in some high-amenity rural communities, and coupled with increased tourism and youth out-migration, this trend has altered community composition. This negatively impacted on place attachment and satisfaction, by reducing perceived safety and personal agency. Changing composition also influenced the historical links with location and other residents that were created over time, which presented conflicting ideals of what the rural environment should represent. This was particularly salient for retirement migrants, who often viewed their rural communities as sites of consumption that reflected their personal values and desired life transitions.

For long-term residents, community demographic and social change across the lifecourse had often embedded them in historical time and place, and created connections with other longer-term residents based on shared experiences. However, the trend of younger cohorts to relocate to urban centres reduced the agency of older people in that they were less able to access support, forcing them to consider relocation. This is problematic, as out-migration of older community members will impact their ability to maintain linked lives, and the ability to relive and further create historical and social connections within rural spaces. Significantly, it will also impact on the capacity of the older people who remain in rural places to maintain their historical and social links.

In conclusion, factors associated with both older people's differing lifecourse trajectories and rural demographic shifts dictate their lifecourse engagement with rural places, and this continued renegotiation of what it means to age rurally can be simultaneously beneficial and unfavourable. As Phillipson (2006) has noted, the individualisation of risks associated with ageing is a key issue, and while older people are often active agents in constructing rural spaces across the lifecourse, certain demographic shifts restrict the agency of specific groups and their historical and social emplacement within rural space. Where these changes cannot be accommodated, certain older people will be at risk of exclusion and placelessness (Relph, 1976). While this research has been conducted in the Australian context, international studies have identified both similar demographic challenges related to rural ageing and the importance of relationships with place in maintaining personal wellbeing (Keating and Phillips, 2008; Walsh et al, 2012). Thus, while findings may be transferable to other rural contexts, the diversity of rural communities across national and international contexts must be considered. Research needs to identify ways in which place attachment and identification can be fostered in the context of demographic change and the urban–rural divide. In response to increasing rural diversity and population ageing, connection to place is critical in ensuring the sustainability of rural places, and the wellbeing of individuals who reside there.

References

Alston, M. (2007) 'Globalisation, rural restructuring and health service delivery in Australia: policy failure and the role of social work?', *Health and Social Care in the Community*, 15, 195-202.

Australian Bureau of Statistics (2009) *Future population growth and ageing*. www.abs.gov.au/AUSSTATS/abs@.nsf/Lookup/4102.0Main+Features10March%202009

Australian Bureau of Statistics (2010) *Regional population growth, Australia, 2008-09*. www.abs.gov.au/ausstats/abs@.nsf/Products/3218.0~2008-09~Main+Features~Main+Features?OpenDocument#PARALINK11

Australian Bureau of Statistics (2011a) *Australian statistical geographical standard (ASGS) volume 1 – main structure and greater capital city statistical areas*. Canberra: Australian Government.

Australian Bureau of Statistics (2011b) *Frequently asked questions*. www.abs.gov.au/websitedbs/D3310114.nsf/home/Frequently+Asked+Questions

Australian Bureau of Statistics (2013) *Where and how do Australia's older people live?* www.abs.gov.au/ausstats/abs@.nsf/Lookup/2071.0main+features602012-2013

Australian Institute of Health and Welfare (2007) *Older Australians at a glance*. Australian Government, Australian Institute of Health and Welfare. www.aihw.gov.au/publications/age/oag04/oag04-c05.pdf

Bengtson, V., Elder, G.H. and Putney, N. (2012) 'The life course perspective on ageing: Linked lives, timing and history', in J. Katz, S. Peace and S. Spurr (eds) *Adult lives: A life course perspective*, Bristol: Policy Press, 9-17.

Black, A. (2005) 'Rural communities and sustainability', in C. Cocklin and J. Dibden (eds) *Sustainability and change in rural Australia*, Sydney: University of New South Wales Press, 20-37.

Bonnes, M. and Secchiaroli, G. (1995) *Environmental psychology: a psychosocial introduction*, London: SAGE.

Bronfenbrenner, U. (1977) 'Toward an experimental ecology of human development', *American Psychologist*, 32, 513-31.

Brown, D., Glasgow, N., Kulcsar, L., Bolender, B. and Arguillas, M. (2008) 'Community challenges and opportunities associated with retirement in-migration', in D. Brown and N. Glasgow (eds) *Rural retirement migration*, New York: Springer, 141-77.

Burholt, V. and Naylor, D. (2005) 'The relationship between rural community type and attachment to place for older people living in North Wales, UK', *European Journal of Ageing*, 2, 109-19.

Costello, L. (2007) 'Going bush: The implications of urban-rural migration', *Geographical Research*, 45, 85-94.

Dannefer, D. and Shura, R. (2009) 'Experience, social structure and later life: Meaning and old age in an aging society', in P. Uhlenberg (ed) *International handbook of population aging*, New York: Springer, 747-56.

Davis, S. and Bartlett, H. (2008) 'Healthy ageing in rural Australia: Issues and challenges', *Australasian Journal on Ageing*, 27, 56-60.

Elder, G.H. (1998) 'The life course as developmental theory', *Child Development*, 69, 1-12.

Giele, J.Z. and Elder, G.H. (1998) 'Life course research: Development of a field', in J.Z. Giele and G.H. Elder (eds) *Methods of life course research: Qualitative and quantitative approaches*, Thousand Oaks: Sage, 5-27.

Gray, I. and Phillips, E. (2001) 'Beyond life in "the bush": Australian rural cultures', in S. Lockie and L. Bourke (eds) *Rurality bites: The social and environmental transformation of rural Australia*, Annandale: Pluto Press, 52-60.

Guba, E.G. and Lincoln, Y.S. (1982) *Effective evaluation*, San Francisco: Jossey-Bass.

Halfacree, K.H. (1993) 'Locality and social representation: Space, discourse and alternative definitions of the rural', *Journal of Rural Studies*, 9, 23-37.

Higgs, P. and Gilleard, C. (2006) 'Departing the margins: Social class and later life in a second modernity', *Journal of Sociology*, 42, 219-41.

Hugo, G. (2012) 'Population distribution and internal migration', in J. Pincus and G. Hugo (eds) *A greater Australia: population, policies and governance*, Melbourne: Committee for Economic Development of Australia, 72-95.

Keating, N. (2008a) 'Revisiting rural ageing', in N. Keating (ed) *Rural ageing: A good place to grow old?*, Bristol: Policy Press, 121-30.

Keating, N. (2008b) *Rural ageing: A good place to grow old?*, Bristol: Policy Press.

Keating, N. and Phillips, J. (2008) 'A critical human ecology perspective on rural ageing', in N. Keating (ed) *Rural ageing: A good place to grow old?*, Bristol: Policy Press, 1-10.

McKenzie, F. and Frencken, M. (2001) 'The lively dying town. Challenging our perspectives of rural ageing', *Australian Planner*, 38, 16-21.

Office for National Statistics (2004) *Rural/urban definition (England and Wales)*. www.ons.gov.uk/ons/guide-method/geography/products/area-classifications/rural-urban-definition-and-la/rural-urban-definition--england-and-wales-/index.html

Patton, M.Q. (2002) *Qualitative research and evaluation methods*, California: SAGE.

Peace, S., Holland, C. and Kellaher, L. (2006) *Environment and identity in later life*, Berkshire: Open University Press.

Perkins, H. (2006) 'Commodification: Re-resourcing rural areas', in P. Cloke, T. Marsden and P. Mooney (eds) *The handbook of rural studies*, London: Sage, 243-57.

Phillipson, C. (2006) 'Aging and globalisation', in J.A. Vincent, C. Phillipson and M. Downs (eds) *The futures of old age*, London: Sage, 201-7.

Polyvore (2014), Australia states territories outline map. www.polyvore.com/australia_states_terriotories_outline_map/thing?id=14072103&p=2

Relph, E. (1976) *Place and placelessness*, London: Pion.

Rowles, G. (1983) 'Place and personal identity in old age: Observations from Appalachia', *Journal of Environmental Psychology*, 3, 299-313.

Rubinstein, R. and Parmelee, P. (1992) 'Attachment to place and the representation of the life course by the elderly', in I. Altman and S. Low (eds) *Place attachment*, New York: Plenum Press, 139-63.

Scharf, T. and Bartlam, B. (2008) 'Ageing and social exclusion in rural communities', in N. Keating (ed) *Rural ageing: A good place to grow old?*, Bristol: Policy Press, 97-107.

Statistics Canada (2013) *Population centre (POPCTR): Detailed definition*. www.statcan.gc.ca/pub/92-195-x/2011001/geo/pop/def-eng.htm

Twigger-Ross, C. and Uzzell, D. (1996) 'Place and identity processes', *Journal of Environmental Psychology*, 16, 205-20.

United Nations (2009) *World population ageing 2009*, New York: Department of Economic and Social Affairs, Population Division.

Victorian Community Transport Association (2014), Community Transport Providers for Hume Region. www.vcta.org.au/ct-services-contacts/hume/

Wahl, H. and Weisman, G. (2003) 'Environmental gerontology at the beginning of the new millenium: Reflections on its historical, empirical and theoretical development', *Gerontologist*, 43, 616-27.

Walsh, K., O'Shea, E., Scharf, T. and Murray, M. (2012) 'Ageing in changing community contexts: Cross-border perspectives from rural Ireland and Northern Ireland', *Journal of Rural Studies*, 28, 347-57.

Wiles, J., Allen, R., Palmer, A., Hayman, K., Keeling, S. and Kerse, N. (2009) 'Older people and their social spaces: A study of well-being and attachment to place in Aotearoa New Zealand', *Social Science & Medicine*, 68, 664-71.

Winterton, R. and Warburton, J. (2012) 'Ageing in the bush: The role of rural places in maintaining identity for long-term rural residents and retirement migrants in north-east Victoria, Australia', *Journal of Rural Studies*, 28, 329-37.

Woods, M. (2005) *Rural geography: Processes, responses and experiences in rural restructuring*, London: SAGE.

Ziersch, A., Baum, S., O'Connor, K., Darmawan, I., Kavanagh, A. and Bentley, R. (2009) 'Social capital and health in rural and urban communities in South Australia', *Australian and New Zealand Journal of Public Health*, 33, 7-16.

Part III

PRACTICAL IMPLICATIONS

NINE

The individual in ageing Germany: how the self-employed plan for their old age

Annette Franke

Introduction

Due to an increasing life expectancy in most Western countries, individuals live longer than their parents and their grandparents did. At the same time, traditional support mechanisms, for example pension schemes and health institutions, are challenged because of demographic changes, tight job markets and altered family patterns. Thus, social and demographic changes have become important structural features of contemporary lifecourses, and welfare states emphasise the importance of individual foresight for later life regarding health and social networks as well as adequate income and housing. Against this background, the topic of retirement planning addresses the individual attempt to tackle uncertainty about the future. It symbolises a complex equation between chances and potentials – but also risks – for retiring comfortably. The questions of 'when' and 'what' in retirement planning depend on individual expectations in old age and planning behaviour as well as socioeconomic conditions and social policy context (Street and Desai, 2012).

From the psychological perspective, retirement planning refers, for example, to the concepts of foresighted decision-making and goal achievement. Following the sociological approach, retirement planning is framed by social institutions and socioeconomic resources such as qualification level or work characteristics (Ruhm, 1990; Settersten, 2003; Cate and John, 2007; Komp et al, 2010; Cobb-Clark and Stillman, 2009; Noone et al, 2012; Radl, 2012). Planning for later life also draws on the concepts of lifecourse approach, life stages, destandardisation and differentiation. While the lifecourse concept examines the holistic, socially embedded individual life history and the influence of prior life experiences on today's outcomes, the concept of life stages focuses on age-related sequential stages, such as childhood, adulthood and old age (Grenier, 2012). Kohli (1985, 2007), developing the idea of an institutionalised lifecourse that is shaped by social institutions and regulations.

In recent years, concepts of destandardisation, differentiation and individualisation of the lifecourse in postmodern societies have enriched academic lifecourse research (Giddens, 1991; Beck, 1992). The concept of destandardisation, for example, describes a reduced influence of social institutions on the lifecourse and the modification of distinct life stages due to increasing flexibility of labour markets and welfare arrangements (Brückner and Mayer, 2005). The approach of differentiation of lifecourses criticises the universal view of life histories and points to the variation of lifecourses as a consequence of different historical and social arrangements (Mayer, 2009). With the concept of individualisation, Beck (1992) underlines the detachment of individuals from traditional social bonds, norms and support mechanisms, which leads to the development of modified forms of integration into social institutions.

The lifecourse approach as a framework is crucial for effective welfare instruments in health care and old-age provision (see also Chapter 13 in this volume by Komp and Marier on lifecourse policy). This chapter focuses on the twin issues of retirement timing and financial planning among the group of older entrepreneurs and self-employed workers in Germany. Germany (together with Italy and Japan) represents one of the 'oldest countries' worldwide (World Bank, 2013). In addition, an increasing rate of interrupted working careers and more temporary, low-paid jobs demand a crucial focus on financial and health security in later life (Eichhorst et al, 2010; Keller et al, 2012).

Against this background, Germany's increasing rate of self-employed work[1] becomes significant. Between 1991 and 2009, the rate of self-employed individuals increased about 25%, in particular the rate of small businesses owners without employees – people who are more likely to have lower incomes and restricted financial resources (Piorkowsky et al, 2010). Many of the people falling into this category became self-employed as a solution to avoiding or tackling unemployment. Hence, self-employment work here often represents an uncertain and unexpected sequence in the lifecourse. Self-employed workers are confronted with new costs, such as business liability insurance, and lack the employer's social security contribution. About 75% of self-employed workers (or 3 million) are not compulsorily integrated into the system of old-age provision (Deutscher Bundestag, 2009). Thus, meaningful options for the self-employed and work-related status changes in the lifecourse are needed, to avoid the risk of poverty in older age due to pension gaps.

How do older self-employees plan their transition into retirement? Which structural influence from previous experiences in working life can be observed? To answer these questions, this chapter presents the results of a qualitative study on entrepreneurs and self-employed individuals aged 50-plus in Germany. The first section describes the current state of research on retirement planning of self-employed workers. Key information on recent trends in the transition to retirement in Germany is presented in the second section. After a brief description of central theories on lifecourse research and retirement planning, the next section is dedicated to the author's empirical findings. Finally, conclusions are offered in the last section.

Current state of research

Several studies underline structural factors that influence the decision of older workers to exit the labour market. These impacts can be divided into 'push' factors (age discrimination in the workplace, health limits, lack of job alternatives) and 'pull' factors (such as generous severance payments), which can also be found in complex combination (Naegele, 1992; Edwards et al, 2001; Aleksandrowicz et al, 2010). Thus, retirement planning is framed by aspects such as financial resources, qualification level, work characteristics and national retirement policy (Ruhm, 1990; Settersten, 2003; Aleksandrowicz et al, 2010; Komp et al, 2010; Maxin and Deller, 2011; Lancee and Radl, 2012; Noone et al, 2012; Radl, 2012).

Apart from institutional aspects, private care obligations or the parallel retirement of the partner can also promote the wish to exit work (O'Rand and Farkas, 2002; Ho and Raymo, 2009). Other studies, which concentrated on individual time aspects and motivation, conclude that individual constructions of endings in the lifecourse (as awareness of retirement age) show a strong impact on personal goals (Neugarten et al, 1965; Carstensen et al, 1999; Lang and Carstensen, 2002; Timmer et al, 2003; Cate and John, 2007). Some evidence can be found that, in this context, the attitudes towards future opportunities are perceived as being limited for older people (Ekerdt and DeViney, 1993; Lang and Carstensen, 2002; Cate and John, 2007; Aleksandrowicz et al, 2010). These results match lower job mobility with increasing age (Blossfeld, 1986; Schils and Muffels, 2003). A German study from Aleksandrowicz et al (2010) provides an interesting insight into the desire of retired workers to return to work. Thus, retirees are more motivated to return to work compared to part-time workers prior to retirement. The authors label this fact with the term 'an a-reflective attitude', which indicates that a future benefit can hardly be estimated in the present.

The individual retirement planning of older self-employed individuals explicitly has received little academic attention so far (Sainsbury et al, 2006; Hochguertel, 2010). Based on data from the US American Health and Retirement Study, Ekerdt et al (2000) found that self-employed workers were less likely to consider their retirement than employees (see also Abraham and Houseman, 2004). Devaney and Haejeong (2003) came to the conclusion that two thirds have no retirement plans – this was more likely for persons without spouses, with health limitations, and with few resources. These results are concordant with the outcomes of the Australian study from Cobb-Clark and Stillman (2009), based on the Household Income and Labour Dynamics in Australia (HILDA) survey. The authors point out that the status of being self-employed reduces the option for concrete retirement plans by about 70%. The British study of Parker and Rougier (2007) found evidence that income plays an important role in staying active in the labour market. In comparison to employees, aspects like gender, health and family do not have an emphasis on retirement planning for business owners. Also the study by Hochguertel (2010) takes a concrete look at the retirement behaviour and wish for future retirement among older self-employed people. Based on SHARE data of male heads of households, Hochguertel concludes that self-employed workers are 10% less likely to have the idea of early retirement. Interestingly, here income does not have a strong impact on retirement plans compared to factors such as education or marital status and health. In other words, unmarried self-employed individuals with a higher qualification level and better health conditions are more likely to stay in the labour market for longer (Hochguertel, 2010). However, due to the limitation of only including male participants, this research provides no information on gender-specific performances of retirement planning among the self-employed. There are still open questions: how the self-employed in the third age view their own future retirement, and how these individual expectations are linked to the occupational status over the lifecourse.

Paths of transition to retirement in Germany

Two aspects of German old-age provision create concerns about the future economic situation of the self-employed (especially for small businesses without employees): the self-employed are not compulsorily integrated into the statutory pension insurance scheme; and access to, and the amount of, benefits depends on the income-related entitlements during the individual employment history. Inconsistent working careers beyond full-time employment over the lifecourse, like unemployment or atypical work, therefore indicate reduced benefits after leaving the labour market.

German old-age provision operates on a three-pillar system:

- the public pension insurance, which comprises statutory pension insurance, the civil service pension scheme and pension schemes for the self-employed in certain professions (farmers, lawyers, artists, and so on);
- the occupational retirement provision as a funding system;[2]
- with increasing importance, voluntary private provision (Ebbinghaus, 2006; Bäcker et al, 2010; Wörz, 2011).

In addition, a minimum tax-based provision is guaranteed for older individuals with low income in need of social welfare. However, old-age provision in Germany is characterised by the dominance of the public pension insurance – and thus the importance of income-related entitlements from the previous employment career. About 35 million employees are covered by the statutory insurance scheme,[3] more than 80% of the population (Deutsche Rentenversicherung Bund, 2012a). The system is based on the pay-as-you-go principle, and the working population's contributions are divided between employee and employer. With the exceptions that apply to most of the self-employed and civil servants, all employees (and recipients of social welfare) are insured compulsorily in the public pension system, regardless of their income. The self-employed can join the public pension fund voluntarily, but have to pay fully for their insurance contribution or have to consider making private provision for old age.

With the public pension reforms of 1992 and 1999, traditional pension policy shifted to a new paradigm of advertising promoting longer working careers (Bundesministerium für Arbeit und Soziales, 2006; Vogel et al, 2012). In addition, the European Union set the 'Stockholm targets' as a strategic goal (employment rate of 50% for people 55-64 years) to meet the international trend of an ageing and shrinking workforce. In 2007, the German government also decided – from 2012 and the birth cohorts from 1947 onwards – to raise the statutory retirement age from 65 gradually to 67 years. By the year 2029 and with the birth cohorts from 1964 the new retirement age will cover the overall population. In addition, early retirement implies actuarial reduction. In fact, there exist various paths of transition into retirement: 'Instead, the majority of individuals leave career jobs well before retirement and enter a transitional jobstopping period composed of some combination of bridge employment, partial retirement, and reverse retirement' (Ruhm, 1990: 494).

According to the specific situation for self-employed workers, official data regarding their transition to retirement are still patchy. The current tendency, based on data from the German Pension Fund, suggests that only half of the population retires directly from employment where contributions are required to be made for statutory social welfare benefits or from other occupational positions with voluntarily entitlements as civil servants or self-employed. However, half of the employees here are involved in partial retirement schemes. Other paths into retirement are previous unemployment or government-funded bridge jobs or retiring after years of homemaking (Zähle et al, 2009; Simonson et al, 2011; Burkert and Hochfellner, 2013).

In addition, the Federal Institute for Population Research in Germany recently published a study (Bundesinstitut für Bevölkerungsforschung, 2014) on the willingness of people aged 55-70 years to work after retirement. According to the results, self-employed workers are most willing to work longer (67%), followed by white-collar workers (48%), blue-collar workers (45%) and civil servants (42%).

Selected gerontological and lifecourse concepts for individual age planning

The aim of this section is to provide a comprehensive historical overview of key theoretical concepts concerning the idea of individual age planning. In light of the aforementioned discussion, the selected concepts contribute to the transition process of retirement and address the aspects of imagining retirement, decision-making and concrete retirement planning (for a detailed overview, see Feldmann and Beehr, 2011; Wang et al, 2011).

Disengagement theory

The disengagement theory posited by Elaine Cumming and William Henry (1961) focuses on the social function and social roles of older people in society and the process of interaction between older and younger actors in their social circle. According to Cumming and Henry, older people tend to voluntarily withdraw stepwise from their social system (for instance the labour market) as they increasingly perceive physical and cognitive limitations with age: 'Aging is an inevitable, mutual withdrawal or disengagement, resulting in decreased interaction between the aging person and others in the social system he belongs to' (Cumming and Henry, 1961: 14). Thus, this theoretical approach stipulates retirement planning as a known consequence of a general decline in older people's competencies and abilities, leading them to adjust future aspirations. Against this background, disengagement theory is controversial, as older people are perceived as increasingly frail and unfit for working society, and thus lifecourse experiences are substantially neglected.

Continuity theory

Robert Atchley's (1971) concept of a 'continuity theory' states that older people try to maintain their lifestyle, previous activities and behaviours even after retirement (Feldmann and Beehr, 2011). Expectations of retirement and concrete plans for the future are contingent on experiences made over the lifecourse. Some studies found evidence for Atchley's approach regarding the motivation of bridge employment, for example becoming self-employed in older age or other gainful activities after retirement (Ekerdt et al, 2000; Kim and Feldmann, 2000; von Bonsdorff et al, 2009).

In addition, Atchley (1976) created a conceptual phase model, which reflects retirement both as a process and a life stage.

- The first phase begins about three years prior to the actual retirement event. Individuals become aware of their future retirement but still have only vague ideas of life as a retiree. However, expectations for leaving the labour market are positive overall ('remote phase').
- As the retirement event approaches ('near phase'), individuals start to calculate financial resources and savings and prepare for general changes in their daily routines. Individual goals and ideas regarding their new life without work swing between realistic intensions and unfeasible illusions.
- The honeymoon phase starts with the final entry into retirement and comprises the first weeks immediately after stopping work. Here, individuals positively perceive the lack of responsibility as similar to vacation and start to establish desired leisure activities (such as travelling or family time). This euphoria ends with a steady feeling of disillusion known as the disenchantment period.
- Hereafter, individuals enter the phase of 'reorientation'. Retirees start to reconsider their resources and try to develop new avenues and strategies for an enjoyable retirement.
- In the fifth phase ('stability'), individuals establish fulfilling routines and activities which help them maintain a feeling of satisfaction and self-affirmation.

- The last phase of termination refers to new experiences with illness, decreasing autonomy, and the need for care.

With regard to the question of retirement planning, the pre-retirement phase in particular is an important stage of thinking about future life. However, the fourth period of reorientation in retirement also contains the expectations of future life and the option of establishing new activities, such as re-employment or self-employment.

Socioemotional selectivity theory

A more recent and cognitive-oriented lifespan view of retirement planning derives from Laura Carstensen, who extends Baltes' model of 'selection optimization and compensation' (Carstensen et al, 1999; Lang and Carstensen, 2002; Carstensen, 2006). According to Carstensen's 'socioemotional selectivity theory', individuals become increasingly aware of their shrinking time horizon and future perspectives. Long-term knowledge-related outcomes become more and more unlikely, thus older individuals develop a new constellation of emotion-related, present-oriented goals, which can be immediately achieved. As a result of this temporal context, they tend to redefine the importance of specific goals that they still want to fulfil in the remaining time and become increasingly selective in their motivation. Activities are more related to positive and enjoyable interactions with the family and invested in their social network. The premise of the socioemotional selectivity theory is the construct of 'future time perspective' (Carstensen et al, 1999; Lang and Carstensen, 2002). This future time perspective describes the aforementioned individual perception of either a boundless or a limited future. According to this bipolar concept, individuals either perceive their future as being filled with opportunities and options for further goals, or they primarily take notice of restrictions and losses (Cate and John, 2007).

Lifecourse theory

Lifecourse theories represent an integrated approach for explaining current outcomes as a sum of personal events and roles in life history. Lifecourse theories further argue that life histories reflect the shaping function of social and structural context (Neugarten et al, 1965; Kohli, 1985; Elder, 1994; Settersten, 2003; Wang et al, 2011). Changes are embedded over a long stretch in a lifetime, so prior life experiences and events have the potential to construct today's outcomes as a domino effect on the individual and family level (Mayer, 2009). This recognition of cumulative advantages or disadvantages is crucial for understanding heterogeneity and social inequality in later life (Grenier, 2012).

The lifecourse perspective encompasses several social circumstances which shape individual lives in contemporary societies (time, location, context, social and cultural units, etc.), and is created as a multidisciplinary approach, involving, for example, sociology, gerontology, psychology, or economics. However, there is still no comprehensive theory which satisfactorily frames the empirical research (Mayer, 2009).

Lifecourse theories point out that perception and decisions of age planning are not created from scratch, but rather are embedded in, and transformed by, conditions and events occurring during the historical and social context in which people live (Grenier, 2012). Kohli (1985, 2007) establishes a model of the institutionalisation of the lifecourse shaped by social institutions and regulations. Thus, the lifecourse acts as a predictable social programme for individual positions and orientations through all stages in age. Elder (1985) elaborates the importance of transitions and trajectories as social organisations. While transitions represent discrete life changes or events (for example, parenthood), trajectories are long-term sequences of linked states within a conceptually defined range of behaviour or development (for example, education and occupational career). The timing of transitions also can decrease the chance of success in a particular trajectory such as, for example, entrepreneurial activities in the third age. Thus, age-related configuration of social roles and social norms over the lifecourse create normative associations for trajectories and life events.

Arguments against universal age-stratification are central in Riley's (1987) model. In her work, Riley points out the increasing diversity of ageing, and how generations or cohorts indicate different resources in terms of other stratification elements such as gender, race or social class. Thus, people of the same age do not necessarily share the same perspectives or resources. As complementary concepts, critical gerontology and political economy emphasise the structural involvement of individuals and outcomes of former lifecourse events in old age (Estes, 1979; Minkler and Estes, 1999; Moody, 1996; Phillipson, 1982; Walker, 1981). The central principle behind this concept is the awareness and reproduction of social inequality and different living conditions with cumulative disadvantages in later life.

In her study, *The Aging Enterprise* (1979), Caroll Estes points out the main concern of the political economy of ageing, apart from strictly individualised approaches: the explanation of other individuals' structural dependency, and thus the shaping character of the structural forces and processes that contribute both to constructions of ageing and social policy. According to Estes, powerful interests and classes define a set of theories of ageing and images of older individuals as different from other members of society. The deviant character of older individuals leads on to a specific social policy for a labelled 'problem' as well as to a certain self-perception of ageing. For example, Estes argues that social policies in the US take certain advantages of poverty in old age as a mechanism of social control – 'a demonstration to the young that they must work hard and save wisely or they too would sink into the pit in old age' (Wilson, 1997: 343). The view of political economy therefore also highlights the interaction of the societal (macro level), the organisational/institutional (meso level), and the individual (micro level) dimensions of ageing (Estes, 2001).

Besides environmental aspects, which contribute to the construction of the lifecourse, individuals are active creators of decisions and goals. Thus, intentional efforts such as agency and personal control influence planning and later outcomes, depending on opportunities (Elder, 1985; Clausen, 1991; Grenier, 2012). From the economic perspective, the lifecycle model assumes that households aspire to a stable standard of living (Ando and Modigliani, 1963). Individuals try to maximise utility from consumption and saving over the lifecourse. Thus, planning and saving behaviour are predicted by the individual goal to maintain the same consumption in retirement as in previous years.

To summarise the aforementioned theoretical concepts, retirement planning from an integrated lifecourse perspective is shaped by social age norms, individual goals, the policy framework, family issues as well as positive or negative experiences in the workplace and planning behaviour. All the different concepts discussed here have been used frequently as theoretical frameworks for several studies on individual age planning. However, these models only symbolise specific blueprints of various theoretical paths towards understanding retirement planning.

Results from a qualitative study on older self-employed in Germany

The presented outcomes in this section are based on a qualitative study on older entrepreneurs and self-employed people in Germany (Franke, 2012). Data from the US show that half of all new businesses are created by people over 45 (Fairlie, 2011). In Germany, nearly every fourth entrepreneur belongs to this age group, and policy makers are paying more attention to the older self-employed as a symbol for productive ageing (Engel et al, 2007).

From a lifecourse perspective, older entrepreneurs and the self-employed constitute an interesting group for research on the outcomes of former employment for the new position of business owner. However, little is known about the motives, satisfaction and attitudes regarding retirement of older entrepreneurs and self-employed individuals. This study focuses on new business owners over 50, based on the grounded theory paradigm (Glaser and Strauss, 2009/1967). The minimum age has been set at 50 as the beginning of self-employment and market entry.

The theoretical sampling was oriented on the analysis of current research as well as data collection and data analysis. This sampling approach provides a recurrent and step-by-step process of collecting, coding and analysing data. All interviews were recorded, transcribed and coded with the computer program MaxQda. In the next step, data was categorised into a three-stage procedure (open, theoretical and selective coding) with the aim of finding a core category in the dataset. Further data collection was completed when the core category had been defined, and more data do not deliver any new insights (Strauss and Corbin, 1990). Qualitative interviews were conducted with 17 older self-employed people

Table 9.1: Interviewees' characteristics

Code	Sex	Age when starting own business	Marital status	Working activity	Education
Ernst	Male	54	Married	Consulting	University degree; Ph.D.
Bernhard	Male	56	Married	Private equity investors	Lower secondary school
Christel	Female	50	Single	Health counselling	University degree
Robert	Male	52	Married	Services of general economic interest	Lower secondary school
Herta	Female	58	Married	Hairdresser	Lower secondary school
Else	Female	55	Single	Trade/retail sector	High school diploma
Annegret	Female	50	Married	Health counselling	Lower secondary school
Jörg	Male	50	Married	Carpenter	Lower secondary school
Julia	Female	50	Married	Trade/catering	High school diploma
Christine	Female	54	Single	City tours/coaching	High school diploma
Ulla	Female	50	Single	Services of general economic interest	Lower secondary school
Ulf	Male	51	Married	Services of general economic interest	University degree
Ursula	Female	50	Single	Coaching	High school diploma
Wolfgang & Karl	Male/ male	51/52	Married/ married	Car garage	Lower secondary school
Rainer	Male	50	Married	Trade/retail sector	Lower secondary school
Selma	Female	50	Married	Fundraising	Univ. degree

(mean age 51, range 50-69 years) in Germany following Flick's model of episodic interviews (Flick, 2009).

Table 9.1 indicates that the gender ratio among the older self-employed is fairly balanced in comparison with the field as a whole in Germany. In addition, better educated older people seem more likely to move into self-employment – many even have a university degree. 'Heterogeneous career biographies' emerged as the core category in this study by forming a pattern for orientation, creation and perception of self-employed work. For example, late start-up plans are usually based on past experiences, knowledge and social networks – so older people are not treading entirely new ground in their self-employment. From the lifecourse perspective, the analysis indicates other key outcomes.

The lifecourse embeddedness of motivation for self-employment

Older self-employed individuals represent a distinct heterogeneous group in the labour market. The variations in motives, attitudes and patterns in their work may result in various lifecourse performances and experiences in their biographies. The main motivation for becoming self-employed in older age is an impulse to change one's own situation. While some understand their unemployment as a chance and develop a high intrinsic motivation for self-employment, others feel that this move is the only way out of unemployment.

Former experiences and conditions in work and family life have a major impact both on the approach and on avoidance motivation to become self-employed. For example, family obligations like childcare, high job satisfaction as an employee, and also the fear of risks or failure can foster a more passive attitude, with low motivation for this step, as suggested by the following direct quotation: 'There is a fear of risk and especially of failure. If this business idea fails, that's also the failure of your life work. There's no way back. And there is also the fear of financial risk when you're older' (Selma).

The results also underline historically determined inequalities between both sexes, which accumulated over the lifecourse. Thus, especially older female entrepreneurs report unstable working careers due to family work, and use self-employment more often as a strategy to gain a small additional household income or to avoid unemployment. Most of the interviewees also stated that they would have not been able to start up a business during their earlier years. The most important factors included acquired competence and experiences with increasing age, family responsibilities, laziness, lack of courage, or the fact that they could not have started their new business without the experiences and contacts gained through their prior employment: "When I was younger, I was not that self confident, neither from my personality, nor regarding my experiences. I think that especially in my job, in psychotherapy, where I have to be responsive to my clients, my age and my life experience play a very important role" (Christel).

The major impact of former work experiences

Long-term acquired experiences, skills and professional networks build up the framework for creating a new business. Thus, the individual work history is reflected in all dimensions of business creation, for example in motives, skills, networks and financial background as older entrepreneurs tend to remain in the branches or sector they are used to and where benefits look promising. In this context, age-related factors accumulated over the lifecourse as life and job experience, pension entitlements and seriousness indicate a highly positive impact: "In the past, that would have never worked out, because I didn't have the experiences, the practical knowledge. Generally, self-employment was always an idea, but today I'm able to combine my desire for social networking, my skills, and my experiences in a very positive way" (Robert).

The former job situation also creates a blueprint for the key do's and don'ts in the new business. For example, interviewees reported that they had been able to avoid the same mistakes they'd experienced in their former work environment: "All these bullying events we have witnessed, particularly with co-workers...We don't need that anymore." (Ulla). However, participants also reported specific negative impacts of ageing, for example an increasing risk of health problems and a perceived decrease in physical strength.

The high satisfaction and contentment with the second career

In this explorative study, the participants reported a high degree of general satisfaction with their decision to move into self-employment. This positive evaluation includes all branches and levels of income. Core aspects are gains in experience, a somewhat higher income, or the chance to change something in society. In this context, individual satisfaction is linked to the initial plans and goals of the new business, the freedom to create daily work, and how former experiences and knowledge can be transferred into the new job.

Aspects like the significance of the work, the locus of control and recognition from others – always reflected by comparing the former and current work – also influence job satisfaction: "I always felt hemmed in my old jobs and that they did not honour my skills" (Ursula). However, aspects like less time for leisure and holidays, high contributions for tax and social security, and more responsibilities are perceived as somewhat critical: "I envy people who have six weeks off per year. This is the only thing I really don't like about being self-employed" (Christel).

High motivation to remain active in the labour market due to financial needs or self-fulfilment

Regarding retirement planning, findings suggest high job identification and less will to retire early. In contrast, nine of the 17 individuals reported a high motivation to continue working even after reaching the statutory retirement age. The most important conditions for continuing work are the individual's health status and enjoyment in his or her tasks. The following quotation illustrates a typical attitude: "Well, as long as I'll stay healthy, I want to work longer than 65 … . Maybe not that much, but surely some hours per day. And when I'm 70 and still fit and enjoying my work … I'm not setting limits" (Christel).

Other interviewed self-employed individuals reported their wish to leave the labour market when reaching statutory retirement age, albeit early retirement was never indicated. The idea of remaining active follows a bipolar path: the intrinsic wish to stay active in the workforce; and financial needs and an additional income resource as a result of low pension claims. "I guess that for me it will never end. I won't get any money. So I always say to myself: I have to work until I die or I will die, when I won't be able to work" (Christine).

Thus, the self-employed are more likely to refuse early retirement, when they indicate good physical health and cognitive abilities, a positive framework and support from their close relatives, freedom in creating their working tasks, a high job identification, a high job satisfaction and benefits from lifecourse experiences. However, financial strain can also predict a choice to stay in the labour market. With regard to financial resources and pension entitlements, it should also be mentioned that the majority of the interviewed persons make thoughtful plans for later life, for example, in terms of private pension insurance or property-based investments. However, some individuals rely solely on the public pension system, with entitlements accumulated from their former job, and refuse to pay for private insurance.

As the study shows, retirement planning of older self-employed individuals is characterised by a remarkable work motivation and uncertainty regarding the right time and the right age to exit the labour market. However, the study also underlines the financial needs for continuing working and some concern about private provision for retirement. Older entrepreneurs/self-employed individuals are considerably less susceptible to age norms, albeit they are noticing age-related future limits (for example regarding financial amortisation in their self-employment). However, they indicate employment-related goals for the future that lead to a postponed retirement.

Conclusion

For working individuals, retirement planning is an ongoing stage in the lifecourse, framed by welfare state instruments, working conditions and individual factors. Preparedness and precautions for life after exiting the labour force become more and more essential in an ageing society, where traditional welfare state instruments are being reduced or are at least subject to reforms.

The aim of this chapter was to provide a deeper understanding of individual retirement planning of older self-employed individuals in Germany. The key results from the qualitative study underline a high job satisfaction and considerably less will for early retirement. The older entrepreneurs and self-employed workers report a remarkable motivation for remaining active in the labour market, which leads to the majority continuing to work after statutory retirement age. This desire arises from individual perception of physical and cognitive conditions, family support, personal fulfilment, and a high degree of independence and job satisfaction. On the other hand, some of the self-employed workers are not confident about whether they will have enough money to retire earlier than the state retirement age. Thus, retirement planning refers to an uncertain stage in the future, regardless of statutory age norms. Time and ageing are important factors and especially older entrepreneurs, who started their business with 50 years or later, complain a shorter future perspective for personal fulfilment and financial amortisation. In addition, diverse biographies and the role of lifecourse embeddedness are highly relevant for understanding both motives and patterns of self-employment and future retirement plans.

These explanations point to the fact that the motives for leaving or remaining in the labour market are complex and variable on the individual and social level. With regard to theoretical concepts – such as future time perspective, political economy and the lifecycle model – planning for later life is framed by gender aspects, social inequality and specific events, as well as experiences and individual conditions in one's personal life. However, the overall results should be read and interpreted carefully due to the country-specific context and the small sample size. Regarding further research on retirement planning, the results suggest a focus on approaches that tackle the question of financial resources, the role of spouses' retirement, and the influence of physical and cognitive abilities among the self-employed.

Against the background of the current public pension system in Germany, it remains a challenge to give concrete answers to the questions of financial resources and retirement provision of self-employed workers. All in all, a lifecourse perspective and the awareness of different resources and inequality remain vital for gaining an accurate insight into this complex process of planning for retirement.

Notes

[1] Self-employed work is defined as work generating the income directly from customers, clients or other organisations as opposed to being an employee of a business. An entrepreneur is a person who recently started their own business.

[2] Since 2002, the build-up of occupational and private pensions has been promoted by tax subsidies and tax breaks.

[3] Plus about 17 million so called 'passive insured', who do not currently contribute to the insurance scheme, but have already accumulated entitlements.

References

Abraham, K. and Houseman, S.N. (2004) *Work and Retirement Plans Among Older Americans*. Upjohn Institute Working Paper No. 04-105. Kalamazoo MI: W.E. Upjohn Institute for Employment Research, http://research.upjohn.org/up_workingpapers/105

Aleksandrowicz, P., Fasang, A., Schönmann, K. and Staudinger, U.M. (2010) 'Die Bedeutung der Arbeit beim vorzeitigen Ausscheiden aus dem Arbeitsleben' [The impact of work on early retirement], *Zeitschrift für Gerontologie und Geriatrie*, 43, 5, 324-29.

Ando, A. and Modigliani, F. (1963) 'The "life cycle" hypothesis of saving: Aggregate implications and tests', *The American Economic Review*, 53, 1, 55-84.

Atchley, R.C. (1971) 'Retirement and leisure participation: Continuity or crisis?', *The Gerontologist*, 11, 1, 13-17.

Atchley, R.C. (1976) *The sociology of retirement*, Cambridge, MA and New York: Schenkmann.

Bäcker, G., Naegele, G., Bispinck, R., Hofemann, K. and Neubauer, J. (2010) *Sozialpolitik und soziale Lage in Deutschland* [*Social policy and social situation in Germany*], Wiesbaden: VS Verlag für Sozialwissenschaften.

Beck, U. (1992) *Risk society*. London: Sage Publications.

Blossfeld, H.-P. (1986) 'Career opportunities in the Federal Republic of Germany: A dynamic approach to the study of life-course, cohort, and period effects', *European Sociological Review*, 2, 3, 208-25.

Brückner, H. and Mayer, K.U. (2005) 'The de-standardization of the life-course: What it might mean? And if it means anything, whether it actually took place?', *Advances in Life Course Research*, 9, 27-54.

Bundesinstitut fuer Bevoelkerungsforschung (2014) *Erwerbsarbeit & informelle Tätigkeiten der 55- bis 70-Jährigen in Deutschland* [*Work and informal activities of people aged 55-70 years in Germany*], Wiesbaden: Bundesinstitut fuer Bevoelkerungsforschung.

Bundesministerium für Arbeit und Soziales (2006) *Kraft der Erfahrungnutzen* [*Using the power of experience*], Berlin: Bundesministerium für Arbeit und Soziales.

Burkert, C. and Hochfellner, D. (2013) 'Berufliche Aktivitätim Ruhestand: Fortsetzung der Erwerbsbiographie oder notwendiger Zuverdienst?' ['Employment related activities beyond retirement: continuance of working career or financial demand?'], *Zeitschrift für Gerontologie und Geriatrie*, 46, 3, 242-50.

Carstensen, L.L. (2006) 'The influence of a sense of time on human development', *Science*, 312, 5782, 1913-15.

Carstensen, L.L., Isaacowitz, D.M. and Charles, S.T. (1999) 'Taking time seriously: A theory of socioemotional selectivity', *American Psychologist*, 54, 3, 165-81.

Cate, R.A. and John, O.P. (2007) 'Testing models of the structure and development of future time perspective: Maintaining a focus on opportunities in middle age', *Psychology and Aging*, 22, 1, 186-201.

Clausen, J.A. (1991) 'Adolescent competence and the shaping of the life course', *American Journal of Sociology*, 96, 4, 805-42.

Cobb-Clark, D. and Stillman, S. (2009) *The retirement expectations of middle-aged individuals*, Bonn: IZA Discussion Paper no. 2449.

Cumming, E. and Henry, W.E. (1961) *Growing old: The process of disengagement*, New York: Basic.

Deutsche Rentenversicherung Bund (2012a) *Rentenversicherung in Zahlen 2012. Statistik der Deutschen Rentenversicherung* [*Rension insurance in number 2012. Statistics from the German statutory pension insurance scheme*], Berlin: Deutsche Rentenversicherung Bund.

Deutscher Bundestag (2009) *Bericht der Bundesregierungüber die gesetzliche Rentenversicherung* [*Report from the German government on the German statutory pension insurance scheme*], Berlin: Deutscher Bundestag.

Devaney, S.A. and Haejeong, K. (2003) 'Older self-employed workers and planning for the future', *Journal of Consumer Affairs*, 37, 1, 123-42.

Ebbinghaus, B. (2006) *Reforming early retirement in Europe, Japan and the USA*, Oxford: Oxford University Press.

Edwards, G., Regan, S. and Brooks, R. (2001) *Age old attitudes: Attitudes towards planning for retirement, means-testing, inheritance and informal care*, London: Institute for Public Policy Research.

Eichhorst, W., Marx, P. and Thode, E. (2010) *Atypische Beschäftigung und Niedriglohnarbeit. Benchmarking Deutschland: Befristete und geringfügige Tätigkeiten, Zeitarbeit und Niedriglohnbeschäftigung*. Gütersloh: Bertelsmann Stiftung.

Ekerdt, D. and DeViney, S. (1993) 'Evidence for a preretirement process among older workers', *Journal of Gerontology, Series B: Psychological Sciences and Social Sciences*, 48, 2, 535-43.

Ekerdt, D., Kosloski, K. and DeViney, S. (2000) 'The normative anticipation of retirement by older workers', *Research on Aging*, 22, 1, 3-22.

Elder, G.H. Jr. (1985) *Life course dynamics*, Ithaca, NY: Cornell University Press

Elder, G.H. Jr. (1994) 'Time, human agency and social change: perspectives on the life course', *Social Psychology Quarterly*, 57, 1, 4-15.

Engel, D., Bauer T., Brink, K., Down, S., Hartmann, J. and Jacobi, L. (2007) *Unternehmensdynamik und alternde Bevölkerung* [*Entrepreneurship dynamics and ageing society*], Berlin: Duncker & Humbot.

Estes, C. L. (1979) *The Aging Entreprise*, San Francisco: Jossey Press.

Estes, C. (2001) 'Political economy of aging: A theoretical framework', in *Social policy & aging: A critical perspective*, Thousand Oaks, CA: SAGE Publications, 1-23.

Fairlie, R.W. (2011) *Kaufmann index of entrepreneurial activity. National report 1996-2010*, Kansas City: Kauffman Foundation.

Feldmann, D.C. and Beehr, T.A. (2011) 'A three-phase model of retirement decision making', *American Psychologist*, 66, 3, 193-203.

Flick, U. (2009) *An introduction to qualitative research*, London: Sage.

Franke, A. (2012) *Gründungsaktivitäten in derzweiten Lebenshälfte. Eine empirische Untersuchung zu Gründern 50plus im Kontext der Altersproduktivitätsdiskussion* [*Entrepreneurship in the second phase of life. An empirical study on older entrepreneurs 50plus in the context of age productivity discourses*], Wiesbaden: Springer VS.

Giddens, A. (1991) *Modernity and self-identity*, Cambridge, UK: Polity Press.

Glaser, B. and Strauss, A. (2009/1967) *The discovery of grounded theory: Strategies for qualitative research*, New Brunswick: Aldine Transaction.

Grenier, A. (2012) *Transitions and the lifecourse*, Bristol: Policy Press.

Ho, J.-H. and Raymo, J.M. (2009) 'Expectations and realization of joint retirement among dual-worker couples', *Research on Aging*, 31, 2, 153-79.

Hochguertel, S. (2010) *Self-employment around retirement age*, Tinbergen Institute: Tinbergen Institute Discussion Papers 10/067-3.

Keller, B., Schulz, S. and Seifert, S. (2012) *Entwicklung und Strukturelemente der atypischen Beschäftigung in Deutschland bis 2010*, WSI Diskussionspapier Nr. 182, Düsseldorf: Hans-Böckler-Stiftung.

Kim, S. and Feldmann, D.C. (2000) 'Working in retirement. The antecedents of bridge employment and its consequences for quality of life in retirement', *Academy of Management Journal*, 43, 6, 1195-210.

Kohli, M. (1985) 'Die Institutionalisierung des Lebenslaufs: historische Befunde und theoretische Argumente' ['The institutionalisation of the life-course – historical evidence and theoretical arguments'], *Kölner Zeitschrift für Soziologie und Sozialpsychologie*, 37, 1, 1-29.

Kohli, M. (2007) 'The institutionalization of the life course: Looking back to look ahead' *Research in Human Development*, 4, 3-4, 253-71.

Komp, K., Van Tilburg, T. and Broese van Groenou, M. (2010) 'Paid work between age 60 and 70 years in Europe: A matter of socio-economic status?' *International Journal of Ageing and Later Life*, 5, 1, 45-75.

Lancee, B. and Radl, J. (2012) 'Social connectedness and the transition from work to retirement', *The Journals of Gerontology, Series B: Psychological Sciences and Social Sciences*, 67, 4, 481-90.

Lang, F.R. and Carstensen, L.L. (2002) 'Time counts: Future time perspective, goals, and social relationships', *Psychology and Aging*, 17, 1, 125-39.

Maxin, L. and Deller, J. (2011) 'Activities in retirement: Individual experience of silver work', *Comparative Population Studies*, 35, 4, 801-32.

Mayer, K.U. (2009) 'New directions in life course research', *Annual Sociological Review*, 35, 413-33.

Minkler, M. and Estes, C. (1999) *Critical gerontology: Perspectives from political and moral Economy*, Amityville, NY: Baywood.

Moody, H.R. (1996) 'Critical theory and critical gerontology', in G. Maddox (ed), *The encyclopedia of aging*, New York: Springer Publishing, 244-5.

Naegele, G. (1992) *Zwischen Arbeit und Rente* [*Between work and retirement*], Augsburg: Maro Verlag.

Neugarten, B., Moore, J. and Lowe, J. (1965) 'Age norms, age constraints, and adult socialization', *American Journal of Sociology*, 70, 6, 710–17.

Noone, J., O'Loughlin, K. and Kendig, H. (2012) 'Socioeconomic, psychological and demographic determinants of Australian baby boomers' financial planning for retirement', *Australian Journal on Ageing*, 31, 3, 194-97.

O'Rand, A.M. and Farkas, J.I. (2002) 'Couples' retirement timing in the United States in the 1990s: The impact of market and family role demands on joint work exits', *International Journal of Sociology*, 32, 2, 11-29.

Parker, S.C. and Rougier, J.C. (2007) 'The retirement behaviour of the self-employed in Britain', *Applied Economics*, 39, 6, 697-713.

Phillipson, C. (1982) *Capitalism and the construction of old age*, London: Macmillan.

Piorkowsky, M.-B., Buddensiek, M. and Fleißig, S. (2010) *Selbständige in Deutschland 2005-2009 – Eine Strukturanalyse von Mikrozensusergebnissen* [*Self-employed in Germany 2005-2009 – a structural analysis of results from the microcensus*], Bonn: University of Bonn.

Radl, J. (2012) 'Too old to work, or too young to retire? The pervasiveness of age norms in Western Europe', *Work, Employment & Society*, 26, 5, 755-71.

Riley, M.W. (1987) 'On the significance of age in Sociology', *American Sociological Review*, 52, 1-14.

Ruhm, C.J. (1990) 'Bridge jobs and partial retirement', *Journal of Labor Economics*, 8, 4, 482-501.

Sainsbury, R., Finch, N. and Corden, A. (2006) *Self-employment and retirement: A report of research carried out by Social Policy Unit*, York: University of York, Department for Work and Pension, Research Report No 395.

Schils, T. and Muffels, R. (2003) *The ageing workforce and labour market mobility: Do mobility patterns differ between age groups and welfare regimes?*, Essex: University of Essex, Institute for Social and Economic Research, EPAG Working Paper No 4.

Settersten, R.A (2003) 'Age structuring and the rhythm of the life course', in J. Mortimer and M. Shanahan (eds) *Handbook of the Life Course*, New York, NY: Kluwer, 81-98.

Simonson, J., Romeu Gordo, L. and Titova, N. (2011) 'Changing employment patterns of women in Germany: How do baby boomers differ from older cohorts? A comparison using sequence analysis', *Advanced in Life Course Research*, 16, 2, 65-82.

Strauss, A.L. and Corbin, J. (1990) *Basics of qualitative research*, Newbury Park: Sage.

Street, D. and Desai, S. (2012) 'Planning for old age', in R. Settersten, Jr and J.L. Angel (eds) *Handbook of Sociology of Aging*, New York: Springer, 379-97.

Timmer, E., Bode, C. and Dittmann-Kohli, F. (2003) 'Expectations of gains in the second half of life: A study of personal conceptions of enrichment in a lifespan perspective', *Ageing & Society*, 23, 1, 3-24.

Vogel, E., Ludwig, A. and Börsch-Supan, A. (2012) *Aging and pension reform: Extending the retirement age and human capital formation*, München: Munich Center for the Economics of Aging (MEA), MEA Discussion Papers 257-12.

von Bonsdorff, M.E., Shultz, K.S., Leskinen, E. and Tansky, J. (2009) 'The choice between retirement and bridge employment: A continuity theory and life course perspective', *International Journal of Aging and Human Development*, 69, 2, 79-100.

Walker, A. (1981) 'Towards a political economy of old age', *Ageing and Society*, 1, 1, 73-94.

Wang, M., Henkens, K. and Van Solinge, H. (2011) 'Retirement adjustment: A review of theoretical and empirical advancements', *American Psychologist*, 66, 3, 204-13.

Wilson, G. (1997) 'A postmodern approach to structured dependency theory', *Journal of Social Policy*, 26, 3, 341-50.

World Bank (2013) *Data sheets on population ages 65 and above*, http://data.worldbank.org/indicator/SP.POP.65UP.TO.ZS

Wörz, M. (2011) *Old-age provisions in Germany. Changes in the retirement system since the 1980s*, Berlin: Social Science Research Center Berlin (WZB), Life Course Risks Working Paper No. 7.

Zähle, T., Möhring, K. and Krause, P. (2009) 'Erwerbsverläufe beim Übergang in den Ruhestand' ['Working careers at the transition to retirement'], *WSI-Mitteilungen*, 62, 11, 586-95.

TEN

Families in ageing Netherlands and ageing China: redefining intergenerational contracts in lengthened lives

Fleur Thomese and Zhen Cong

Introduction

As populations age, the structure of families and associated roles are altered in ways that can affect our view of the lifecourse. This change can be clearly seen in family relations. Families can comprise up to seven generations as some people can live as long as a hundred years or more. As a consequence of decreasing fertility, families tend to have more members who are older and fewer who are younger. The pyramid-shaped family structure is growing ever more vertical, like a beanpole. As a consequence, the linkages between the lives of family members become more complex. For example, people in middle age may now have adult children starting a family, parents needing help, while they themselves may be starting or ending a partner relationship. Greater diversity of family arrangements, within and between generations, exacerbates the increasing complexity of family structures (Cherlin, 2010). These changes call for renegotiation and redefinition of intergenerational relations. People are confronted with changing needs for, and availability of, intergenerational support where traditional arrangements may not provide guidance, like when stepparents become frail. Structural changes also open up more possibilities for material and immaterial intergenerational support, because it can skip a generation.

This chapter examines key challenges to the intergenerational contract posed by recent changes in the lifecourse. It considers the intergenerational contract as a loosely defined, yet powerful obligation to mutual support between generations. This contract exists both at the micro level of families and at the macro level of populations and states. Both levels presuppose and influence each other (Walker, 2002). The obligations between generations, and the actual support emanating from them, differ across families, social and cultural groups, and social contexts (Bengtson and Achenbaum, 1993). In general, the youngest and oldest generations, typically being the most in need of support, should be able to count on the support of their parents and children, respectively. Parental responsibility and filial piety form the core of the intergenerational contract, where parental responsibility may extend well into the early adulthood of their children. However, the lengthening of life implies that more parent and child generations may co-exist, and may also change their needs and opportunities for support. Put simply, the longer lifespan prompts a redefinition of generations and their mutual obligations in the context of family solidarity, while the verticalisation of families implies a redistribution of those needing support and those available to provide it.

The next section elaborates this argument, using theoretical perspectives from lifecourse and family solidarity frameworks. Then, this chapter looks into changes in family structures and in intergenerational solidarity in two distinct contexts: the Netherlands, a small, developed, and mainly urban European country; and China, a developing country with stark contrasts in wealth and in rural–urban conditions.

Theoretical background

Family solidarity: complexity and ambivalence

A wealth of theoretical approaches describes the ways in which relatives may be obliged to support other generations. Two important features stand out. First, obligations are negotiated (Finch and Mason, 1993). Second, the intergenerational contract is embedded in a multidimensional construct of family solidarity (Bengtson and Roberts, 1991).

The negotiated nature of the intergenerational contract results from the assumption that values and norms, like family obligations, do not determine behaviour but function as guidelines that people use to coordinate their actions. They reflect what is approved in large parts of a society, rather than prescribing specific behaviours (Hammarström, 2005). Cultures and nations differ in the way that – and the extent to which – intergenerational obligations are institutionalised. The Netherlands is among the cultures where family obligations are weakly felt and hardly sanctioned at the individual and family levels, but at the same time extensive intergenerational support is provided at the macro level as part of a strong welfare state (Lowenstein and Daatland, 2006). A well-developed pension system and high levels of collective long-term care provide for much of the basic needs of older generations that would otherwise have been the responsibility of adult children. China, by contrast, has strong family obligations, which are supported by legal duties of children towards their parents (Deutsch, 2006; Chou, 2010); alternatives to family support are weakly developed.

The concept of intergenerational ambivalence (Luescher and Pillemer, 1993) further points to the fact that intergenerational support is negotiated in the context of different, and sometimes conflicting, norms and expectations between generations. People have to deal with three types of ambivalence when confronted with intergenerational norms: the simultaneous desire for autonomy and need for dependence on both sides; conflicting norms (for example to look after oneself well and not to be a burden on one's children); and conflicting solidarities, such as with one's parents and one's children. Ambivalence is inherent in the complexity of social roles and interactions, where multiple perspectives and contexts are always involved. It may be more strongly felt in late modern societies, where traditions and social contexts offer less guidance for behavioural choices, and behavioural choices are seen as the responsibility of the individual (Van Tilburg and Thomese, 2010).

The theoretical framework of family solidarity (Bengtson and Roberts, 1991) explains the embeddedness of the intergenerational contract in other dimensions of family solidarity. The framework of family solidarity distinguishes six dimensions: associational, structural, affectual, functional, normative and consensual solidarity. The intergenerational contract is on the normative dimension. It is embedded in a family structure with specific types of contact between relatives (associational), where people have emotional bonds (affectual), help each other (functional), and may or may not share the same (religious) outlook on life (consensual). The dimensions are not independent, and the framework of family solidarity is particularly well suited to show how change in one dimension may affect others.

Thus, the effect of verticalisation, a structural characteristic of family solidarity, on intergenerational support (functional solidarity) can be either aggravated or compensated by the other dimensions. In Western societies like the Netherlands, affective bonds and frequent contacts compensate in part for the decreased availability of adult children for needy parents and a lessening of normative solidarity (Van der Pas et al, 2007): the fewer available children are willing to do more for their parents if they feel emotionally connected. When parents separate, another structural change, the emotional bond becomes crucial to continued contact (associational solidarity) and support (functional solidarity). Divorced fathers, in particular, find that their adult children are less inclined to continue bonds with them, because their relationship has been more structural than affectual (Tomassini et al, 2004; Kalmijn, 2007).

In China, verticalisation was strongly accelerated by the one-child policy that was put into effect in 1979. The policy was most effective in urban areas, where the benefits of compliance, in terms of rights to schooling and welfare, were higher and control was easier than in rural areas, where people needed children as an old-age provision (Deutsch, 2006). Here, the lower availability of children to ageing parents may even have strengthened the moral and consensual solidarity, in so far as single children feel even more obliged towards their parents. At the same time, the labour migration of rural adults to urban areas aggravates the structural lack of children to care for ageing parents.

Lifecourse: changing generations and life stages in the face of changing demographics

Complexity and ambivalence are thus inherent to intergenerational solidarity, because of its negotiated nature, its multidimensionality, and the interdependencies between macro and micro levels. With increasing life expectancy, another source of complexity and ambivalence emerges in the guise of changing generations.

By 'generation' we mean family generations, seen in the context of successive life stages in the standard tripartite lifecourse, which dominated most of the 20th century (Kohli, 2007; Mayer, 2009).

The standard lifecourse consists of three stages: youth, adulthood and old age. These life stages were more or less aligned with generations at the micro level of families and at the macro level of social institutions – if not in practice, then in ideals as expressed by individuals and in social institutions (Kohli and Meyer, 1986; Settersten and Hagestad, 1996; Liefbroer and Billari, 2009). Youth was defined by living with one's parents and preparing for one's own family by learning in school or through apprenticeship. Starting a family roughly coincided with earning a living and/or running a household, which means leaving the parental household and its concomitant dependency on parents. Thus preparing to become – or becoming – a parent generation also marked the onset of adulthood. Adulthood, in turn, was the life stage of providing for one's family by earning money and raising children. Caring for ageing parents was considered to be part of adulthood as well (Brody, 1990). When paid work and raising children come to an end, later life commences. Retirement and emptying the nest are considered important markers of the onset of later life for men and women, often closely followed by the imminent end of the most economically productive years of adulthood (Chudakoff and Hareven, 1979; Komp et al, 2009). Old age then remains as the final stage of life, void of major obligations. People may become the grandparent generation, which in developed nations is not an obliging social role (Kemp, 2004). It is also a life stage where the people who once provided support to other generations turn into those needing help, and their adult children are expected to care for them.

Changes in the lifecourse and family structures

Table 10.1 shows some key characteristics of the changes that have occurred in the standard lifecourse model and their consequences for family structures. In 1950, just before the 1956 policy that installed the Dutch state pension, less than 8% of the population was over the entitlement age of 65. In 2010, it was 15%. This is partly caused by a swift decrease in fertility after the introduction of the contraceptive pill in 1967. Fertility rates dropped from around 3 before 1967 to under 2 in the 1970s. Consequently, within less than 20 years, the 65+ population will rise from almost 17% in 2013 to over 24% in 2030. Moreover, the proportion of the population who are expected to survive to older ages continues to increase. Some predict that over half the children born today in developed nations could live until age 100 or older (Christensen et al, 2009). In China, both longevity and fertility changed even more drastically. Life expectancy was 39 for men and 42 for women in the 1950s, just after the People's Republic of China was established in 1949. It has now increased by about 35 additional years. After 1979, fertility dropped from about 3 children to 1.7 now. Yet the share of older

Table 10.1: Demographic and lifecourse changes in the Netherlands and China, 1950-2010

	The Netherlands		China	
	1950	2010	1950	2010
Life expectancy (men/women)	70/73	79/83	39/42	72/77
Population aged 65+ (in %; men/women)	7/8	14/17	5	8/10
Number of children per woman	3	2	8	2
Women's age at first birth	25	29	–	–
Four grandparents alive at birth (in %)	27	50	–	–
Number of divorces per 100 couples	3	10	–	2

Note: – = no data

Sources: Statline CBS, Chinese National Bureau of Statistics, United Nations

people rises similarly to that in the Netherlands, with a steep increase towards about 25% over age 65 in the coming decades.

Causes of lifecourse stretching and verticalisation also include delays in the age at which women have their first child. In the Netherlands, women around 1950 had their first child on average four years earlier than women in 2010, and the average number of children almost halved by 2010. As noted, the Chinese one-child policy caused a dramatic drop in family size in China after 1979. Age at first birth in China has fluctuated since 1950: policies first aimed at increasing the age of childbearing by setting a minimum marriage age up to the age of 25. It decreased after policy changes in 1980, but increased again in recent years, possibly because of socioeconomic change (Morgan et al, 2009; Jiang and Sánchez-Barricarte, 2011). Western children today have at least three living grandparents for most of their childhood (Murphy, 2011). Chinese grandchildren can expect to share over 30 years of life with at least one grandparent (Jiang and Sánchez-Barricarte, 2011).

At the same time, family diversity increased. Divorces almost tripled in the Netherlands between 1950 and 2010. Although Chinese divorce rates are low compared to the Netherlands, they more than tripled between 2001 and 2009 (Ministry of Civil Affairs of China, 2011), suggesting a similar trend. Rural to urban migration in China rocketed. Internal migration was strongly curtailed after 1949, and only since 1978 have policies enabled rural–urban migration. About a quarter of the rural labour force, 118 million rural residents, left farms around the turn of the 20th century to look for employment in economically burgeoning cities (Carillo Garcia, 2004). These migrants often left behind their children and their ageing parents. Rural to urban migration is less of an issue in the Netherlands, although there is extensive foreign immigration, adding ethnic and linguistic diversity. This is only beginning to touch older generations, because most immigrants are still under 60 years of age. The picture is more varied across developed nations, but significant numbers of migrants ageing in their adopted nation is new to most societies (Warnes et al, 2004).

Living longer has become increasingly normal throughout the 20th century. Consequently, the character of life stages, interrelations and expectations of age norms may change as well. At first, existing life stages grew longer: adulthood was postponed by prolonged education and delay of family formation (Furstenberg, 2010). Old age has become a regular phase of life, catching the first larger cohorts of older adults as 'surprised survivors' (Hagestad, 1998). In the late 20th century, particularly developed societies witnessed further differentiation of life stages: a prolonged adolescence is sometimes seen as a new stage between childhood and adulthood, where young adults may finish education and leave home, but do not yet settle in steady jobs and relationships. The third age as a life stage between middle adulthood and very old age has been widely discussed as a product of affluent societies pushing old-age-as-dependency to later years (Laslett, 1991; Gilleard and Higgs, 2005). This differentiation of the lifecourse occurs alongside increased diversity. More people do not experience the transitions in the standard lifecourse (for example, they remain single), or they experience transitions at different times in their lives (for example, youth unemployment), or they experience transitions that are not part of the standard lifecourse (for example, divorce and remarriage, long-term unemployment).

This implies that the age at which family members from different generations experience important transitions can also change, and the conditions under which relatives may be called on for support may also change alongside this. Grandparents help the growing numbers of parents who have difficulty balancing work and family. But given the longer life expectancy, many grandparents, both in the Netherlands and in China, may also have parents who are in need of care. Where Elaine Brody (1990) before worried about middle-aged mothers as women wedged in between caring for dependent children and ageing parents, we now see an increase in very old (grand)parents being cared for by children who are ageing themselves (Grundy and Henretta, 2006). Thus, a three-generation model no longer matches the typical lifecourse constellation of families. There is an increase in so-called Janus generations (Herlofson and Hagestad, 2012): people with one or more generations above *and* below them. Any of these generations may be free from (other) work or family obligations, but may also be working and caring for others. At the same time, younger generations have become smaller, and older people in need of care have become more numerous. The question is: who comes first, either as a recipient or a care provider? This complexity is further corroborated by the blending of families through divorce and remarriage across generations. The ways in which people negotiate family obligations between stepfamily and family members who have left the household is largely unexplored.

Such changes are not merely a new way of classifying life stages. Lifecourses are socially structured, and the paths people choose are preconditioned by the opportunities and constraints imposed by social structures. When discussing the intergenerational contract and ambivalence, the role of welfare state structures stands out. In the Netherlands, welfare state arrangements have played a major role in shaping the options and choices that people have over the lifecourse. In China, the absence of many of these arrangements has shaped lives and fostered interdependence among family members. Families and local communities have been at the heart of Chinese welfare, as documented thousands of years ago in the writings of Confucius and through to the present time.

Grandparenting and elder care as sources of ambivalence in the Netherlands

Intergenerational solidarity in the Netherlands is embedded in a welfare system that can be characterised as a continental welfare regime (Esping-Andersen, 1990): a high level of income support and medical and social care builds on a mix of universal provisions and occupational insurance. Many arrangements are based on the male breadwinner model, which implies that women are available to provide for children and other relatives who need care. With growing female labour market participation, women in particular have to balance work and family commitments, which in the Netherlands results in high levels of women working part-time, and fragmented childcare provision (Saraceno, 2008). The Netherlands has among the highest levels of public home and residential care in Europe: 2.2% of the gross domestic product is spent on long-term care, reaching almost 70% of the 65+ population with care needs (Rodrigues and Nies, 2013). Even this generous formal system relies heavily on informal care, which accounts for the large majority of long-term care provision (Suanet et al, 2012). Informal care is predominantly provided by spouses and children.

The biggest challenge for the Dutch system is its sustainability in the light of population ageing and verticalisation: the greater demand for care in combination with the lower number of younger people available to support the system will significantly raise its costs in the near future. The national government is searching for ways to manage budgets, leaving less intensive types of care to the market and to families. Decentralisation of long-term care provision is putting the responsibility for realising cuts and curtailing entitlements on municipalities. This will bring about greater diversity in a country that has been accustomed to universal care provision.

While families are ageing, growing smaller and more complex, the government is increasing its appeals to provide informal care to older relatives. This puts pressure on the 'crowding in' of formal and informal care typical of the Dutch system: good formal care enables more families to provide informal care than would be the case if these families had to do more (Suanet et al, 2012).

Grandparenting can be seen as a key example of such 'crowding in' across European welfare states: almost twice as many grandparents provide childcare in countries with better formal childcare, but the intensity of childcare is much lower than in countries where parents have little alternative (Hank and Buber, 2009). The percentage of Dutch grandparents providing regular childcare has risen from about 15% in 1996 to about 30% in 2006 (Geurts, 2012). This indicates the greater number of grandparents in good health and with spare time. It also signals the importance of grandparents for dual-earner families. Families that can rely on care from grandparents have higher fertility and mothers work longer (Thomese and Liefbroer, 2013). Thus, the third age is partly used for a new role in the family.

Because grandparenting as a form of informal childcare is relatively new, we do not know how this will play out in intergenerational obligations. Gender differences do stand out, however. Grandparents often provide childcare together, if they are a couple, but it appears that grandmothers are in the lead (Glaser et al, 2013). Personal care to parents is mostly provided by daughters. Taking into account the growing demand for informal long-term care combined with recent raising of the pension age and cuts in public childcare funding, women are increasingly challenged to weigh roles inside and outside the family against each other. Where younger mothers have to balance childcare and paid work, mid-life women now have to balance paid work against care for parents or grandchildren. This increases ambivalence. On the other hand, British results indicate that men may be increasingly at risk of spending late life with little informal care available, either because they remain single or because relationships with children have deteriorated after divorce (Demey et al, 2011). For them in particular, adult children may deal with ambivalence by tightening the boundaries of what constitutes family and who is entitled to intergenerational care (Seltzer and Bianchi, 2013).

Grandparenting and elder care as sources of ambivalence in China

Rural people in China are more disadvantaged than their urban counterparts, because of the household registration system. This system was developed in the 1950s to prioritise the development of urban areas, by separating urban and rural residents and limiting rural-to-urban migration. Consequently, rural residents have been greatly disadvantaged concerning income and educational opportunities, as well as access to pension and medical insurance (Sicular et al, 2007; Zimmer et al, 2010).

In addition to the social welfare programme that provides basic necessities for a strictly defined population with no alternative sources of income, only about 5% of rural older people receive a pension, compared to 74% of urban older people (China Research Center on Aging, 2009; Chou, 2011). Likewise, urban older people usually have access to medical insurance funded by employers and government (Blumenthal and Hsiao, 2005). After 1949, rural residents enjoyed low-cost care through a cooperative care system, but with the privatisation of the system they became responsible for paying for almost all the costs (Beach, 2001; Zimmer et al, 2010). Recently, the New Cooperative Medical Scheme has brought significant changes to the lives of rural residents. It is generally regarded as affordable and has facilitated access to health care (Sun et al, 2009; Dai et al, 2011).

Overall, the social welfare system is changing, and the gradual development of a social insurance system reduces older people's dependence on their adult children. However, care from children and grandchildren will remain vital to many people, especially in rural areas. This necessity is corroborated by the instalment of a law in July 2013 obliging children to keep in touch with their parents. As in the Netherlands, the Chinese government thus tackles a structural lack of availability of informal care with a moral – even legal – appeal which goes against the ambivalence that is also growing in Chinese families. Adult children are not only diminishing in availability, but they also increasingly have to juggle filial piety against pressures to make the most of their own lives (Cameron et al, 2013; Yang et al, 2012).

More grandparents than ever are available to provide care for their grandchildren. The extreme case of 4-2-1 families is described as the consequence of the one-child policy: to each child there will be two parents and four grandparents (Jiang and Sánchez-Barricarte, 2011). The need for grandchild care is increasing, too. Rural-to-urban migrants are faced with great barriers to bringing their children with them, such as the household registration system of 'Hukou', a shortage of adequate housing, and difficulties in obtaining low-cost childcare (Wang and Fan, 2006). Consequently, in rural areas with high migration rates, about 20% of older people live in skipped-generation households, where grandparents take full custody of their grandchildren (Silverstein et al, 2006). The effects of divorce on this pattern are not yet known.

The increased needs for grandparenting – and the availability of grandparents to provide help – may bring substantial changes to intergenerational relationships. Upstream intergenerational transfers are considered manifestations of the cultural norm of filial piety and a form of altruism on the part of children. Yet older adults' help with grandchild care is a pivotal reason for receiving transfers and negotiation of responsibilities to older parents among adult children (Cong and Silverstein, 2010, 2011). This kind of exchange is not limited to financial returns; other benefits of providing childcare include increased emotional closeness, hands-on support, and help with farm labour from children who receive the service (Shi, 1993; Yang, 1996; Hermalin, 2002). This suggests that the negotiation of filial piety norms is based on reciprocity considerations. Where filial piety becomes less reliable and grandparents' support to their children's families grows in importance, reciprocity could offer families a new basis for finding a balanced solution to intergenerational obligations.

However, it will not be a solution to the fast diminishing availability of children and grandchildren to growing numbers of dependent older people (Liu et al., 2009; Peng et al, 2010). Long-term facilities are just beginning to emerge in urban China; they are rare in rural areas (Chan, 2002; Chou, 2010). Also, people are still reluctant to be taken care of in institutions. A national survey found that only 20% of older adults in urban and 17% in rural areas are willing to live in eldercare institutions (Chou, 2010). Thus long-term care responsibilities are placed on the shoulders of spouses, who are often frail themselves, and children.

Intergenerational co-residence is usually adopted to take care of older parents. In rural China, co-residence with a married son is culturally preferred. Co-residence greatly increases the chance that older parents receive instrumental assistance, even compared to non-co-residing parents with children living nearby. Urban Chinese are increasingly tolerant to older adults co-residing with their married daughters. It is estimated that 15-25% of urban couples have ever co-resided with the wives' parents (Pimentel and Liu, 2004). Like other transfers from children, the co-residence is becoming less dependent on norms, but more dependent on negotiation, such as the needs of older parents and adult children, which adds further ambivalence to intergenerational relationships (Cong and Silverstein, 2010, 2011).

Discussion

In spite of many differences, families in China and the Netherlands are faced with similar changes and challenges caused by increased longevity and verticalisation. Most notably, ageing and old age become a larger part of family life, both in the guise of grandparents taking part in raising children, and a longer period where older relatives need care. Three important consequences play out differently in the Netherlands and in China.

Transformation of grandparenting

First, the emergence of grandparenting is a timely relief for working children. In China, families transform an existing tradition of co-residence and multigenerational childcare, thus enabling their children to take part in the economic growth and improve their life chances and those of their children, that is, the grandchildren. Often, the economic success of children flows back to grandparents in the form of financial remittances. In the Netherlands, with its tradition of two-generation living, grandparenting as a substantive element of childrearing is relatively new. It resembles a new lifestyle in the third age, expressing one's individual identity in a consumer society (Gilleard and Higgs, 2005). This greater disconnection from intergenerational solidarity compared to China may explain why grandparental childcare in the Netherlands does not appear to pay off in terms of informal care later in life (Geurts et al, 2012). In both countries, the stretching of the lifecourse results in stretching of reproductive responsibilities over more generations: women have fewer children, but they extend their childcare responsibilities to their children's children (MacInnes and Perez Diaz, 2009). This grandparental support could limit the fertility drop occurring in both countries. Chinese urban women also appear to postpone childbearing for economic reasons (Morgan et al, 2009).

Longer duration long-term care needed

Second, greater longevity lengthens the demand for informal care on smaller and sometimes more blurred families. Because of the one-child policy, this change will be most prominent in China. In both countries, families remain the main source of long-term care, and governments can only provide for part of the growing needs. The Chinese government is trying to deal with this change by increasing the provision of formal care to 'crowd in' existing intergenerational solidarity: virtually no formal system has been put in place, with the exception of expensive private residences and services that older adults can pay for out of their own pocket. The Dutch government is trying to cut back on a well-developed system that may soon become unaffordable. The growing pressure on families for long-term care will increase ambivalence. Family obligations have become less clear to younger generations in China, mostly because filial obligations compete with values and roles aimed at improving the family's economic position. As in the Netherlands, blended families also blend family borders and family values. Obligations to care for the older generation compete with obligations towards the younger generation, in particular grandchildren.

In China, this predicament may partly be solved by stretching the obligations to care for the old over multiple generations: grandchildren are also called on to care for ageing grandparents. This is not yet common in the Netherlands, but as current generations of caring grandparents age, their adult grandchildren could also take on caring responsibilities. Such generation blending is reminiscent of Caribbean family patterns, where caring is shared over multiple generations (Zontini and Reynolds, 2007).

Another solution that families seek is to rely more on reciprocity norms. Again, the Chinese example shows clearly that reciprocity may inform the enactment of family obligations, which are negotiated among those who share a bond. When the obligations themselves become unclear because of conflicting roles or blurring family boundaries, reciprocity may become more important in deciding who to care for and when. In the long run, this could individualise the informal care relationship, which is now enacted in the context of family solidarity (Bordone, 2012). Individual resources and credits gathered over the lifecourse will then increasingly determine entitlements to informal care in later life.

Changing inequalities

Finally, lifecourse stretching in the context of verticalisation can reshuffle inequalities. Greater reliance on reciprocity within the family will increase inequalities due to social skills and other resources. In China, this may result in growing numbers of older people not getting any care at all, unless the formal system can catch up very quickly. Rural older people now count on their (migrant) children. When the one-child policy reaches older generations, the number of childless people – or people with no children able or willing to care for them – will grow fast. They must depend on their network for informal care. In the Netherlands, relatives and non-kin are not used to providing care with the intensity that may be needed in the near future. With no tradition behind them to guide normative choices, personal considerations will play a major role in the decision to care (Van der Pas et al, 2007). This will cause inequalities based on social capital.

Besides inequalities arising from social capital differences, gender inequalities may change as well. Most notably, a new sandwich generation of women could emerge, who need to balance care for grandchildren and parents with paid work. Even if care responsibilities upward and downward can be spread over the lifecourse, gender inequalities will deepen. This appears to be more pronounced in China than in the Netherlands (Cook and Dong, 2011). Yet, particularly Western women have to juggle longer work life and childcare (Gray, 2005). Grandparents in China, where the third age is rare, often face a trade-off between childcare and their own health. The vulnerability of older Chinese men has, to our knowledge, not been explored, but in countries like the Netherlands it clearly increases after divorce.

Similar changes in the lifecourse, caused by longevity and verticalisation, play out differently in the distinct cultural and welfare contexts of China and The Netherlands. This in turn imposes different pressures on the intergenerational contract in each country. It is to be expected that intergenerational solidarity will survive population ageing, but it may go through important changes in the near future.

Acknowledgement

The authors wish to thank Dr Aaron Hagedorn for his comments and improvements to the text.

References

Beach, M. (2001) 'China's rural health care gradually worsens', *Lancet*, 358, 9281, 567.

Bengtson, V. and Achenbaum, W.A. (eds) (1993) *The changing contract across generations*, New York: De Gruyter.

Bengtson, V.L. and Roberts, E.L. (1991) 'Intergenerational solidarity in aging families: An example of formal theory construction', *Journal of Marriage and Family*, 53, 4, 856-70.

Blumenthal, D. and Hsiao, W. (2005) 'Privatization and its discontents. The evolving Chinese health care system', *The New England Journal of Medicine*, 353, 11, 1165-70.

Bordone, V. (2012) 'Social norms and intergenerational relationships', *International Studies in Population*, 100, 159-78.

Brody, E.M. (1990) *Women in the middle. The parent care years*, New York: Springer.

Cameron, L., Erkal, N., Gangadharan, L. and Meng, X. (2013) 'Little emperors: Behavioral impacts of China's one-child policy', *Science*, 339, 953-7.
Carillo Garcia, B. (2004) 'Rural-urban migration in China: Temporary migrants in search of permanent settlement', *Portal*, 1, 2, 1-26.
Chan, J.P. (2002) 'From elderly care institutions to long-term care policy: Evolution of nursing homes in the United States and China', *DAI*, 63, 03A, 336.
Cherlin, A.J. (2010) 'Demographic trends in the United States: A review of research in the 2000s', *Journal of Marriage and Family*, 72, 403-19.
China Research Center on Aging (2009) *Data analysis of the sampling of survey of the aged population in China*, Beijing: China Biaozhun Publication.
Chou, R.J.-A. (2010) 'Willingness to live in eldercare institutions among older adults in urban and rural China: A nationwide study', *Ageing and Society*, 30, 4, 583-608.
Chou, R.J.-A. (2011) 'Filial piety by contract? The emergence, implementation, and implications of the "Family Support Agreement" in China', *The Gerontologist*, 5, 1, 3-16.
Christensen, K., Doblhammer, G., Rau, R. and Vaupel, J.W. (2009) 'Ageing populations: The challenges ahead', *The Lancet*, 74, 1196-208.
Chudakoff, H.P. and Hareven, T. (1979) 'From the empty nest to family dissolution: Life course transitions into old age', *Journal of Family History*, 4, 69-83.
Cong, Z. and Silverstein, M. (2010) 'Which sons live with their older parents in rural China? The role of migration and intergenerational exchanges', *Family Science*, 1, 1, 67-71.
Cong, Z. and Silverstein, M. (2011) 'Custodian grandparents and intergenerational support in rural China', in K. Mehta and L. Thang (eds) *Experiencing grandparenthood: An Asian perspective*, New York: Springer, 109-27.
Cook, S. and Dong, X. (2011) 'Harsh choices: Chinese women's paid work and unpaid care responsibilities under economic reform', *Development and Change*, 42, 947-65.
Dai, B., Zhou, J., Mei, Y.J., Wu, B. and Mao, Z. (2011) 'Can the new cooperative medical scheme promote rural elders' access to health-care services?', *Geriatrics and Gerontology International*, 11, 3, 239-45.
Demey, D., Berrington, A., Evandrou, M. and Falkingham, J. (2011) 'The changing demography of mid-life, from the 1980s to the 2000s', *Population Trends*, 145, 1-19.
Deutsch, F.M. (2006) 'Filial piety, patrilineality, and China's one-child policy', *Journal of Family Issues*, 27, 366-89.
Esping-Andersen, G. (1990) *Three worlds of welfare capitalism*, Cambridge: Polity Press.
Finch, J.D. and Mason, J. (1993) *Negotiating family responsibility*, London: Routledge.
Furstenberg, F. (2010) 'On a new schedule: Transitions to adulthood and family change', *The Future of Children*, 20, 67-87.

Geurts, T. (2012) *Grandparent-grandchild relationships in the Netherlands: A dynamic and multigenerational perspective*, Dissertation, Amsterdam: VU University.

Geurts, T., Poortman, A.R. and Van Tilburg, T.G. (2012) 'Older parents providing child care for adult children: Does it pay off?', *Journal of Marriage and Family*, 74, 239-50.

Gilleard, C. and Higgs, P. (2005) *Contexts of ageing*, Cambridge: Polity Press.

Glaser, K., Price, D., Ribe Montserrat, E., Di Gessa, G. and Tinker, A. (2013) *Grandparenting in Europe: Family policy and grandparents' role in providing childcare.* London: Grandparents Plus.

Gray, A. (2005) 'The changing availability of grandparents as carers and its implications for childcare policy in the UK', *Journal of Social Policy*, 34, 4, 557-77.

Grundy, E. and Henretta, J.C. (2006) 'Between elderly parents and adult children: A new look at the intergenerational care provided by the "sandwich generation"', *Ageing and Society*, 26, 707-22.

Hagestad, G. (1998) *Towards a society for all ages: New thinking, new language, new conversations.* Keynote Address, United Nations, 1 October.

Hammarström, G. (2005) 'The construct of intergenerational solidarity in a lineage perspective: A discussion on underlying theoretical assumptions', *Journal of Aging Studies*, 19, 33-51.

Hank, K. and Buber, I. (2009) 'Grandparents caring for their grandchildren. Findings from the 2004 Survey of Health, Ageing, and Retirement in Europe', *Journal of Family Issues*, 30, 53-73.

Herlofson, K. and Hagestad, G.O. (2012) 'Transformations in the role of grandparents across welfare states', in S. Arber and V. Timonen (eds) *Contemporary grandparenting. Changing family relationships in global contexts*, Bristol: Policy Press, 27-50.

Hermalin, A.I. (2002) *Well-being of the elderly in Asia: A four-country comparative study*, Ann Arbor, MI: University of Michigan Press.

Jiang, Q. and Sánchez-Barricarte, J.J. (2011) 'The 4-2-1 family structure in China: A survival analysis based on life tables', *European Journal of Ageing*, 8, 2, 119-27.

Kalmijn, M. (2007) 'Gender differences in the effects of divorce, widowhood and remarriage on intergenerational support: Does marriage protect fathers?', *Social Forces*, 85, 1079-104.

Kemp, C.L. (2004) '"Grand" expectations: The experiences of grandparents and adult grandchildren', *The Canadian Journal of Sociology*, 29, 499-525.

Kohli, M. (2007) 'The institutionalization of the life course: Looking back to look ahead', *Research in Human Development*, 4, 253-71.

Kohli, M. and Meyer, J.W. (1986) 'Social structure and social construction of life stages', *Human Development*, 29, 145-80.

Komp, K., Van Tilburg, T. and Broese van Groenou, M. (2009) 'The influence of the welfare state on the number of young old persons', *Ageing and Society*, 29, 609-24.

Laslett, P. (1991) *A fresh map of life*, Cambridge: Harvard University Press.

Liefbroer, A. and Billari, F. (2009) 'Bringing norms back in: A theoretical and empirical discussion of their importance for understanding demographic behaviour', *Population, Space and Place*, 16, 287-305.

Liu, J., Chi, I., Chen, G., Song, X. and Zheng, X. (2009) 'Prevalence and correlates of functional disability in Chinese older adults', *Geriatrics and Gerontology International*, 9, 3, 253-61.

Lowenstein, A. and Daatland, S.O. (2006) 'Filial norms and family support in a comparative cross-national context: Evidence from the OASIS study', *Ageing & Society*, 26, 203-23.

Luescher, K. and Pillemer, K. (1993) 'Intergenerational ambivalence: A new approach to the study of parent-child relations in later life', *Journal of Marriage and the Family*, 60, 413-25.

MacInnes, J. and Perez Diaz, J. (2009) 'The reproductive revolution', *The Sociological Review*, 57, 262-84.

Mayer, K.U. (2009) 'New directions in life course research', *Annual Review of Sociology*, 35, 413-33.

Ministry of Civil Affairs of China (2011) *National civil affairs statistics*. http://cws.mca.gov.cn/article/tjsj/qgsj/

Morgan, S.P., Zhigang, G. and Hayforth, S.P. (2009) 'China's below-replacement fertility: Recent trends and future prospects', *Population and Development Review*, 35, 605-29.

Murphy, M. (2011) 'Long-term effects of the demographic transition on family and kinship networks', *Population and Development Review*, 37 (supplement), 55-80.

Peng, X., Song, S., Sullivan, S., Qiu, J. and Wang, W. (2010) 'Ageing, the urban-rural gap and disability trends: 19 years of experience in China – 1987 to 2006', *PLOS One*, 5, 8, e12129.

Pimentel, E.E. and Liu, J. (2004) 'Exploring non-normative coresidence in urban China: Living with wives' parents', *Journal of Marriage and Family*, 66, 3, 821-36.

Rodrigues, R. and Nies, H. (2013) 'Long-term care in Europe: Improving policy and practice', in K. Leichsenring, J. Billings and H. Nies (eds) *Long-term care in Europe. Improving policy and practice*, Basingstoke: Palgrave Macmillan, 191-212.

Saraceno, C. (ed) (2008) *Families, ageing and social policy: Intergenerational solidarity in European welfare states*, Cheltenham: Edward Elgar.

Seltzer, J.A. and Bianchi, S.M. (2013) 'Demographic change and parent-child relationships in adulthood', *Annual Review of Sociology*, 39, 275-90.

Settersten, R. and Hagestad, G. (1996) 'What's the latest? Cultural age deadlines for family transitions', *Gerontologist*, 36, 178-88.

Shi, L. (1993) 'Family financial and household support exchange between generations: A survey of Chinese rural elderly', *Gerontologist*, 33, 4, 468-80.

Sicular, T., Yue, X., Gustafsson, B. and Shi, L. (2007) 'The urban-rural income gap and inequality in China', *Income and Wealth*, 53, 1, 93-126.

Silverstein, M., Cong, Z. and Li, S. (2006) 'Intergenerational transfers and living arrangements of older people in rural China: Consequences for psychological well-being', *Journal of Gerontology: Social Sciences*, 61, S256-66.

Suanet, B., Broese van Groenou, M. and Van Tilburg, T. (2012) 'Informal and formal homecare use among older adults in Europe: Can crossnational differences be explained by societal context and composition?', *Ageing and Society*, 32, 491-515.

Sun, X., Jackson, S., Carmichael, G. and Sleigh, A.C. (2009) 'Catastrophic medical payment and financial protection in rural China: Evidence from the new cooperative medical scheme in Shandong Province', *Health Economics*, 18, 1, 103-19.

Thomese, F. and Liefbroer, A. (2013) 'Child care and child births. The role of grandparents in The Netherlands', *Journal of Marriage and the Family*, 75, 2, 403-21.

Tomassini, C., Kalogirou, S., Grundy, E., Fokkema, T., Martikainen, P., Broese van Groenou, M. and Karisto, A. (2004) 'Contacts between elderly parents and their children in four European countries: Current patterns and future prospects', *European Journal of Ageing*, 1, 54-63.

Van der Pas, S., Van Tilburg, T. and Knipscheer, K. (2007) 'Changes in contact and support within intergenerational relationships in the Netherlands: A cohort and time-sequential perspective', *Advances in Life Course Research*, 12, 243-74.

Van Tilburg, T.G. and Thomese, F. (2010) 'Societal dynamics in personal networks', in D. Dannefer and C.R. Phillipson (eds) *The Sage handbook of social gerontology*, London: Sage, 215-25.

Walker, A. (2002) 'The politics of intergenerational relations', *Zeitschrift fur Gerontologie und Geriatrie* [*Journal of Gerontology and Geriatrics*], 35, 297-303.

Wang, W.W. and Fan, C.C. (2006) 'Success or failure: selectivity and reasons of return migration in Sichuan and Anhui, China', *Environment and Planning*, 38, 939-58.

Warnes, A.M., Friedrich, K., Kellaher, L. and Torres, S. (2004) 'The diversity and welfare of older migrants in Europe', *Ageing and Society*, 24, 307-26.

Yang, H. (1996) 'The distributive norm of monetary support to older parents: A study in China', *Journal of Marriage and the Family*, 28, 2, 404-15.

Yang, T., Rockett, I.R.H., Lv, Q. and Cotrell, R. (2012) 'Stress status and related characteristics among urban residents: A six-province capital cities study in China', *PLOS One*, 7, e30521.

Zimmer, Z., Kaneda, T., Tang, Z., and Fang, X. (2010) 'Explaining late life urban vs. rural health discrepancies in Beijing', *Social Forces*, 88, 4, 1885-908.

Zontini, E. and Reynolds, T. (2007) 'Ethnicity, families and social capital: Caring relationships across Italian and Caribbean transnational families', *International Review of Sociology*, 17, 257-77.

ELEVEN

Social care in ageing Sweden: learning from the life stories of care recipients

Stina Johansson

Ageing and diversity

As a society ages, this diversity causes tension in the welfare structures of the society, because more and more older people are sharing the available care resources. In Sweden, cuts in welfare funding are taking place, and the coverage of public home help and residential care has become less generous over the last 15 years. During this period of cutbacks, public care has become more stratified, based on class, gender and ethnic dimensions (Szebehely, 2012).

The cutbacks are severe when considering how much help people over 75 will now receive compared to previous years. People who received their first public home care visit in 2008 were older than those who had received their first public home care visit in 1980, and women have been the most affected. The sensitivity to individual needs has also been replaced by a practice guided by standards and routines instead of by the needs of the individuals (Lindelöf and Rönnbäck, 2004). All of this has happened without any changes in legislation.

In the 20th century, the sociopolitical discourse changed from a view of older adults as dependent, isolated and passive to a group expected to be active, independent, healthy and well-integrated consumers. This change in the view of older people was followed by the expectation that they should be resourceful enough to purchase care services previously offered by public care (Prop 1987/88:176: 27). When the threshold to qualify for care increases, people are more likely to buy services on the market, and this favours people with higher socioeconomic status. People in economic hardship, who are often women and less educated, must ask for help from family members who are also often women. Family-based care has increased and, regardless of national origin, women have become the ones most likely, whether paid or unpaid, to support their older family members.

Universalism, the cornerstone of Swedish social policy, means that basic social benefits and services are designed for all citizens, and in practice a large majority of citizens use these benefits and services. The benefits and services are uniform rather than tailored to specific groups (Sainsbury, 1996). The social security system, including pensions and other financial aid, with its base in full employment, created a situation where an individual's welfare is linked to the individual's participation in paid work. This could be a problem for women with many years of lower work participation due to providing informal care for their families and for older immigrants, who have relatively low levels of work participation to fall back on when they retire (Statistiska Centralbyrån, 2013). The change has resulted in a split between the universal social policy devoted to healthy and independent people, including things like pensions, and the social care for dependent older adults.

Some people experience the tension in the welfare system more strongly than others. In this chapter, the life histories of some older women who immigrated to Sweden late in life are described. The following story of a woman interviewed in 2009 (with her son, Mr Chung, as the interpreter) illustrates this concept:

> Mr Chung, a refugee from Vietnam, arrived in Sweden in 1984. He immediately found a job where he still is fully employed on a permanent basis. He also runs a private company. His elderly mother and his disabled sister came in 1996 as family reunification cases. At first his mother lived in an apartment of her own and received public home care, but she chose to move into her son's house. The public home help then ceased to be provided. The family is occasionally visited by relatives from Vietnam who can stay 3 + 3 months without residence status. Their care for the mother is priceless. Mr Chung's mother (born in 1927), who never earned wages in Sweden, is entitled to a guaranteed pension. A means-tested 'cash for care' paid to Mrs Chung enables her to provide compensation to her relatives who help her. Such a solution is preferred by immigrants. Swedish care managers, however, have questioned this practice. The manager's argument has been that there is a risk of isolation in her son's home. The Vietnamese family found that their mother was more isolated in her own apartment receiving public home care in Swedish than when living with her family. She has a 'translocal' identity, and she often speaks with relatives in Vietnam on Skype. (Mrs Chung, interviewed by the author)

Mrs Chung found her own solution and was, contrary to the welfare state expectations, happy with her life. To relieve her isolation, she moved to her son's house and she also received some economic support from the municipality to pay cash within the family for her care.

International migration research has highlighted immigration as a challenge to universal welfare systems. One argument is that welfare goods can be shared only within a bounded group. This logic can be explained with the concepts of 'bounded universalism' (Benhabib, 2002) and 'normative consensus' (Freeman, 1986). In contrast, Crepaz (2008) has argued that good and rapidly established welfare systems can result in successful integration outcomes. Koopmans (2010) has suggested that the combination of generous welfare politics and multicultural politics without strong incentives to learn the language of the country receiving immigrants or to socialise across ethnic boundaries creates a situation where the immigrants become dependent on the welfare state and also become economically marginalised (see Brochmann and Hagelund, 2011). Anttonen (2002) asked whether: 'universalism might mean uniformity instead of diversity, conformity instead of pluralism and absolutism instead of relativism. Does this mean that the Nordic welfare state model, with its strong emphasis on universalism, is not sensitive to pluralism, differences and diversities?'

Sweden and migration

During the 20th century, Sweden changed from being a country of emigration to a country of immigration. At the beginning of the 20th century, a constant flow of immigrants from the Nordic countries dominated the group of people born outside Sweden. After World War II and until the mid-1970s, the dominant stream of immigration to Sweden was caused by labour market demands (Regeringskansliet, 2005). The restrictions on immigration were minimal at that time (Crepaz, 2008). When the majority of immigrants were labour immigrants, Sweden operated a policy that required the welfare state to take care of the immigrants' particular needs as newcomers and as cultural minorities. Restrictions on immigration increased at the end of the 1960s.

A third phase of immigration began in the 1970s with the reception of refugees from Chile, Vietnam, Eastern Europe, Iran and Iraq. Immigration from Finland continued, but Sweden ended its most ambitious multicultural objectives for minority rights in the mid-1980s. At the beginning of the 1990s, the pattern of Nordic migration was broken due to the waves of refugees, that is, people from non-Nordic European countries and non-European countries (Statistiska Centralbyrån, 2005). An additional stream[1] of immigrants came to Sweden in order to be reunited with their families[2] (Corman, 2008), and the number of asylum seekers in Sweden increased from about 5,000 in 1984 to 24,804 in 2012 (Migrationsinfo, 2013).

In 1997, the goal to move away from targeting immigrants as a particular group was formulated. Compared to other Scandinavian countries, Sweden has the largest population of immigrants and their descendants. In 2008, this group (both first and second generation) made up 18% of the population (Brochmann and Hagelund, 2011). The labour immigrants from the mid-1950s had at that time reached retirement age. Almost 6% of all the people who immigrated to Sweden in 2000 were 55 years of age or older. Ten years later, official statistics showed that 6% of immigrants living in Sweden at that time had immigrated to Sweden when they were 65 years of age or older (Statistiska Centralbyrån, 2013). Thus, it is clear that the number of people migrating to Sweden later in life has increased, and the need for long-term assistance has increased for those who have been in Sweden for a relatively short time, especially in the case of non-European immigrants (Socialstyrelsen, 2009; Palme et al, 2002).

A Swedish discourse about immigrants

Scuzzarello (2010) compared how immigration policies were constructed in policy documents and narratives in local communities in Sweden, Britain and Italy. In Sweden, she interviewed policy officers, local councillors, trade union representatives and others, and she found a devaluation of unpaid care work carried out in the private sphere. The interviewees talked about employment and community engagement, the employed immigrant, competitiveness, and immigrants as strangers in need of help to become integrated. Scuzzarello found that those who, for one reason or another, did not participate in the labour force were not mentioned in these interviews and that older immigrants were excluded. Therefore, life histories collected among older immigrants can broaden this discourse.

Migration and care in literature

Literature related to migration and elder care is concerned with children caring for their older parents who have been left behind in their home country (Baldassar et al, 2007). Another issue described in research is the care chains developed when people move from one country to another to earn their living (Hochschild, 2000). Isolation is a risk for older people (Steptoe et al, 2013), and providing social spaces for transnational meetings is one concept that has been explored in the research on immigrants (Pries, 1999; Faist et al, 2013). The focus of this chapter is on social care especially for migrants late in life and its challenge to the universalist ambitions that have historically characterised the Swedish welfare system (Esping-Andersen, 1990).

Older immigrants as care recipients

In Sweden, Szebehely (2009) found that people born outside the Nordic countries, and especially outside Europe, receive help from public home care to a lesser degree than native Swedish people. Although the variation among older people has increased, the services offered have become more standardised. Care needs of older recipients are often expected to be similar, and to fit within the standard services offered by the organisation. Services that are important for a minority group might be removed from the range of possible services, and this might be perceived as unfair (Andersson and Johansson, 2010). Dilemmas with the standardised system have been described, and researchers have discussed how far older people, especially immigrants, can go in asking for other, more personal services than the standard package allows. One extensive debate is whether the municipality should offer the option to hire relatives as caregivers (Torres, 2006; Andersson and Johansson, 2010). Another question is whether the care recipient should have the right to choose the person who will come to take care of them in their home (Andersson and Johansson, 2010).

'Special needs'

From the work of Torres (2006), we can conclude that special needs are often associated with family cultures and gender equality norms. Immigrants are often cared for by their relatives and, therefore, are underrepresented in nursing homes. The underlying philosophy of care provided by the Swedish social service has been to maximise the individual's independence from their family. For example, the tradition of family care in many immigrant families, such as Mrs Chung's family mentioned in the introductory section, can be interpreted as the repression of women in the Swedish context. On the surface, it might be taken as a lack of trust in the system to ask for an attendance allowance, which is a less common solution for municipalities to provide (Johansson et al, 2011). An important difference is that Swedish women have acted from a secure position in the labour market, but this has not been the case for immigrants (Forssell, 2004). For those who arrive in the country later in life, the Swedish language can also be an obstacle to communication and can lead to isolation in one's home.

Narratives about caring experiences

Magnússon and Mahin (2011) studied how a number of late-in-life Iranian female immigrants based their everyday lives around improvised day-centre care activities organised by an Iranian-Swedish association in Malmö. Their narratives of loneliness, failing health and their desire for integration into Swedish society reflected an image that differs from the common assumptions among social care workers that older immigrants are passive bearers of cultural characteristics. Those women tried their best to participate in Swedish society on their own terms.

Naldemirci (2013) investigated the caring experiences of Turkish immigrants in a Swedish context, and he concluded that 'in order to understand the possible expectations of older migrants when it comes to decisions about and needs of care, it is crucial to consider their experience of having lived and aged in diaspora space'. Building trust in the Swedish health and care system is important, because trust is not immediately present. Naldemirci argued that it is important to recognise the local and the lived experiences of older immigrants who came from diaspora space rather than, as is often done today in Sweden, to assume that there are cultural differences within these communities and then let these stereotypes form the basis for culturally competent care.

After a brief description of Sweden as an ageing multicultural society, the life history data from strategically selected individuals who participate in the special care solutions that are available to them are presented, to show the constraints and opportunities related to care and welfare in the country if one has immigrated there as an older adult.

Late-in-life immigrants as a litmus test

This chapter focuses on women who have immigrated to Sweden late in their lives. All of these women immigrated in order to be reunited with their families, and none of them had earned wages in Sweden. They form a minority among immigrants from a demographic perspective, but they are a statistically visible group in Swedish society.

This chapter sets out to answer the following questions. In what way, and to what extent, are these women integrated into Swedish society? How does the caring sector respond to the needs of these immigrant women? In what ways are their needs for help and care met? How can the lifecourses of immigrant women contribute to the development of the caring sector in order to meet new challenges?

In this study, evidence that the welfare sector is divided became visible when no older immigrants were found in the registers of recipients of public home care in the municipality where the data were collected. These immigrants were not members of pensioners' organisations, and other sources such as churches and trade unions were unable to find any links to them. After a long search, most of the informants were identified through the PREI (PREparation for Integration) programme. Some informants, such as Mrs Chung, were identified through the author's private network. As with Scuzzarello (2010), many of the informants in this study presented their needs in a way that excluded them from the assistance that the municipality has reserved for 'older care recipients'. Local social services seemed to be organised for people who were financially independent (via pensions) and who had a high level of trust in public welfare arrangements.

Collecting life histories

To collect the life histories discussed in this chapter, participants in a multicultural care facility were asked if they would be interviewed about their life histories. Only a few people volunteered for the interviews. The informants were all women, and few of them could speak Swedish or English. The interviews were conducted through an interpreter chosen by the informant, and in all cases the interpreter also participated in the multicultural care programme and was trusted by the informant. Table 11.1 provides information on the language used in the different interviews and on the interpreter who was used. The women were asked open-ended questions about their childhood (family situation, memories about parents and other relatives, memories from school, and friends), their adolescence (family situation, school and friends), their adulthood (raising their family, children, education, work and relationships), and their later life as immigrants in Sweden. The informants told their stories relatively freely in the initial interview, and they were willing to be interviewed again at a later stage to elaborate their story. This chapter focuses on their situations in later life.

In parallel with the interviews, written stories from a larger group of participants were collected and submitted to the manager, Ayana. These stories were written in the language with which the informants were most comfortable, and they were not readable by the author without interpretation. Ayana – who mastered several languages – wrote a summary together with each informant, and these were discussed with the author in an interview that was held after the preliminary analysis was made and when the themes were identified. The themes from the interview were compared with the themes in the larger number of written stories. The consistency was high, but the examples from the women's experiences of dealing with Swedish social care were more richly described in their written stories.

After a broad description of the institutional context, this chapter ventures deeper into some women's life stories to understand the interaction between traditional Swedish norms for welfare distribution and the expectations of immigrants moving to Sweden late in life.

A case study: PREI – a space for multicultural care

The PREI (PREparation for Integration) programme was founded in 1990 and operates in several cities in Sweden, but its presence is stronger in some regions than in others. PREI, which is a partly volunteer-based and partly publicly supported, is independent of religious and political attachments, and works to influence policies on a national level. It operates democratically with a board, open meetings, and decisions made by majority votes. Its objectives are to help immigrants integrate into Swedish society and to work for equality and against isolation. Among the target groups are immigrants and other groups who are at risk of isolation, especially older immigrants.

PREI advocates 'Swedes and immigrants together hand-in-hand'. Its homepage states: 'PREI fights against the age-specific mentality in the Swedish society, that is, we promote and encourage close and open interactions among people of all ages' (PREI, 2013). PREI specifically tries to help isolated immigrants and older immigrants who feel excluded or 'left out'. Discussing politics or religion, or using alcohol and drugs in the public meeting places, is strictly prohibited. The women's life stories provide information about their autonomy in relation to family, finances and society, and about their participation and feelings of belonging in their new home country.

The informants

In Table 11.1 and Table 11.2 the reasons for the informants' migration to Sweden are presented as well as their present kin networks. Most of them need social support according to Swedish public needs assessment, and these needs are also described in Table 11.1. If we exclude Ayana, the manager, all of the informants came to Sweden for family reunification. They were all between 68

Table 11.1: The women interviewed

Name	Country of origin	Age	Reunification and kin networks	Dependency/social needs[1] (social needs defined as something society is responsible for)
Amina	Iraq[2]	72	Reunification with son	In severe need of help. Receives home care daily.
Mrs Chung	Vietnam[3]	82	Reunification with son	In severe need of help. Receives some cash from the local government to pay her relatives for care.
Du	China[4]	68	Reunification with husband. Quite independent from other family members	Still healthy. Her needs for social help are not considered sufficiently comprehensive for publicly provided care.
Henryka	Poland[5]	78	Reunification with daughter. Family members both in Sweden and Poland	In severe need of help
Li	India/ China[6]	75	Grandparenting. Her 10 siblings live in Sweden, India, Canada, Taiwan, Austria and the US. With extensive planning they can meet regularly, even if it does not happen every year	Minor need for help. Problem with sight and back pain. Receives home help services from PREI.
Ayana[7]	Ethiopia	Not known	Professional manager. Provides support to many of the visitors at PREI. Her position is partly paid and partly voluntary and unpaid. Studied sciences in Poland. Speaks many languages.	Not known

Notes:

[1] All except the manager receive a guaranteed pension; [2] Interviewed in English; [3] Interviewed with help of her bilingual Swedish-Vietnamese son as interpreter; [4] Interviewed with help of a Chinese friend with good knowledge of Swedish; [5] Interviewed with help of a PREI member with knowledge of Polish and Swedish, neither of which were the interpreter's first language; [6] Interview in Swedish; [7] Collected written stories from a larger number of PREI visitors and made a summary that was discussed in this interview.

Table 11.2: Present family, education, occupational and migration history

Name	Present family	Occupational history	Education	Migration history
Amina	Married, one son.	Followed her husband in his international career	Academic education in sciences	Lived in more than one country before coming to Sweden. Good knowledge of English.
Mrs Chung	Widow, one son and one disabled daughter.	Not known	Not known	Experience of children living under asylum. in Sweden
Du	Married, two children, one in China and one in Europe	Language teacher in China until retirement. Cared for her mother until she died and Du was free to reunite with her husband	Academic education in languages	Her husband made an international career in science.
Henryka	Widow and divorced from her second husband. Three children, of which one is no longer alive. Family members live in both Poland and Sweden.	Hard work in labour camps behind the 'Iron Curtain'	No higher education	Lived in more than one country before coming to Sweden.
Li	Three children one in Sweden and two in India	Professional dressmaker until her back pains and bad sight interrupted her work	Artisan	Grew up in a Chinese migrant family in India.

and 82 years of age when the interviews were conducted, and Table 11.1 provides information about the different languages the interviews were performed in and who interpreted the conversations.

Background stories: continuity and discontinuity

The women who participated in this study immigrated to Sweden in their old age, which marked a step of discontinuity in their life stories. They had all immigrated from the Far East, Middle East or European countries affected by war from societies at different stages of modernisation. The migration also marked a step of continuity, when they were reunited with family members in Sweden.

Many of the women had participated in higher education, and even those who had not still had well-educated family members (see Table 11.2). Many of them also had significant work experience and several of them had experience of living abroad. For example, Du (68 years) and Li (75 years), both Chinese, experienced two totally different situations in Sweden, and this can be understood in terms of their early family history. Li, who was the most international person among the interviewees, was brought up in a migrant family in India and easily adapted to life as an immigrant in Sweden. She knew what was required in a new country, and she got her husband's support to learn Swedish. Du, the youngest of the informants, never went abroad before she was reunited with her husband in Sweden. She came to Sweden because of her husband's desire to stay in Sweden after his international career ended. She said that she "would like to return to China but my husband does not want to. He enjoys living in Sweden. He has lived outside China for 20 years, and he lived in the US for 10 years before he came to Sweden."

Adaptations to the view of the older care recipient

This section is based on the experiences of late-in-life migrants living in Sweden, which is a society with other expectations for them than the society in which they grew up. It covers four broad themes:

- perceived difficulties as an immigrant;
- personal adaptations;
- care and support;
- personal social needs in contrast to social needs as defined by society.

Theme 1: Perceived difficulties as an immigrant

Under the theme of perceived difficulties as an immigrant, three subthemes were identified: 'isolation'; 'language problems'; and an 'unclear social situation'. An overview of the informants' difficulties can be found in Table 11.3.

The experiences of isolation in Swedish society varied. Mrs Chung, for example, found herself in a situation that was quite unstructured and she was disconnected from people in the local community other than her son and his family. She felt very isolated during her separation from her relatives and friends in Vietnam, especially during her transition from living with her son's family, then staying in her own apartment, and then moving back to her son's family. She did not feel comfortable with the care she was offered by the Swedish welfare representatives, and she felt at a disadvantage, because she could not communicate with authorities in her own language. Compared to that experience, Mrs Chung did not feel isolated staying in her son's house.

Du and Li admitted in their interviews that they felt insecure and had had great difficulty in finding a role in their community. Li felt isolated, and mentioned that in India she had had "a lot of friends hanging in her shop every day". Due to her lack of language skills, she could not initially speak to anybody outside her family. Li's husband agreed to take responsibility for the grandchildren while she studied Swedish at SFI (Swedish for Immigrants). After that, she wanted to get a job to break the isolation, but she was told that as a retiree she did not need to work. She chose to visit PREI during its open meetings, to practise her Swedish and to have some social contact.

Table 11.3: Perceived difficulties and personal adaptations

Name	Perceived difficulties in the migrant situation (special needs)	Personal adaptations
Amina	Without language skills in Swedish and with limited knowledge about Swedish society, her stay has been difficult. Wants contact with relatives in Iraq and brothers in Canada and France.	Wants to learn how to use Facebook. Totally dependent on her son to be able to use community services like transportation.
Mrs Chung	Language is a barrier.	Help from a huge family network in Vietnam and Sweden. Uses Skype and satellite to watch Vietnamese television.
Du	Du and her husband do not expect help from their children, which is contrary to the tradition in their culture. Financial problems. Does not trust the Swedish welfare system.	Tried to learn Swedish but found it too difficult. Found PREI, and this helped her to counter her isolation.
Henryka	Traumatizing memories from a lost happy family life. Grew up in a quite rich family. Her father lost everything during WWII. Hard life in labour camps behind the Iron Curtain.	The manager Ayana is like a daughter to Henryka. Ayana is available for Henryka almost around the clock. For the past 8 years they have met on a daily basis.
Li	Limited social network.	A resource for PREI. She helps her fellow migrants from China by interpreting. More of a care giver than a care recipient.

Theme 2: Personal adaptations

The informants had to adapt as strangers in the Scandinavian welfare system, which depends on a strong relationship between labour market participation and welfare benefits. Under the theme of personal adaptations, the subthemes were identified as 'finances' and 'distrust of welfare offers'.

The informants did not expect to get financial support or care services from Swedish authorities, but all of them are entitled to a guaranteed pension, a form of basic protection (which is also low for Swedes). Some of them had their own savings (such as Du and her husband), but in the global world the cost of living varies and the exchange rate often makes savings worth less in the new country. Li's role in childcare as a grandparent in exchange for free care in old age could also be viewed as saving for the future.

Du's husband was 67, and his employment would soon end. However, his international life will not have benefited him. His earnings in Sweden have qualified him to withdraw money from the guaranteed pension, which will be reduced until the balance is reached. Du has her own pension from China but, when exchanged into Swedish crowns, it does not cover her living expenses. Moving back to China is not a good solution, because her husband has been abroad too long to get a pension there. They would not get health care or health insurance in China, but her husband is entitled to health care in Sweden. Du became entitled to health care one year after her immigration to Sweden. Du was worried that their savings would prevent them from receiving a housing allowance from the social services: "We have not applied for it because we are afraid that they will reduce our pension if they find that we have savings". The couple had not applied for a housing allowance (*bostadsbidrag*), because they were afraid that their application would be denied. (Their distrust is unfounded, and they are entitled to housing allowances.)

Li has found a good balance in her life with small living expenses, because she lives with her son's family.

Amina rents a small apartment. Due to her financial situation, she is basically trapped in the city where she lives right now. Her son recently moved to another city, and Amina would like to move there as soon as possible, because she has no other connections to the city where she is now living.

Trust in the public welfare system was not in these women's imagination due to their upbringing, and they were relying rather on the types of solutions that they had used earlier in their lives.

New technologies were easy to use for those who wanted to keep in contact with relatives and friends in their home countries.

Theme 3: Care and support

The subthemes identified under the theme of care and support included: 'different roles in caring activities'; 'own solutions'; 'intergenerational exchange'; and 'dependency'.

The women had different roles in providing care, and they were receiving different types of care. Li cared for her grandchildren and also received home care services from a company managed by Ayana, the manager of PREI. Du had applied for public home care, but was not assessed as needing such help. Amina, Du, Mrs Chung and Henryka were all in need of support from their families as well as from volunteer services. None of the women could find support from public services that fitted their needs, which was partly connected to their lacking knowledge of Swedish and Swedish society and partly connected to their unusual expectations and their lack of trust in public support. Their stories described a wide variety of situations and gave meaning and understanding to the concept of 'special needs'. For them, the 'special need' could be a need for social contact, or the right not to receive care in a language they did not understand, or help with things that are not relevant in their everyday lives, for example receiving standard food rather than the type of food they are used to, which Mrs Chung mentioned.

The two Chinese women, Li and Du, acted out their personal preference differently in relation to intergenerational exchange. For Li, there was an agreement about reciprocity within her family, and she expected some care from her family when she needed help as an old woman. The strict age limits for work and retirement in Sweden surprised Li: "In India I would have had to work if I had been able to because India has no universal pension system". Li decided to follow the family tradition and take care of her grandchildren and to become financially dependent on her son.

In Du's story, there was no such agreement. Du and her husband have not told their children about their situation, and their children have had no chance to help them. The reason for this is that they do not want to involve their children in these issues; they wish their children to "live independent from them". Their attitudes blend well with Swedish norms. Dependency on family members, as well as receiving volunteer care as a standard procedure, is far from the thinking behind the universal welfare system. Without having participated in wage work in Sweden, to which individual welfare is linked, Du was excluded from the solutions that would guarantee independence. Her background as a wage earner and caring for her old mother in China limits her chances for an independent life. Unfortunately, she has not learned to trust governmental solutions.

For Amina, a woman with no family members or relatives in Iraq who could help her as she aged, the decision to immigrate to Sweden can be seen as being strongly influenced by her son's decision. She never mentioned any alternative, and the decision to immigrate seems to have been made immediately after her husband died. Moving to Sweden with no language skills and no knowledge about Swedish society has been difficult for Amina, because she now has to rely on her son to be able to use community services.

PREI was important in many of the women's stories. One of Du's language teachers recommended that she go there for social interaction. PREI was also important for Henryka and gave her support after some turbulent years in Sweden. She sees the manager every day and gets a lot of help, and she said that the manager, Ayana, is "better than my own daughter". When Henryka is ill, Ayana comes to help her: "PREI is my home and the manager is my daughter".

Theme 4: Personal social needs in contrast to social needs as defined by society

The general picture from the interviews and the written histories (Table 11.4) can be described as follows. Some of the rules and regulations in Sweden can be difficult to understand and to live up to, and the immigrants have had to build new, concrete and trustful relations. One difficulty is that the care recipients have no say about who will provide care in their home, and they have to accept the fact that in Sweden both women and men can provide care. Help performed by family members or by friends, and financed by public means, is not preferred by public authorities, because such relations within public social care can come into conflict with the underlying goal of universal access. Personal isolation is looked on as a problem, and the solution is participation in public arrangements. In that respect, language skills will be important, especially because the women also mentioned that a lack of language skills was a barrier to social interactions.

Subthemes identified in the interviews included: "standardised solutions"; "voluntary work"; "family-based care"; and "dependency". The informants discussed how they found situations that better suited their needs than standardised solutions. Having control over what happens in everyday life is important and cannot be easily included in standard care packages. Ayana said: "People in need of home help services have a strong desire to choose for themselves the person who will come to their home. The personal relation is the most important." PREI stresses that it is important to show respect for the person and to be kind and to care about the person's social needs. It is important that the contact is reciprocal and that there is an effort to find the right person in the group of available volunteers. The stories of the women expressed their dependency on voluntary and unpaid help from Ayana. At PREI, the informants could receive help that they would not have been entitled to in the standardised public home care system. Ayana, who also sells standardized home care services to the municipality, volunteered during her spare time to assist the women with their 'special needs' – needs that were not found to be 'legitimate' by the public home services.

Table 11.4: Themes related to care provision. PREI compared to public service norms.

Theme	PREI	Public service norm
Relationships	Relationships are the primary goal.	Service is more important than relationships, which can lead to injustice and exploitation of staff.
Language	Important but subordinate to the goal of relationships.	Problems when it is difficult to match people, and exploitation of staff can happen when the language is the primary link between the care recipient and the care provider.
Gender of the care provider	Women want to be cared for by women and men by men (if no daughter is available). Staff and volunteers of both genders are available.	In a gender-equal society, it does not matter if a man or a woman provides care. This is not a question of free choice. Staff of both sexes are assigned regardless of the sex of the recipient.
Family members and friends as care providers	Possible to nominate a preferred person to provide care. This is a trusted person with patience who can show respect. Not always a family member.	A family member or a friend as care provider is not preferred within public home care.

Learning from life histories

The informants in this chapter were well educated, and some were linked to family members all round the world (Table 11.2). That makes this relatively small group interesting, because they can be expected to vocalise the issues they are faced with to a greater extent than other immigrants in a similar situation. They were also quite old. They described their expectations and needs of help from local services that were not included in the standard care offered to them. They also described their financial problems, interdependency within families, and dependency on special volunteers. One observation was that socialisation into the role as an old person as well as a welfare recipient was important. Some desires were fulfilled, but others were not. The support for independent living that is embedded in the welfare structure is difficult to obtain without having participated in working life, because such participation determines what one is entitled to later in life. Du wanted to live independently from her family, but she was not able to make the correct risk calculations and her guaranteed pension was not enough for the life she preferred to live. Li did not expect any pension and was happy with her guaranteed pension, which was enough together with the support her family gave. With reference to Benhabib (2002) and her concept of 'bounded universalism', we agree that welfare cannot fully be shared with people who do not belong to a bounded group. Independence from a supporting family without any financial base was one such desire that was not supported by the Swedish welfare system.

The language is crucial when negotiating what services will be needed. When standardised support is offered, the applicant must be able to give an exact description of their social needs. One question that needs to be addressed is if the women interviewed would have been less dependent on the welfare state and less economically marginalised (argued by Koopmans, 2010), if they had been speaking Swedish. The problem is that the service they wanted was not available. Ayana stressed that having a language in common is important in this context, but its degree of importance "cannot compete with the individual commitment" to whatever language might be used. She mentioned that people often want to be helped by a person of the same sex and that for both sexes receiving help from a daughter is also highly desired. Ayana also emphasised that "knowledge is essential for the performance of good quality care".

All of the informants experienced a change in their living conditions late in life, and the experiences of discontinuity and adaptation were different for people at this stage in life than for those of younger ages. Their interactions with others depended mainly on giving and receiving care. They found various ways of relating to their family, ranging from declaring total independence to accepting total dependence. This made them very different compared to traditional Swedish society.

The women received no formal recognition for the informal care that they provided within their families. Scuzzarello (2010) described a devaluation of the unpaid care work performed in the private sphere and found that paid professional care is valued more highly than voluntary or family-based care. This also means that PREI's initiatives are undervalued. That kind of lower-valued care work is actually what the women said would better suit their needs – and was even the reason for living in Sweden in some cases. The stories revealed gaps between one group of minority women and the universal welfare structure. The informants described how they have used their agency to have their needs met at PREI and how the manager acts as a bridge between that space and the universal welfare system.

The development of special places where one's needs can be met is one example of how an individual's agency can bring about structural changes. Similar to the conclusions of Naldemirci (2013), the life stories described here reveal the importance of finding ways to connect local welfare practices with the lived experiences of older immigrants in diaspora, both those arriving early and those arriving late in their lives. For the women, PREI represented something familiar and trustful, and they used their agency to create a space that corresponded to their wishes. For them, PREI became the social network they had lost in their migration and became something to which they could link their lives. To paraphrase Anttonen (2002), to recognise informal contributions could be a way to build trust in the Swedish public welfare system, to accept diversity instead of uniformity, pluralism instead of conformity, and relativism instead of absolutism.

Erel (2007) discussed how marginalised people's agency can be taken into account, and how this gives them an opportunity to contribute to a more nuanced understanding of their situation. The interviews exemplified how an ageing society with an increasing number of minority groups presents significant challenges for a universal welfare model. Diverse needs create a demand for less-standardised social services. The life stories described here indicate that diversity brings more tension among groups and a greater demand for changes in the roles of minorities as consumers of welfare services as well as increased emphasis on overall flexibilisation, pluralisation and individualisation. The migrants' stories provide a deeper understanding of the underlying contradictions in the Swedish welfare structure. PREI represented a higher acceptance for different attitudes to gender equity and family cultures, and the manager acted as a bridge between that pluralist programme and the conformist universal welfare system. A better balance between the majority and minority groups must be seen as an opportunity for the future and not as a failure of the universal welfare model.

Acknowledgement

This chapter is a publication from the research project 'Power and influence in elderly care – Structural conditions and individual expressions' that was funded by the Swedish Research Council (421-2007-7231). I want to express my deep gratitude to Marie-Louise Snellman from Umeå University for her valuable contribution to this chapter. She also co-wrote an early draft of the chapter.

Notes

[1] According to a statistical investigation carried out in 2004, the largest non-Swedish groups in Sweden came from Finland, former Yugoslavia, Iraq, Bosnia-Herzegovina, Iran, Poland, Norway, Denmark, Germany and Turkey (Statistiska Centralbyrån, 2005).

[2] Since 15 April 2010, the requirements for family reunion are that the person living in Sweden must be employed and have acceptable housing to host the family member moving to Sweden (Riksdagen, 2011).

References

Andersson, K. and Johansson, S. (2010) 'Valfrihetsom dilemma [Choice as a dilemma]', in S. Johansson (ed) *Omsorg och mångfald* [*Care and diversity*], Malmö: Gleerups, 116-31.

Anttonen, A. (2002) 'Universalism and social policy: A Nordic-feminist revaluation', *NORA – Nordic Journal of Feminist and Gender Research*, 10, 2, 71-80.

Baldassar, L., Baldock, C.V. and Wilding, R. (2007) *Caring across borders*, New York: Palgrave Macmillan.

Benhabib, S. (2002) 'Transformations of citizenship: The case of contemporary Europe', *Government and Opposition*, 37, 4, 439-65.

Brochmann, G. and Hagelund, A. (2011) 'Migrants in the Scandinavian welfare state. The emergence of a social policy problem', *Nordic Journal of Migration Research*, 1, 1, 13-24.

Corman, D. (2008) 'Sveriges invandring och utvandring [Swedish immigration and emigration]', in M. Darvishpour and C. Westin (eds) *Migration och etnicitet* [*Migration and ethnicity*], Lund: Studentlitteratur, 175-92.

Crepaz, M.M. (2008) *Trust beyond borders*, Ann Arbor: University of Michigan Press.

Erel, U. (2007) 'Constructing meaningful lives: Biographical methods in research on migrant women', *Sociological Research Online*, 12, 4.

Esping-Andersen, G. (1990) *The three worlds of welfare capitalism*, Cambridge: Polity Press.

Faist, T., Fauser, M. and Reisenauer, E. (2013) *Transnational migration*, Cambridge: Polity Press.

Forssell, E. (2004) *Skyddandets förnuft. En studie om anhöriga till hjälpbehövande äldre som invandrat sent i livet* [*The logic of protection: A study of informal caregiving to older family members in immigrant families*]. Doctoral thesis, Stockholm: Department of Social Work, Stockholm University.

Freeman, G. (1986) 'Migration and the political economy of the welfare state', *The Annals of the American Academy of Political and Social Science*, 485, 1, 51-63.

Hochschild, A.R. (2000) 'Global care chains and emotional surplus value', in W. Hutton and A. Giddens (eds) *On the edge: Globalization and the new millennium*, London: Sage, 130-46.

Johansson, L., Long, H. and Parker, M. (2011) 'Informal caregiving for elders in Sweden: An analysis for current policy developments', *Journal of Aging & Social Policy*, 3, 4, 335-53.

Koopmans, R. (2010) 'Trade-offs between equality and difference. Immigrant integration, multiculturalism and the welfare state in cross-national perspective', *Journal of Ethnic and Migration Studies*, 36, 1, 1-26.

Lindelöf, M. and Rönnbäck, E. (2004) *Att fördela bistånd* [*Distributing assistance to the elderly*], Umeå: Umeå University.

Magnússon, F. and Mahin, K. (2011) 'Integration mot ohälsa. Äldre iranska kvinnor i Malmö' [Integration against danger to health. Old Iranian women in Malmö], *Socialmedicinsk tidskrift*, 3, 88.

Migrationsinfo (2013) *Migration: Sverige* [*Migration: Sweden*]. www.migrationsinfo.se/

Naldemirci, Ö. (2013) *Caring (in) Diaspora. Aging and caring experiences of older Turkish migrants in a Swedish context*, Gothenburg: University of Gothenburg, Department of Sociology and Work.

Palme, J., Bergmark, Å., Bäckman, O., Estrada, F., Fritzell, J., Lundberg, O., Sjöberg, O. and Szebehely, M. (2002) 'Welfare in Sweden: Balancing the books for the 1990s', *Journal of European Social Policy*, 12, 4, 329-46.

PREI (2013) *Projekt för integration* [*Project for integration*]. http://prei-umea.se/sv/

Pries, L. (1999) 'New migration in transnational spaces', in L. Pries (ed) *Migration and transnational social spaces*, Aldershot: Ashgate, 1-35.

Prop (1987/88) *Äldreomsorgen inför 90-talet. Regeringens proposition* [*Elder care on the brink of the 90s. The Government's Bill*], Stockholm: Gotab, 176

Regeringskansliet (2005) *Arbetskraftsinvandring till Sverige.* [*Workers' migration to Sweden*], Stockholm: Regeringskansliet.

Riksdagen (2011) Socialförsäkringsutskottets betänkande 2011/12:SfU12 'Anhöriginvandring' [Report 2011/12: SfU12 of the social committee 'Immigration of relatives']. www.riksdagen.se/sv/Dokument-Lagar/Utskottens-dokument/Betankanden/Anhoriginvandring_GZ01SfU12/

Sainsbury, D. (1996) *Gender, equality, and welfare states*, Cambridge: Cambridge University Press.

Scuzzarello, S. (2010) *Caring multiculturalism*, Lund: Lund University, Faculty of Social Sciences.

Socialstyrelsen (2009) *Folkhälsorapport 2009* [*Public health report 2009*], Stockholm: Socialstyrelsen.

Statistiska Centralbyrån (2005) *Efterkrigstiden in- och utvandring* [*Postwar immigration and emigration*], Stockholm: Statistiska Centralbyrån.

Statistiska Centralbyrån (2013) Låga pensioner *risk för utrikes födda* [*Low pensions are a risk for people born abroad*], Stockholm: Statistiska Centralbyrån.

Steptoe, A., Shankar, A., Demakakos, P. and Wardle, J. (2013) 'Social isolation, loneliness, and all-cause mortality in older men and women', *Proceedings of the National Academy of Sciences of the United States of America*, 110, 15, 5797-801.

Szebehely, M. (2009) 'Omsorgsmönster bland kvinnor och män' [Caring patterns among women and men], in E. Gunnarsson and M. Szebehely (eds) *Genus i omsorgens vardag [Gendered caring]*, Stockholm: Gothia.

Szebehely, M. (2012) 'Universell eller skiktad äldreomsorg – vem vinner och vem förlorar?' [Universal or stratified elderly care – who are the winners and the losers?], in L. Andersson (ed) *Jämlik ålderdom?* [*Equity in later life?*], Malmö: Liber.

Torres, S. (2006) 'Elderly immigrants in Sweden: "Otherness" under construction', *Journal of Ethnic and Migration Studies*, 32, 1341-58.

TWELVE

The labour market in ageing Sweden: lifecourse influences on workforce participation

Mikael Stattin and Daniel Larsson

Introduction

Among the array of challenges that arise in the wake of population ageing, one of the most topical is probably the question about the length of working life. Increasingly, extending working life is believed to be a necessary measure for maintaining economic competitiveness, since predictions suggest that the labour force in many countries will decrease, or at least stop growing. Governments in most Western countries have concluded that the prospect of retaining acceptable levels of productivity and economic growth and, consequently, the ability to maintain previous levels of welfare provision and general standards of living, requires the mobilisation of all available labour resources (Organisation for Economic Co-operation and Development, 2006).

One key target in that context has been older workers, and many countries have adopted strategies to increase labour force participation in old age by decreasing the prevalence of early retirement and by raising the official pension age above the age of 65. However, scholars are questioning whether such measures will be sufficient to achieve these policy goals (Dragano et al, 2011). Even if supply-side measures such as pension age reforms, given increased life expectancy, seem reasonable and rational, it is likely that such measures to prolong working life will have behavioural effects mainly for a certain selected part of the workforce – that is, employees in privileged social positions, who have favourable working conditions and are in good health. The main reason for this is that the question of how, when and why people depart from paid labour is a profoundly complex one that involves a very broad set of determinants that are related to macro, meso and micro levels of explanation. Together, conditions at these levels define what we may call an opportunity structure surrounding the decision to retire and leave work (Wang et al, 2011).

At the macro level, populations and individuals are influenced through incentives and disincentives in social policies, social norms, the economy and demography, whereas at the meso level influence is exerted through work experiences, work organisations and family. The micro level concerns the individual's physical and mental health, and financial and social situations. All of these levels are of importance in defining the opportunities and constraints that affect individuals' subjective evaluation and capabilities regarding the prospect of retiring or remaining active in the labour market.

How long individuals work and their decisions about when to retire should therefore not be regarded as merely their responses (at a given point in time) to the opportunities and constraints presented by the design of welfare provisions or pension programmes. Instead, we need to view major transitions in life (such as retirement) and the lifecourse as 'institutionally embedded and multi level in form' (Silverstein and Giarrusso, 2011: 38). Such an institutional approach to the lifecourse takes into account how various institutions of society influence 'orderly transitions in role and status positions across the life span by fostering collective expectations for an orderly life path, and by providing incentives and disincentives for particular actions' (Silverstein and Giarrusso, 2011: 37). The institutional lifecourse perspective focuses on how lifespans are associated with, and shaped by, social institutions such as welfare state regulations, work, family and leisure, and how these multi-level institutions jointly and dynamically influence each other over the lifecourse. From this perspective, institutions are considered to be dynamic, changing with individuals and societies over time, and each of the three levels is mutually dependent on the other two. Analysing the issue of labour force participation in old age from an institutional lifecourse perspective can potentially provide us with new understandings about how individual capabilities in old age are shaped. This is important, since the way we understand what determines exit from work directly affects our ideas about how to intervene in order to promote a longer working life.

In this chapter, we aim to explore the complex multi-level web of factors that influence labour force participation in old age. As indicated earlier, this is a highly complex matter and we do not aspire to cover all potential facets involved, but rather to selectively describe the macro, meso and micro mechanisms from a Swedish perspective. Second, and in relation to our descriptions of the different analytical levels, we will present examples of empirical studies that illustrate how an institutional lifecourse perspective may be used in research. However, it should be emphasised that a full-scale analysis of all three levels requires extensive data sets that are not often available. Therefore, our examples should be considered limited illustrations that intend to show that lifecourse analyses need to take social contexts into consideration, especially social contexts that change over time.

The macro level: characteristics and effects

The supply side

At the macro level, we identify both an institutional (macro) and a normative context. The institutional level refers to the welfare state as well as labour markets (Ebbinghaus, 2006; Edlund and Stattin, 2013). The former, also often described in terms of protection pull factors, highlights the importance of the design and configuration of welfare state provisions, laws and regulations that define the individual's scope of action and thus people's behaviour. One actual mechanism concerns the incentive/disincentive trade-off within retirement options as individuals assess the relative gains and costs of retirement as compared to remaining in paid work. This means that the income levels in pension benefits are a crucial and decisive factor. The more generous the benefits, the greater the likelihood that people will choose to retire. Even if it is hard to determine the relative importance of the economic rationality argument, the empirical evidence demonstrating the relevance of this argument is strong (Esser, 2005; SOU, 2013). Consequently, contemporary pension age reforms rely quite strongly on expected incentive effects.

From an institutional protection pull perspective, however, it is not only replacement rates that are of importance. The availability of different pathways to work exit is highly relevant in this context (Ebbinghaus, 2006). First and foremost, many countries have specially designed early retirement programmes that enable people to leave the labour market before they are eligible to receive an old age pension. Throughout Europe, millions of working-age people have permanently left the labour market by means of social security schemes that were originally designed to handle rare and occasional events, such as disability benefits/pensions,[1] and sickness and unemployment benefits. Such programmes have regularly been used (or misused) as pre-retirement programmes and have actually played a crucial role in decreasing labour force participation in old age and in lowering the average exit age despite increased life expectancy and improved health in populations (Marin, 2003).

Another important aspect in relation to the macro-level concerns eligibility criteria in different social security programmes. Broad eligibility criteria automatically include more potential applicants in the programmes. For example, during the 1980s and 1990s, many countries increasingly relaxed access to disability programmes, often making them accessible for reasons other than ill health (Stattin, 2005), which has opened up for a large outflow of working-age people into inactivity.

It is thus quite clear that macro-level characteristics, such as welfare state arrangements, are of crucial importance in encouraging people to extend their work careers. This was also an important point of departure when the Swedish government changed the old age pension and disability benefit programmes in the late 1990s. These reforms addressed both economic incentives and a number of alternative exit pathways.

The new old age pension programme, which came into effect in 2001, is designed to cope with demographic challenges, which the old system was unable to do. In particular, the new programme has ended the old system's tendency to pass on pension costs to future generations, and it has adjusted compensation levels to create a financially sustainable system. Compensation levels are on average 5% lower than in the previous programme, given unchanged pension behaviour.

However, a long working career is favoured, since the actual pension received depends on the total income during the entire working life and the age at which pension payments start to be drawn. The longer an individual works, the higher the pension will be, and every additional year at work increases pension income by roughly 9–10% (SOU, 2013).

Another feature in the system is that there is no longer a formal pension age. Instead, a flexible pension age has been introduced, so that it is possible to begin drawing a pension from the age of 61 to 67. One important objective of the Swedish pension reform was to offer increased economic incentives to prolong working life and, by means of a flexible pension age, to affect social norms concerning the timing of retirement. Indeed, there is evidence that the changes have had some real effects, as labour force participation rates in old age have increased over the past decade. The extent to which this is due to the pension reform is not entirely clear, however. Such development might also be a result of cohort effects or a reflection of occasional phenomena. It is, however, quite possible that the former system did come with some degree of institutional discrimination, as people were not allowed to work after the age of 65. As this restriction has now been removed, it is likely that at least some employees have postponed their retirement just because it is possible to do so.

Another important recent macro-level change in Sweden concerns the disability benefit programme, which was radically changed in 2003. Prior to the reform, Sweden scored very highly in international comparisons of annual inflow into the programmes. A disability benefit decision often meant a permanent departure from the labour market, a one-way trip, as return to work from the programme was extremely low. Most recipients instead left the programme by reaching the age of eligibility for the old age pension. Changes to the programme have dramatically decreased the number of recipients. This can mainly be explained as an effect of the introduction of new eligibility criteria in the programme. The disability benefit programme is basically designed to provide economic compensation to individuals whose working capacity has become limited due to ill health. However, previously, the programme had sometimes also accepted unemployment and various social circumstances as eligible criteria to qualify for the benefit. Also, the criteria were relaxed for older workers in disability benefit decisions. All such considerations were abandoned in the 2003 reform (SOU, 2013), and now, only medical reasons are accepted as legitimate. The disability benefit programme was also moved from being a part of the pension programme to become part of the sickness benefit scheme, in order to give the benefit a less permanent character. In parallel with the reform of the disability benefit programme, the possibility of receiving sickness benefits for longer periods has been quite heavily restricted. These changes in social security programmes actually mean that health-related social security benefits in Sweden are now much less functional as pathways towards premature and permanent withdrawal from work.

The demand side

The macro level also concerns rules and regulations that apply to the functioning of labour markets – the demand side. The workings of labour market regulations may, to various degrees, work in favour of a prolonged working life. Examples are employment protection laws. In Sweden, the Employment Protection Act is designed in a way that shelters older workers. Together with legislation about age discrimination, the Employment Protection Act regulates lay-offs and restricts employers' free choice when it comes to hiring and firing practices, and thus protects older workers in cases of organisational downsizing or restructuring. Given such restrictions on replacing existing workers with new hires, employers may become more engaged in skills training for workers they currently employ. As a result of such skill investments, older workers thus become more valuable to the employer (Hall and Soskice, 2001).

Legislation regulating the relationship between employers and employees is another important aspect of institutional conditions in the labour market. The relative strength of the unions in Sweden is one example, as unions have historically struggled for improved co-determination, employee participation and influence in workplaces. Unions have also engaged in the improvement of working conditions, job flexibility, skills enhancement and employment security, which in turn may affect employees' working conditions, workers' health and opportunities and their motivation to work into older age.

It is also important to recognise different structural and environmental constraints defined by the functioning of the labour market. The speed of technological and organisational change may affect demand for certain skills and competences. Older workers may face difficulties, given obsolete education or skills. Here, strategies and resources, concerning both general legislation and active labour market and reintegration policies, are important aspects in relation to older workers' chances of continued labour force participation.

The high level of labour force participation in Sweden among workers aged 60 and older is an indication that the aspects presented have had an effect on the incentives to stay in the labour force even when getting older. As can be seen in Figure 12.1 and Figure 12.2, labour force participation among men and women aged 60 to 64 has been substantially higher in Sweden than the average in the EU 15, and has been so for more than 20 years. When it comes to labour force participation among people aged 65 and above, the difference is smaller, but there is a slight tendency for the difference between Sweden and the EU 15 average to increase, especially among women. Also taking the whole OECD into account, there are only a few countries that have higher labour force participation than Sweden (for example, Japan and the US).

There is reason to believe that the trend of increasing labour force participation in old age will continue as an effect of reformed old age pension programmes

Figure 12.1: Labour force participation among men 60-64 and 65+ years old, 1990-2012, EU 15 and Sweden

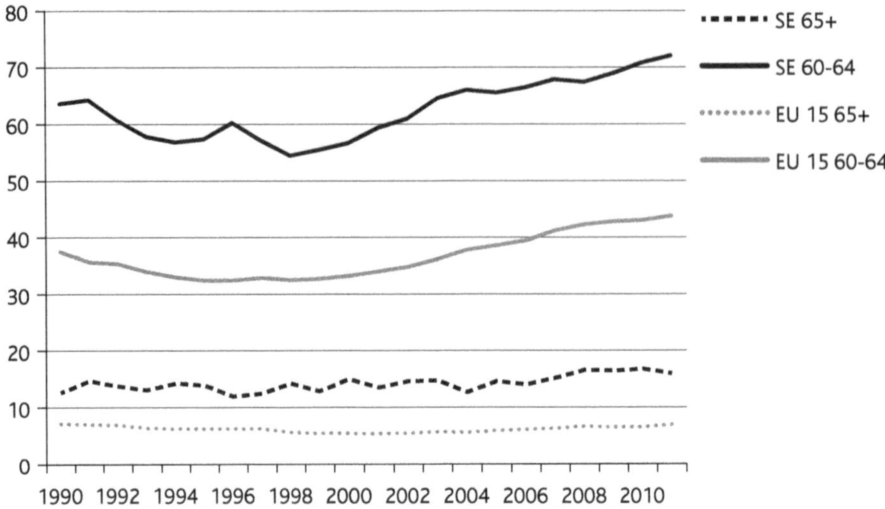

Source: http://epp.eurostat.ec.europa.eu/portal/page/portal/statistics/search_database

Figure 12.2: Labour force participation among women 60-64 and 65+ years old, 1990-2012, EU 15 and Sweden

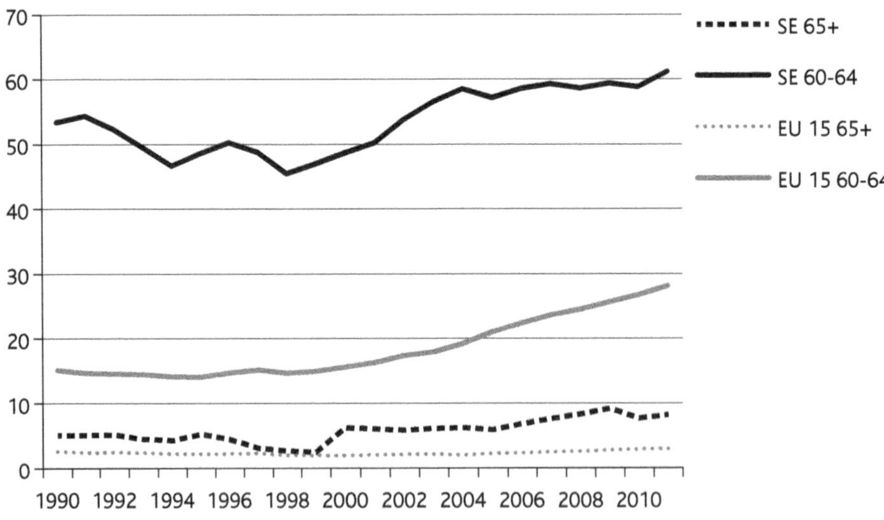

Source: http://epp.eurostat.ec.europa.eu/portal/page/portal/statistics/search_database

and restricted access to programmes that enable premature exit from work (SOU, 2013). Today, the most common way to permanently leave the labour market is through the old age pension; less than 10% of workers leave through the disability pension programme.

The normative context

At the macro level, we also need to consider a normative context. This refers to generalised norms and values in society that may have an impact on individual behaviour. It is important to emphasise that the decision to leave work is not based solely on economic considerations, but also on the extent to which work is perceived as an attractive and desirable activity vis-à-vis other activities, such as leisure and hobbies, voluntary work or family activities. Of particular significance in this context is the argument that specific public policy arrangements and practices may foster country-specific 'age cultures' (Maltby et al, 2004), and scholars have highlighted the possibility of a normative shift in relation to work in old age.

The basic assumption in this argument is that the considerable outflow and outplacement of large numbers of working-age people during the 1970s and 1980s may have institutionalised a perceived right to leave work earlier in life (Maltby et al, 2004). Research has observed both late-exit cultures, characterised by norms of active ageing and older workers' right and duty to participate in the labour market, and early-exit cultures, with norms of the ageing worker's right and duty to leave the labour market relatively early. In such cases, the 'right to exit early' has replaced the right, or duty, to work (De Vroom and Guillemard, 2002: 202). Such early-exit cultures or similar value patterns may very well be one obstacle to extending working lives. It is therefore an important aspect that needs to be accounted for in any analyses of determinants of labour force participation into older age.

As demonstrated earlier, there are a number of strong arguments supporting the idea that conditions at the macro societal level have the power to shape individual-level behaviour as well as social norms and attitudes. These arguments support the idea of a complex and dynamic relationship between different analytical levels in influencing labour force participation in old age (Svallfors, 2010). We now proceed by presenting two studies that try to scrutinise this dynamic relationship empirically.

Empirical illustration 1: the dynamic relationship between macro and micro levels

A recent study analysed possible effects of the Swedish old age pension reform on individual retirement preferences, that is at what time employees prefer to retire (Örestig et al, 2013). The data covered employees aged 55-64 years, and individual retirement preferences were measured in cross-sectional studies at two points in time: first in 2002-03, when most potential retirees were covered by the former old age pension programme; and then in 2010-11, when the new pension programme was up running and in effect for the majority of the subjects.

Figure 12.3 shows retirement preferences divided into three categories: a preferred retirement age below the age of 65, at 65 and later than 65. The first

Figure 12.3: Preferred retirement age among Swedish employees 55-64 years of age at two points in time

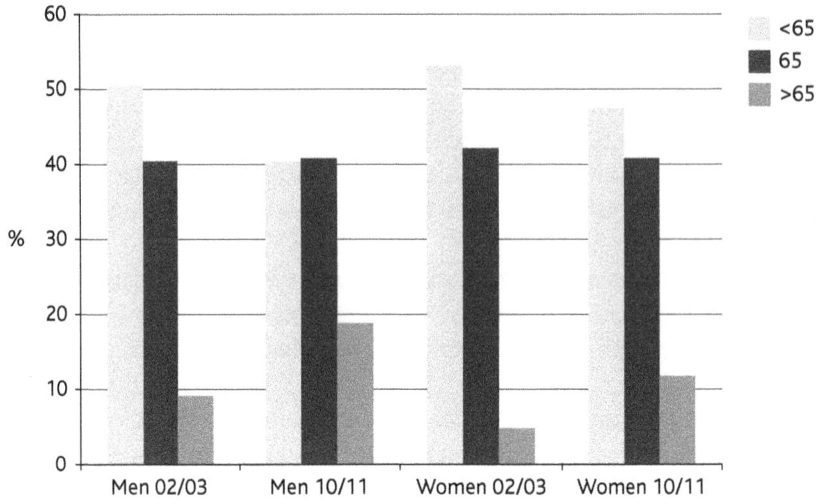

Source: Stattin, 2013

thing to note from Figure 12.3 is that the age of 65 seems to hold as a significant social norm regarding exit age. But even more common is a preference for an early retirement, which is before the age of 65. A rather small part of the sample reports a retirement preference later than the age of 65. These results might be an indication of an existing early-exit culture in Sweden. However, more interesting here is the fact that the relative number of respondents reporting a late retirement preference, later than 65, has increased over time. For men, it has increased from 9% to almost 20% and for women from 4% to nearly 12%. The number of respondents preferring to retire before the age of 65 had decreased significantly, whereas small changes were observed regarding 65 as a preferred retirement age. To assess whether this preference pattern was related to the macro-level changes, a time period variable was included as an indicator of the contextual (or macro) effect of the new pension system, and the result showed that the period effect significantly correlated with a preference to retire after the age of 65. This turned out to be a very robust result, and it also held when individual/micro-level aspects (health, education, and so on) as well as the organisational/meso-level aspects (working conditions) were taken into account.

The conclusion that can be drawn from this study is that the extensive old age pension reform in Sweden did actually have an impact on preference changes at an individual level. This study is an illuminating example of how the understanding of a phenomenon of great relevance to ageing research may benefit from an institutional lifecourse perspective. The study shows how micro and macro dimensions are interwoven in a dynamic change over time. When synthesising these dimensions in empirical studies, we thus make visible social processes and transformations of great importance in relation to policy objectives such as a prolonged working life.

Empirical illustration 2: the dynamic relationship between macro and micro levels

In our second empirical illustration we again draw attention to an analysis of the relationship between the macro and micro levels. This empirical example concerns an analysis of the relationship between retirement transitions and post-retirement health (Halleröd et al, 2013). This question has been extensively researched, but social gerontological studies have reached differing conclusions. There are findings suggesting that retirement is basically good for individual health, but the exact opposite result has also been empirically supported (Nordenmark and Stattin, 2009; Westerlund et al, 2009). Yet other studies find that retirement has virtually no implications at all for pensioners' health and wellbeing (Salokangas and Joukamaa, 1991; Kim and Moen, 2001). This inconclusiveness may be attributed to differing theoretical and empirical approaches in the studies. But, and more importantly in this context, it may also be an effect of selection bias. This is especially relevant in relation to exit due to ill health, and recent studies have questioned the welfare and health gains of premature departure from work and have even suggested that disability pension/benefits are associated with increased mortality (Wallman et al, 2006). Given that the main aim of such welfare state provisions is to assist people with disabilities to live socially and economically satisfactory lives, freed from exposure to employment health hazards, thus avoiding any further decline in health, research results suggesting the opposite effect are indeed challenging.

This was also the central point of departure in the study presented here, and the aim was to analyse whether – and to what extent – different and complex exit pathways per se were associated with subsequent states of health and wellbeing. In order to control for selection bias, such a study requires first and foremost a longitudinal design with an observation window in which it is possible to observe an ordered sequence of events. First, health is measured prior to the start of the retirement transition process (t0). The phase following that covers the extent to which subjects have received social security benefits from different programmes, and the final phase measures health after the subjects have begun to receive the old age pension (t1) (see Figure 12.4).

As background to the study it is important to note that during the past decades, exit transitions have become more heterogeneous, as a palette of different pathways are often used in the transition process. This change is largely due to changes at the macro level, as new exit pathways have been introduced and the relative numbers of employees who leave the labour market through a straightforward and abrupt transition from work to old age pension have decreased. Instead, the transition is often more complex, as people tend to move into and out of different types of income protection schemes. Therefore, a number of different exit pathways

Figure 12.4: Design of the study of determinants of post-retirement health

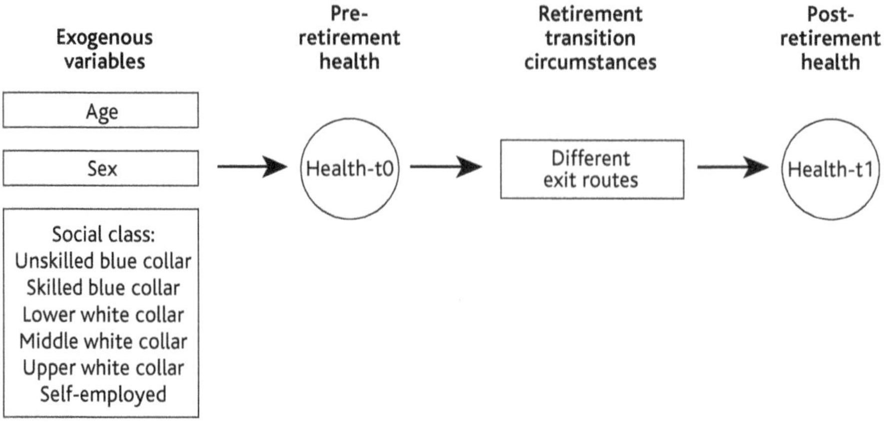

Exogenous variables | Pre-retirement health | Retirement transition circumstances | Post-retirement health

Age

Sex

Social class:
Unskilled blue collar
Skilled blue collar
Lower white collar
Middle white collar
Upper white collar
Self-employed

→ Health-t0 → Different exit routes → Health-t1

Source: Halleröd et al, 2013

were identified through information about incomes from various social security benefit schemes. Five different pathways were defined:

- people who made a straightforward transition from work to retirement, that is, who received no transfer income;
- people who received only sickness benefits;
- people who received a combination of the disability pension and sickness benefits;
- people who received transfers related to unemployment;
- people who, prior to retirement, received a mixture of health- and unemployment-related transfers.

The analyses were based on structural equation modelling and included a number of background variables in order to assess the influence of exit pathway on health. Health was measured as an index variable including both indicators of somatic health and of psychosocial wellbeing. Table 12.1 shows the coefficients for initial

Table 12.1: Associations between different exit pathways and health at t1: unadjusted coefficients and multivariate coefficients with control for sex, age, social class, health-t0

Exit patterns	Bivariate coefficients	Multivariate coefficients
No benefit dependency	0.114	0.001
Sickness benefit	0.272***	0.1*
Disability and Sickness benefit	0.386***	–0.063
Unemployment	–0.009	–0.036
Health at t0	0.830***	0.890***

Note: *p \ 0.05; **p \ 0.01; ***p \ 0.001

Source: Halleröd et al, 2013

health and different exit pathways; positive coefficients indicate higher levels of ill health at t1. At the bivariate level, it appears that an exit route that included income from sickness benefits or disability benefits was related to a high degree of post-retirement health problems. But what happens if pre-retirement health is controlled for in the analyses? This is displayed in the third column in Table 12.1. Here it becomes clear that the effects related to exit pathway disappear when controlling for pre-retirement health. This means that post-retirement health should largely be regarded as a reflection of pre-retirement health and not as a consequence of atypical exit transitions. Further, the analyses also showed a significant correlation between pre-retirement health and retirement transition circumstances, suggesting that welfare state provisions such as disability benefit programmes are successful in singling out those individuals most severely affected by ill health.

This example resembles our first illustration, but here we did not focus on the effects of changes in societal institutions but rather on changes at the individual level. Here, the link between micro and macro levels concerned how the configuration of available exit from work pathways might affect individual health over time – a research question that clearly seeks to bridge multi-level dimensions of explanations. The conclusion from the study was that involvement in social security programmes enabling early retirement does not seem to have any additional negative consequences for post-retirement health. On the contrary, the programmes seem to work as intended, as they manage to single out those most affected by ill health. This is indeed an important result. The study also illustrates the importance of access to high-quality data in order to assess the effects of macro-level conditions and sort these out from other explanatory mechanisms, such as health selection bias effects.

The meso level: characteristics and effects

The meso level refers to different social institutions, such as family and work (Silverstein and Giarrusso, 2011). Since we are occupied in this chapter with the issue of labour force participation in late age, we will discuss the meso level with a focus on the importance of work organisation. We argue that if a sustainable change towards increased working careers in old age is to be realised, the role of organisations and workplaces needs to be taken into account. In terms of interventions, quite a lot has been done on the supply side to enhance older workers' careers, while very little has been done on the demand side, that is, with respect to organisational and workplace conditions.

It is actually in the workplace where a substantial part of basic prerequisites for a long and healthy work career are defined. Still, there is a considerable scarcity of knowledge about human resources policies and strategies aimed at encouraging older workers to remain in paid work. Such strategies might range from age discriminatory to inclusive, and may be expressed in workplace cultures and leadership styles. Organisations and leaders practising age-flexible human resource policies may determine workers' decisions to quit or stay at work (Furunes and Mykletun, 2011), but how leadership styles and human resource practices are related to prolonged working careers is not very well studied.

A particular issue for investigation is whether organisations are willing to employ-to-retain the older worker, and if employers are, for example, adjusting salaries, bonuses, work content, flexibility, working hours and physical training in relation to the special needs of older workers (Mykletun et al, 2012). Several studies indicate that this might not be the case, and it seems to be a discrepancy between policy ambitions to delay retirement and employers' attitudes to older workers (Van Dalen et al, 2010). A study that surveyed 28,000 employers in 25 different countries showed that 14% of employers had a strategy for recruiting older workers and 21% had designed strategies for retaining older workers (SOU, 2013). A recent Swedish study reported that a substantial proportion of employees (25% of women and 33% of men) regard attitudes towards older employees as an obstacle to a prolonged working career and only 45% of the employers say that they think employees older than 60 should stay on longer. Substantial shares of the employers also regard younger employees as better educated, more productive and better able to adapt to technological and organisational change.

One key component enabling older employees to stay in work is competence and human capital (Ilmarinen, 2006). Competence may be regarded as a responsibility shared by the employer and the employee, and if attended to by both sides in the long term, makes an individual employable during major changes and redesigns of the workplace. Tacit knowledge and social networks, which may be the experience-based strength of the ageing worker, make these employees strong assets to the workplace as long as these competences are valid, relevant and appreciated (Furunes and Mykletun, 2011). However, while policy makers aim to delay retirement, employers have largely failed to value the qualities of mature workers. Despite an emerging and strong consensus around the need to prolong working lives, the response from much of industry has been generally unenthusiastic (Taylor, 2008).

However, although not very well documented, there are signs that employers are growing more aware of the consequences of the ageing society. In labour market sectors where labour shortages are becoming more frequent, there are several examples of employers implementing measures aimed at retaining older workers and also at re-employing already retired employees. There are also examples of organisations that systematically engage older employees as mentors in order to transfer key competences to younger, less experienced employees. But according to a recent governmental report (SOU, 2013), more needs to be done in order to increase work participation in old age. The report therefore suggests a number of measures that are of relevance at the organisational level. First and foremost, these concern a broad and long-term initiative for improved working conditions that will provide increased resources for research and the development of knowledge in the area. They also concern increasing resources for training managers and disseminating knowledge about how workplaces can be adapted to better accommodate an older workforce. The report also suggests strengthened legislation to combat age discrimination and measures that would help people to maintain and develop their skills and competences throughout their working life.

Empirical illustration 3: the dynamic relationship between meso and micro levels

Here we would like to draw attention to how characteristics at the meso level may affect the chances for a long working life at an individual level. The empirical example presented here concerns the understanding of occupation as a risk factor for early retirement and thus exclusion from the labour force.

Research has demonstrated that there are huge differences between occupations and early withdrawal from the labour force (Stattin, 1998; Sjögren-Lindqvist, 2013). How can such differences be explained? The answer is by no means self-evident, since the explanatory mechanisms behind such patterns are rather complicated. An occupational title in itself provides very limited information about actual mechanisms in play. Therefore we need to go beyond occupational titles and search for properties and traits that may provide us with a substantial understanding of what is causing differences in early exit risk in various occupations. An occupation may be associated with high rates of early exit as a result of certain characteristics associated with the employees in the occupation. Employees' age, working capacity, education and so on may explain differences in relative early exit risk in occupations, which means that the reason for an increased risk is explained by the composition of the individuals in the occupation. This composition is affected by recruitment strategies and turnovers.

Recruitment of, for example, individuals of above-average good health, especially for jobs with high physical demands, is reflected in lower rates of ill health. We will get similar results if a large share of employees leaves the occupation as a result of impaired health. Such selection processes may heavily distort our conclusions and interpretations of the occupation as a causal risk factor.

The second explanatory mechanism concerns properties and characteristics that are typical for the occupation and that might affect employees' capability and motivation to work. Employees in an occupation are exposed to specific working conditions, and these vary between occupations. They may concern differences in working time, work environment, career prospects and so on. Of special interest in relation to exit from work is the physical and psychosocial work environment, since research has shown that these aspects heavily affect health and wellbeing, causing short- and long-term sickness absences. The work environment can thus be regarded as a specific feature closely related to occupations – that is, conditions that can be defined as meso-level characteristics. The strong association between work environment and health may thus be a mechanism that helps us to understand differing exit risks in occupations. To empirically test this properly requires data that include information on exit from work and antecedent exposure to various work environmental factors. We review here an example of such a study (Stattin and Järvholm, 2005). The study is based on a historical cohort of construction workers that consists of almost 400,000 subjects who participated in health examinations and in surveys on working conditions. Almost 68,000 of them received a disability pension during the study period.

An initial observation in the study was a considerable variation in disability pension risks between occupations in the construction industry. The results demonstrated clear associations with both physical and ergonomic factors. Analyses of psychosocial work environment dimensions according to the well-known demand-control model (Karasek and Theorell, 1990) were also performed. The demand-control model is basically a model that captures two important dimensions in the psychosocial work environment. It states that certain combinations of the dimensions are especially harmful to health and wellbeing; a combination of low levels of control and high levels of demand have proven to have a negative effect on health and to cause high levels of stress. Figure 12.5 shows the result of the analyses.

Figure 12.5 shows a clear association between psychosocial strain and risk of disability pension. The highest relative risk (odds ratios) is observed for those who have experienced low control and high demands as compared to those reporting high control and low demands. For all levels of demand, the relative risk increases with decreasing levels of control. The relationship is linear except for the category

Figure 12.5: Risk of disability pension in different combinations of demands and control

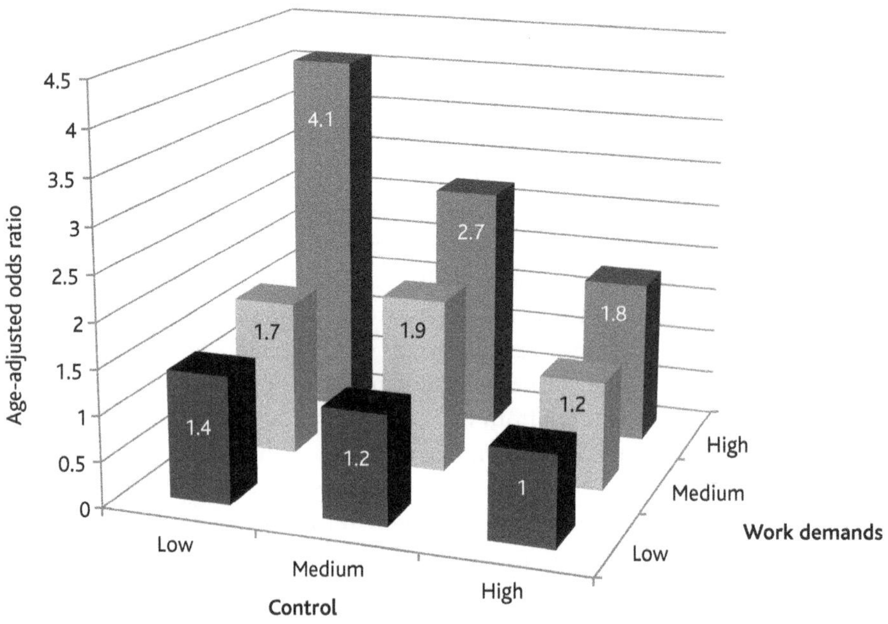

Source: Stattin and Järvholm, 2005: 89

with medium levels of demands. The study thus shows that psychosocial factors are important risk factors in relation to disability pensions in Sweden.

From an institutional lifecourse perspective, this analysis may be imperfect. An analysis of how changes over time in exposure to work environment strain – or of cumulative exposure to it – affect the likelihood of early exit through disability pension would have provided more dynamic insight into the matter. However, it is an illustration of how conditions at the meso level interact with individual work careers. Studies like this are surely valuable, as they provide us with an insight into explanatory mechanisms related to different analytical levels and they pinpoint potential areas of intervention for stakeholders with the aim of prolonging working careers.

Concluding remarks

This chapter has been devoted to furthering understanding of conditions that shape prerequisites for labour force participation in old age. We have stressed that this is indeed a highly complex issue. In line with the institutional lifecourse perspective, we have discussed different levels of opportunities and constraints that either promote or limit older workers' ability to remain active in work at late ages. By means of empirical examples we have illustrated that all these levels are interwoven in a complex web of interactions and reciprocal influence.

Our main message is that the recognition of this complexity is crucial – not least in relation to policy interventions. We argue that this has not been the case in most of the policy reforms in the area. Even if Sweden had been at the forefront in reforming old-age policies, policy reforms have been concerned mainly with economic incentives and downsizing and abolishing early retirement options. This may have effects for some, but there is an obvious risk that it may jeopardise the welfare of less privileged people. In order to promote long working careers also for those with reduced working capacity (which is quite common among people in their late sixties), or for those whose work is heavy and strenuous, we need to, in parallel with pension reforms, ask how to adjust working life and working conditions in accordance with the needs of an ageing workforce. This is actually a highly neglected area of research, which is somewhat peculiar since, after all, it is within the workplace that much of the action has to take place in order to adjust conditions to better fit an ageing workforce.

In line with the institutional lifecourse perspective, we argue that we need a broader interventional perspective that takes into account not only supply-side factors but also demand-side factors in the struggle to adjust retirement age upwards. It is therefore indeed promising that a recent governmental report (SOU, 2013) on older workers' labour market competitiveness in Sweden actually addresses these issues in terms of a very broad and wide-reaching strategy that involves all different analytical levels discussed in this chapter as well as an awareness of the complex interplay between the societal-macro, institutional-meso and individual-micro levels.

Notes

[1] The terminology in this context varies between countries. Here, the terms 'disability pension' and 'disability benefit' refer to social security programmes that cover income loss resulting from long-term absence due to disability.

References

De Vroom, B. and Guillemard, A.M. (2002) 'From externalisation to integration of older workers: Institutional changes at the end of the worklife', in J.G. Andersen and P.H. Jensen (eds) *Changing labour markets, welfare policies and citizenship*, Bristol: Policy Press, 183-208.

Dragano, N., Siegrist, J. and Warendorf, M. (2011) 'Welfare regimes, labour policies and unhealthy psychosocial working conditions: A comparative study with 9917 older employees from 12 European countries', *Journal of Epidemiology and Community Health*, 65, 793-9.

Ebbinghaus, B. (2006) *Reforming early retirement in Europe, Japan and the USA*, Oxford: Oxford University Press.

Edlund, J. and Stattin, M. (2013) 'Age and work in different labour market contexts', in P. Taylor (ed) *Older workers in an ageing society*, Cheltenham: Edward Elgar, 68-88.

Esser, I. (2005) *Why Work? Comparative studies on welfare regimes and individuals' work orientations*, Doctoral Dissertation, Stockholm: Stockholm University.

Furunes, T. and Mykletun, R.J. (2011) 'Managers' decision latitude for age management: Do managers and employees have the same (implicit) understanding?', in R. Ennals and R. Salomon (eds) *Older workers in a sustainable society. Great needs and great potentials*, Frankfurt: Peter Lang, 107-16.

Hall, P. and Soskice, D. (2001) *Varieties of capitalism. The institutional foundations of comparative advantage*, Oxford: Oxford University Press.

Halleröd, B., Örestig, J. and Stattin, M. (2013) 'Leaving the labour market: The impact of exit-routes from employment to retirement on wellbeing in old age', *European Journal of Ageing*, 10, 1, 25-35.

Ilmarinen, J. (2006) 'The ageing workforce – challenges for occupational health', *Occupational Medicine*, 56, 6, 362-4.

Karasek, R. and Theorell, T. (1990) *Healthy work: Stress, productivity, and the reconstruction of working life*, New York: Basic Books.

Kim, J.E. and Moen, P. (2001) 'Is retirement good or bad for subjective wellbeing?', *Current Directions in Psychological Science*, 10, 3, 83-6.

Maltby, T., De Vroom, B., Mirabile, M.L. and Øverbye, E. (eds) (2004) *Ageing and transition to retirement. A comparative analysis of European welfare states*, Aldershot: Ashgate.

Marin, B. (2003) 'Transforming disability welfare policy. Completing a paradigm shift', in C. Prinz (ed) *European disability pension policies. 11 country trends 1970–2002*, Aldershot: Ashgate, 1-54.

Mykletun, R.J., Furunes, T. and Solem, P.E. (2012) 'Managers' beliefs about measures to retain senior workforce', *Nordic Journal of Working Life Studies*, 2, 3, 109-27.

Nordenmark, M. and Stattin, M. (2009) 'Psychosocial wellbeing and reasons for retirement in Sweden', *Ageing and Society*, 29, 413-30.

Örestig, J., Larsson, D. and Stattin, M. (2013) 'Retirement preferences before and after pension reform: evidence from a Swedish natural experiment' [preprint], www.diva-portal.org/smash/record.jsf?pid=diva2%3A651597&dswid=-3410

Organisation for Economic Co-operation and Development (2006) *Live longer, work longer*, Paris: OECD Publishing.

Salokangas, R.K. and Joukamaa, M. (1991) 'Physical mental health changes in retirement age', *Psychotherapy and Psychosomatics*, 55, 100-7.

Silverstein, M. and Giarrusso, R. (2011) 'Ageing individuals, families and societies: Micro-meso-macro linkages in the life course', in R.A. Settersten, Jr and L.J. Angel (eds) *Handbook of Sociology of Ageing*, Springer Science+Business Media.

Sjögren-Lindqvist, G. (2013) 'Om effekter på arbetsutbud och pensionering av förändringar av pensionsåldern – en forskningsöversikt in SOU (2013) Åtgärder för ett längre arbetsliv', *Slutbetänkande av Pensionsåldersutredningen SOU 2013:25* [On the effects on labor supply and retirement of changes in the retirement age – a research review, in SOU (2013). *Measures for a longer working life*, Final report of the retirement age Inquiry], Stockholm: Statens offentliga utredningar.

SOU (2013) Åtgärder för ett längre arbetsliv. *Slutbetänkande av Pensionsåldersutredningen SOU 2013:25* [*Measures for a longer working life. Final report of the retirement age Inquiry*], Stockholm: Statens offentliga utredningar.

Stattin, M. (1998) *Yrke, yrkesförändring och utslagning från arbetsmarknaden: en studie av relationen mellan förtidspension och arbetsmarknadsförändring* [*Occupation, occupational change and exclusion from the labour market — a study of the relationship between disability pension and labour market change*], Doctoral thesis, Umeå: Umeå University, Department of Sociology.

Stattin, M. (2005) 'Retirement on grounds of ill health', *Occupational and Environmental Medicine*, 62, 135-40.

Stattin, M. (2013) 'Svenskabefolkningens inställning till sin pensionsålder 2002/2003 och 2010/2011', *Working papers series. Welfare studies* [*The Swedish population's attitude towards retirement age 2002/2003 and 2010/2011*], Umeå: Umeå University, Department of Sociology.

Stattin, M. and Järvholm, B. (2005) 'Occupation, work environment and disability pension – a prospective study of construction workers', *Scandinavian Journal of Public Health*, 32, 1-7.

Svallfors, S. (2010) 'Policy feedback, generational replacement, and attitudes to state intervention: Eastern and Western Germany, 1990–2006', *European Political Science Review*, 2, 1, 119-35.

Taylor, P. (2008) 'Introduction: the promise of ageing labour forces' in P. Taylor (ed) *Ageing Labour Forces. Promises and Prospects*, Edward Elgar Publishing Limited.

Van Dalen, H.P., Henkens, K., Henderikse, W. and Schippers, J. (2010) 'Do European employers support later retirement?', *International Journal of Manpower*, 31, 3, 360-73.

Wallman, T., Wedel, H., Johansson, S., Rosengren, A., Eriksson, H., Welin, L. and Svardsudd, K. (2006) 'The prognosis for individuals on disability retirement: an 18-year mortality follow-up study of 6887 men and women sampled from the general population', *BMC Public Health*, 6, 103.

Wang, M., Henkens, K. and van Solinge, H. (2011) 'Retirement adjustment: A review of theoretical and empirical advancements', *American Psychologist*, 66, 3, 204-13.

Westerlund, H., Kivimäki, M., Singh-Manoux, A., Melchior, M., Ferrie, J.E., Pentti, J., Jokela, M., Leineweber, C., Goldberg, M., Zins, M. and Vahtera, J. (2009) 'Self-rated health before and after retirement in France (GAZEL): a cohort study', *The Lancet*, 374, 1889-96.

THIRTEEN

The state in ageing Canada: from old-age policies to lifecourse policies

Kathrin Komp and Patrik Marier

Introduction

Population ageing directs the attention of policy makers to older people. Policy makers increasingly have to ponder what today's older people need and how existing institutions can adapt in order to accommodate an ageing population. However, when doing so, policy makers cannot focus on older age alone. After all, experiences during one's youth and middle age can have a profound impact on one's situation in old age. To address population ageing effectively, policy makers would therefore need to account for long-term effects on old age. Long-term effects that unfold over a person's life are called 'life-course effects' (Grenier, 2012).

While considering lifecourse effects in policy-making sounds like a small step, it in fact has major implications. Traditional old-age policies treat older people as a separate and distinct population group, whereas policies embracing the lifecourse perspective see old age as a stage that (almost) everybody reaches at some point in time. Consequently, old-age policies explicitly address older people, while lifecourse policies take a much broader approach (Anxo et al, 2010). On the one hand, they strive to shape the situation in old age by influencing people at earlier ages. On the other hand, they strive to address the phenomenon of population ageing by reassessing the needs and potentials of all age groups. Thus, lifecourse policies address the entire population over longer periods of time.

This chapter explores how lifecourse effects can be incorporated into policies for old age. It explains what this shift in perspective entails and why it is advantageous, and it gives examples of policies that reflect this idea. To reach these goals, this chapter proceeds in five steps. First, it presents theoretical reflections on the character and specificities of lifecourse policies. Then it compares lifecourse policies with old-age policies. Subsequently, this chapter discusses stumbling blocks on the road towards introducing lifecourse policies. Then, it presents examples of lifecourse policies from Canada, where policy makers are currently implementing lifecourse approaches in a number of new programmes. Finally, this chapter discusses advantages and limitations of lifecourse policies.

Understanding lifecourse policies

Lifecourse policies follow individuals from the cradle to the grave, supporting and stimulating them whenever needed. By intervening, these policies strive not only to solve current problems, but also to prevent hardship at later ages. Thus, lifecourse policies account for effects that unfold over longer periods of time (Esping-Andersen et al, 2002; Komp, 2013). In this sense, lifecourse policies can be seen as an extended version of old-age policies. They expand the idea of traditional old-age policies, in that they add considerations of lifecourse effects on old age to measures directly targeting older people. In doing so, these policies draw on three central concepts in current sociological and social policy-related discussions: lifecourse effects; cumulative advantages and disadvantages; and social investment policies.

The first central concept is the one of lifecourse effects. The lifecourse describes the time from birth to death as a progression of experiences, activities and social roles. It captures, for example, how people leave their family of birth and subsequently form their own family (Grenier, 2012; Settersten and Mayer, 1997). Interestingly, lifecourses do not unfold randomly. Instead, a person's situation and experiences at one point of time can influence how their life progresses for decades (Elder, 1994). For example, the education that people receive during their youth can influence how their working careers progress, and at what age they retire from work (Gouldner, 2001). Such long-term influences are called 'life-course effects' (Elder, 1994).

How lifecourse effects unfold is described by the second concept, which is labelled 'cumulative advantages and disadvantages'. Phrased in lay terms, this concept states that good things will come to those in privileged situations, while bad things will come to those in precarious situations (Dannefer, 2003). Researchers hold opportunities, acquired attitudes and capabilities responsible for this mechanism (O'Rand, 2002). Because of the accumulation of advantages and disadvantages over the lifecourse, social problems might aggravate and social inequalities might deepen over time. For example, people who become unemployed are particularly likely to also become unemployed again at a later point of time and to continue to feel less happy and less healthy than their continuously employed peers (Clark et al, 2003; Strandh and Nordlund, 2008).

The third concept, the one of social investment policies, responds to lifecourse effects and to the accumulation of advantages and disadvantages. Social investment policies are rooted in the idea that political interventions can have both short- and long-term pay-offs. In addition to resolving precarious situations in the present, such interventions can also help to create positive developments in people's lives that prevent social problems from manifesting again in the future (Jensen and Saint-Martin, 2003). Social investment policies achieve these beneficial long-term effects by helping people to develop their skills, instead of merely supporting them through transfers in cash or kind (Morel et al, 2012). For example, supporting a high level of education among youths can help these individuals to gain and remain employed during their middle age and, subsequently, to avoid poverty in old age (Esping-Andersen, 2002a).

How old-age policies and lifecourse policies go together

Old-age policies and lifecourse policies take different, although complementary, approaches. Both kinds of policies are similar, in that they provide tools to handle ageing populations. However, in doing so, old-age policies adopt a narrower perspective and a smaller range of tools. Reasons for the divergence are: differences in the target group; the mode of intervention; the time-horizon adopted; and the consideration of social inequalities.

The first difference between old-age policies and lifecourse policies is the target group. While old-age policies focus their activities on older individuals, lifecourse policies target everyone. Thus, old-age policies strengthen age stratification in societies, especially between the younger and older segments of the population, while lifecourse policies do not. Moreover, old-age policies label older people as a group of individuals who cause pressure on society and, hence, need to be influenced. Such labelling is a form of stigmatisation, which can create clear boundaries between social groups, form group identities and lead to blame-shifting between social groups (Goffman, 1963; Moulaert and Biggs, 2013). For example, the United States is often accused of having an 'elderly bias', because many of their fiscal and social policies are advantageous to their older population (Kotlikoff and Burns, 2005; Lynch, 2006). Lifecourse policies, in contrast, stress that people pass from one age group to the next as their lives progress. Thus, age is not seen as an absolute identification point but as a temporary marker. Consequently, policies that benefit a specific age group, for example children below 5 years or individuals older than 65 years, will in the long run benefit everybody – only at different points of historical time (Morel et al, 2012).

The second difference between old-age policies and lifecourse policies lies in the mode of intervention. While old-age policies focus on the redistribution of resources between age groups, lifecourse policies try to guide the lives of people to minimise the need for redistribution (Anxo et al, 2010). Old-age policies try to optimise two kinds of redistribution between age groups. On the one hand, they redistribute resources between young and old people at specific points in time. For example, pay-as-you-go financed pension schemes use this approach. They collect contributions from middle-aged people and distribute exactly these contributions to retirees at the same point in time. When today's middle-aged people retire, they will not receive benefits that were paid by themselves at an earlier point in time, but benefits that are paid for by people who are middle-aged at exactly that point in time (Myles, 2002). On the other hand, old-age policies redistribute resources during an individual's lifetime, from a young age to old age. This kind of redistribution is, for example, used in capital stock-based pensions. Here, middle-aged people contribute to their personal pension funds, which will be disbursed to them only on retirement (Myles, 2002). Lifecourse policies, in contrast, strive to intervene at decisive times in people's lives and, thereby, help to guide lives towards empowerment, activation and self-help. Thus, helping citizens through periods of hardship is just a means to an end; the ultimate goal is to prevent the need for redistribution in old age. For example, facilitating a young person's education might result in a continuous working career during middle age and a stable financial situation in old age (Esping-Andersen, 2002a, 2002b). In this way, the need for welfare state provisions to redistribute from people in financially stable situations to older people in precarious situations decreases.

The third difference between old-age policies and lifecourse policies concerns the time-horizon adopted. While old-age policies work with short- to long-term perspectives, lifecourse policies mainly adopt a long-term perspective. In the most extreme case, the time-horizon of lifecourse policies might be an entire lifetime (Anxo et al, 2010). A short time-horizon means that redistribution occurs between age groups at one point in time. An example for such redistribution is the Belgian Federal allowance for older people, where general taxation finances long-term care services for older people with low income (Organisation for Economic Co-operation and Development, 2011). A long time-horizon, on the other hand, means that redistribution occurs across the lifecourse. An example of this redistribution is the capital stock-based pension described previously.

For example, both policy approaches would adopt drastically different strategies to combat old-age poverty. Old-age policies would, for example, utilise programmes that transfer financial resources to older people, such as social security or pension schemes. Lifecourse policies, by contrast, would stress the persistence of poverty throughout the lifecourse and, as a result, they would begin by lifting households with children out of poverty (Esping-Andersen, 2002a).

The fourth difference concerns the consideration of social inequalities among people. Old-age policies and their analyses usually emphasise one-size-fits-all models, where older citizens are considered as a homogeneous group. This critique has been well formulated in the past by, for example, Guillemard (1980), who condemned French statistical authorities for ignoring the past origins of retired workers, as if the importance of social classes disappeared with retirement. The use of the highly popular dependency ratio faces similar critiques (Ervik, 2005). With a strong focus on youth, most notably education, the social investment literature also underestimates the diversity within each age group. For example, a 'massive investment' in the development of social skills and education of younger individuals is considered necessary to face the challenges of an older population (Lindh, 2012: 281). In contrast, lifecourse policies stress the fact that individuals are engaged in very different career and life paths. As a result, lifecourse approaches are not as sensitive towards the age of the target population, but instead focus on critical junctures where individual paths may face important challenges with long-term implications. For example, rather than devising a single programme to reintegrate older workers into the workforce, a lifecourse approach would develop more individualised efforts to consider the unique trajectory of each older worker. Table 13.1 summarizes the differences between old age policies and life-course policies.

Table 13.1: Comparison between old age policies and lifecourse policies

	Old age policies	Lifecourse policies
Target group	Older people	Everybody
Mode of intervention	Transfers between age groups	Steer lives to minimise need for redistribution
Time-horizon	Short term to long term	Long term
Social inequalities	Not central	Central

Stumbling blocks in the introduction of lifecourse policies

During the past 30 years, many scholars have embraced the assessment that the welfare state 'has grown to limits' (Flora, 1986) and that policy makers operate within a crowded policy space. Thus, new policy ideas are introduced within a process of policy succession (Hogwood and Peters, 1982), where the inheritance of previous policy legacies looms large in their development (Rose, 1990; Pierson, 1994). Accentuating these difficulties further, the acquisition of knowledge by public officials tends to focus on resolving ongoing issues related to current policies and programmes (March, 1991) and they prefer to rely on their own internal sources of knowledge (Boswell, 2009). As a result, novel ideas face tremendous administrative and political obstacles in their development, even when they have been firmly embraced by political authorities.

In this context, the adoption and implementation of lifecourse policies remains a treacherous road. First, citizens and elected officials tend to be short-sighted. At the individual level, studies in psychology and economics demonstrate that humans have a short-term bias and underestimate long-term costs for many situations when they are making intertemporal choices (see Loewenstein and Thaler, 1989; Laverty, 1996). With a strong focus on their re-election, politicians are likely to engage in activities that provide short-term pay-offs at the expense of long-term benefits, as hypothesised in the political business cycle (Nordhaus, 1975). As a result, it remains quite difficult for policy makers to develop and successfully implement long-term policies, the effects of which may not be visible for decades (see, for example, Jacobs, 2011). Adding to these difficulties, benefits from lifecourse policies are diffused and difficult for the average voter to measure and comprehend, which seriously limits their appeal for politicians, who need to account for the effects of their activities at the end of their term in office (Komp, 2013).

Second, the political coalition required to embrace lifecourse policies must be quite large to result in legislation. This implies dealing with veto players in parliament (Tsebelis, 1999) and institutionalised interest groups that may act as veto points (Immergut, 1990).

Finally, and related to the previous point, welfare states that are biased towards older people (Lynch, 2006), such as in the United States, are unlikely to experience a transition towards policies that no longer benefit older people exclusively. In line with the literature on policy feedbacks, organisations for older people are known for being highly mobilised and resistant to change (Pierson, 1994), and their positive social construction is an important source of power from which to draw generous benefits (Schneider and Ingram, 1993). This would apply strongly to lifecourse policies, since they could potentially threaten or dilute generous programmes targeted primarily at the older population (such as Medicare in the US), by seeking a more universal approach across all ages. This is also reflected by the lack of attention devoted to the older population within the social investment perspective. This lack of attention is caused by two facts: first, older people have few years of life left, which means that they are unlikely to fully experience the beneficial long-term effects of political intervention; and second, older people are sometimes considered frail and beyond their productive years, which makes them unattractive for policies that strive to increase activity (Edmondson, 2013). However, the adoption of preventative measures at the beginning of old age can still have tremendous impacts for the remainder of one's life in retirement. Thus, it is important to stress that a lifecourse perspective can also target older individuals to nudge them towards beneficial changes.

There are also multiple administrative problems related to the implementation of lifecourse policies. First, existing administrative structures are likely to exert a specific bias related to the primary programmatic responsibility of a department or ministry. In Canada, a common complaint has been the predominance of institutionalised health at the expense of preventative measures, which are the privileged policy tools in lifecourse approaches to health (Boychuck, 2008). Second, many of the lifecourse policies require substantial policy coordination across departments such as health and education. Under the best circumstances, policy coordination is a key challenge in the development and implementation of public policies (Peters, 1998). These difficulties can be accentuated if there is more than one level of government involved. Third, it is very difficult for a new administrative office to compete with more powerful and established departments, such as health and education, which expanded during the golden age of the welfare state. These departments are likely to have multiple programmatic responsibilities and an easier time in justifying their budget with finance officials.

As a result of all these hurdles, we expect that the introduction of lifecourse policies geared towards an ageing population will be slow and incremental. Policy innovation with lifecourse approaches is akin to the introduction of social investment strategies, where new policies targeting younger populations have been implemented parallel to existing ones (Hudson and Kuhner, 2009; Nygård and Krüger, 2012).

From old-age policies to lifecourse policies in Canada

As a result of its advocacy role in the international arena, Canada gives us an excellent opportunity to observe how lifecourse approaches are introduced. Canada has been participating in the development of various World Health

Organization (WHO) programmes such as 'Active Ageing' and 'Age-Friendly Cities'. Both programmes stress the existence of lifecourse effects and propose that we should consider these effects when developing policy. Thus, in Canada we can currently observe what often goes unnoticed: how and where lifecourse policies are implemented, and what struggles and effects the introduction of such policies brings about. While the case for using policy lenses to analyse the lifecourse has been clearly made, at least at the federal level, the introduction of policies along these lines has proved difficult. In this sense, Canada is a case study par excellence for this chapter.

Lifecourse research through policy lenses

The utilisation of the lifecourse perspective in policy development is a very recent phenomenon (Marshall and McMullin, 2009). The federal government in Canada devoted resources in the early 2000s to enhance research in this area, which led to multiple publications on the connection between the lifecourse and public policies, including a special issue in *Canadian Public Policy* (vol. 37, s1) derived from special collaborations between civil servants and university researchers. Beyond a reference to policies aimed at reducing poverty and social exclusion and their beneficial impact on the lifecourse, the contributions focused primarily on how current policies affect the lifecourse by enhancing (or worsening) situations when individuals face various experiences throughout their lives (McDaniel and Bernard, 2011).

Nonetheless, as discussed later, institutional and policy changes towards older populations are increasingly incorporating lifecourse elements. Institutionally, there has been a growing focus on developing separate healthy ageing agencies; this represents a noticeable break from the biomedical model that dominates health departments in Canada. This matters greatly, since the biomedical paradigm is biased towards favouring interventions once a person has been deemed sick or injured, while healthy ageing agencies embrace a long-term view emphasising the benefits of prevention and social investments. Thus, these institutional battles are rooted in a conflict of guiding principles with regard to the fundamental approaches that different bodies adopt in dealing with an ageing population. In terms of policy, the focus is not on the entire lifecourse, but policies are nonetheless increasingly focused on ageing as a continuous part of the lifecycle rather than a specific and somewhat homogeneous period of time. All of these changes have been strongly influenced by various campaigns launched by the WHO.

The WHO's campaigns on active ageing and age-friendly cities

The WHO has been an active campaigner for the development of lifecourse approaches, most notably to favour the development of health prevention strategies. The policy framework on active ageing sought to introduce a lifecourse perspective to make it easier for individuals to transition into old age. In this framework, the WHO embraced a holistic view of health involving multiple sectors and a variety of actors stressing that healthy older individuals represent a benefit for families, communities and economies (WHO, 2002). The policy document focuses strongly on the older population, but its policy recommendations are nonetheless clearly aligned with the lifecourse approach. For example, it encourages governmental authorities to adopt policies that reduce the risk of major disease and attenuate the burden of disabilities, chronic disease and premature mortality. It also includes measures to provide a better learning environment and to reduce gender inequalities (WHO, 2002).

Following closely in the footsteps of active ageing, the WHO also launched the 'Global Age-friendly Cities' initiative. With continuing urbanisation and the presence of increasingly older individuals, this initiative aims to develop age-friendly cities. This implies, for example, the development of city parks that are geared towards citizens of all ages, as opposed to being targeted exclusively towards children and families (WHO, 2007). There are currently 18 countries involved in the WHO 'Global Network of Age-friendly Cities and Communities'.[1] As demonstrated by the Canadian example, the implementation of these strategies faces many of the hurdles described in the previous section.

Canada represents an interesting case study for these international efforts for multiple reasons. First, Canadian authorities have contributed strongly to the development of both of the WHO's initiatives in multiple ways, such as hosting international conferences on the subject. In addition, the health department of the Canadian government (Health Canada) supported all phases of the WHO's Active Ageing project. Second, as a result of this input, Canadian authorities were quick to embrace and implement the WHO recommendations. For example, 13 of the 103 cities in the WHO 'Global Network of Age-friendly Cities and Communities' are Canadian.

The primary responsibilities for health remain with the provinces, and this is where attempts to introduce a lifecourse dimension have occurred.[2] This is hardly surprising, since two thirds of services and most policy developments occur in the Canadian provinces (McArthur, 2007). A key dilemma has been whether to integrate lifecourse strategies within existing health ministries or to create separate agencies. Health ministries have often been criticised for their emphasis on hospital care at the expense of preventative measures. This explains why advocates for a preventative approach to health and groups of older citizens have long campaigned for the creation of agencies or offices outside the health department.

Lifecourse initiatives

While this section demonstrates stronger considerations for lifecourse initiatives, the evidence suggests that these are implemented to coexist and to complement previous policy approaches. The WHO's 'Active Ageing' and 'Age-friendly Cities' initiatives were highly influential in the development of strategies and frameworks with similar goals in mind in most provinces. It is important to stress that these are recent developments and that it will take many years before their success can be fully assessed.

The first wave of reform followed up from discussions surrounding a 'National Framework on Aging' (Health Canada, 1998), which was followed by similar developments at the WHO, resulting in the 'Active Ageing Initiative' (WHO, 2002). A second wave of initiatives coincided with the launch of the WHO's 'Age-friendly Cities' (WHO, 2007), which included discussions on how to adapt this vision to rural and remote communities (FTP Seniors, 2007). A stronger emphasis on healthy living, along the lines advocated by lifecourse approaches, became rapidly noticeable across all 10 provinces. First, multiple provinces set up consultations with advisory committees, experts and even the public at large to discuss the introduction of a healthy living/ageing strategy. This included extensive efforts in Nova Scotia (2004), Québec (2004/05), Newfoundland and Labrador (2006), British Columbia (2006) and most recently New Brunswick (2012).

Second, long-term strategies and frameworks related to healthy living/ageing were formally introduced in many of the provinces. These strategies involved the participation of multiple ministries, jurisdictions and community groups, and some even featured clear guidelines for the development of future policies. For example, Alberta launched a 10-year strategy as early as 2002 and Nova Scotia developed a 'Positive Aging Framework' in 2005. The latter featured traditional 'old age policy' elements, such as a focus on celebrating seniors and pensions, but it also included goals associated with lifecourse approaches, such as improving life transitions and health/wellbeing prevention.

Third, many provinces set up new, independent offices to implement these strategies related to healthy living/ageing, most notably Newfoundland and Labrador (Office for Aging and Seniors), Manitoba (Seniors and Healthy Living Secretariat) and British Columbia (Seniors' Healthy Living Secretariat). The creation of healthy living/ageing secretariats achieved the twin objective of developing separate entities devoted to prevention and to seniors. Provinces already equipped with a seniors' secretariat simply granted the additional mandate of engaging within healthy living to these offices. These were often accompanied by the creation of a new ministerial position. For example, Newfoundland and Labrador opted to create the 'Office for Aging and Seniors' in 2007 to implement their healthy living strategy. To ensure that the new office would be able to secure and maintain appropriate funding, it was located within the Department of Health and Community Services. The Office for Aging and Seniors was given a clear mandate and lots of independence, to protect it from prevailing hospital care approaches permeating the health department.

Finally, and most importantly, multiple (and very similar) policy initiatives emerged across the country. The primary focus has been on avoiding accidents, illnesses and the abuse of older people, on promoting age-friendly communities (including transportation issues), and on developing long-term care strategies with an emphasis on keeping older individuals in their homes. Unfortunately, as a result of their limited budgets, these offices remain extremely constrained in their capacity to enact their own projects, since they do not have programmatic responsibilities and new projects usually require a sponsor or strong partners (Marier, 2014).

After more than a decade of institutional and policy reforms across all 10 Canadian provinces, the key question for this chapter is whether or not lifecourse approaches are strongly anchored within the policy process. To date, there is limited evidence to support this idea. First, the new secretariats maintain a mandate focused on the older population. This includes constant interactions with old-age interest groups and their attention remains primarily on current developments, such as cuts to health care services or pensions. Second, in part due to their novelty, there is limited evidence regarding the effectiveness of the new actions stimulated by lifecourse initiatives. For example, British Columbia's progress report (Government of British Columbia, 2011) consists primarily of enumerating new or old government actions and it does not feature any programme evaluation. In addition, many of the programmes launched by healthy ageing/living secretariats involve policy tools, such as grants and partnerships with other actors that are responsible for managing and maintaining initiatives, which have important limitations. For example, an early assessment of Québec's age-friendly cities emphasises its limited budget (Can$1 million annually for the entire programme), the lack of action on valorising the contributions of older people, a focus on a few specific priorities, and a lack of coordination between municipal and provincial authorities (Rochman and Tremblay, 2010).

Discussion and conclusions

Population ageing is a global phenomenon that will certainly persist for the foreseeable future. This implies a strong constituency of older voters that are already well organised to protect current benefits and the way in which they are delivered (Pierson, 1994). This political environment makes it difficult to introduce substantive lifecourse policies, since previous policy legacies remain strongly embedded. In addition, the diffused nature of the benefits and their long-term perspective present large obstacles for lifecourse approach advocates for two reasons. First, these characteristics lead to a time lag between the introduction and the full effectiveness of a policy, which exceeds the time-horizon during which policy makers need to present the effects of their activities. Second, the characteristics make it difficult to pinpoint the effects of lifecourse policies, which additionally hamper their justification in heated political debates. Nonetheless, our case study of Canada demonstrates that some policy change is going on despite the relatively marginal financial commitment for these initiatives. Still, there are indications that a lifecourse approach can help governments to design more effective policies for old age.

Lifecourse policies conceive population ageing as an issue for the entire population, instead of one focused on older people only. These policies counter social hardships experienced by people of all ages, emphasising the long-term effects of interventions at specific points in time (Anxo et al, 2010). To reach this goal, policy makers need to supplement measures supporting people in need with measures to enable these people to help themselves. For example, unemployed individuals might need financial support during the spell of unemployment, help to find a job and further qualification in job-related skills. Because lifecourse policies support individuals from an early age, they can attenuate many root causes for social risks at later ages (Anxo et al, 2010). This is particularly true for two of the core concepts associated with lifecourse approaches: lifecourse effects and social investment. Consequently, lifecourse approaches might reduce the support for political intervention into old age.

Lifecourse policies also have a major disadvantage for older people. Instead of just reducing the need for support in old age, these policies might also cut support programmes for older people where such programmes are still needed. While it is true that people nowadays remain healthy until a later age than a few decades ago, they nevertheless experience many years of life in poor health. Moreover, older people are heterogeneous, with some of them needing care and support for extended periods of time, be it because of disabilities or because of unemployment spells before the mandatory retirement age. Hence, older people might experience situations that cannot be remedied anymore. In this case, lifecourse policies fall short and traditional old-age policies are needed, such as for health care services or pension benefits. Unfortunately, the idea of enabling and activating individuals entails that frail older individuals might also be considered responsible for their own difficulties, such as poverty in old age. Consequently, policy makers and the public might approve of cutbacks more easily in policy areas supporting older people.

The evidence presented in this chapter supports the thesis of a policy succession (Hogwood and Peters, 1982), where lifecourse initiatives are added on top of existing policies. In Canada, the budgetary efforts devoted to these initiatives remain modest and they have not replaced old-age policies targeted at older citizens. In many cases, as a result of limited financial capabilities, successful efforts involve the development of a partnership to complement previous efforts. This finding is in line with previous work on social investment policies in industrialised countries (Bonoli, 2007). Therefore, we expect other countries that introduce the lifecourse perspective into policy-making to also marry this perspective with existing policies and institutions. Consequently, the development of lifecourse approaches in national policies will probably reflect the overall history and political system of each specific country. Additionally, the emerging lifecourse initiatives will probably differ markedly between countries.

To sum up, lifecourse policies contain many measures that can improve the situation of older people. Policy makers can combine these measures with existing old-age policies to meet the needs of ageing populations more effectively. This combination of policy approaches is particularly attractive, because it simultaneously supports frail older people and strives to activate healthy older people. Since ageing populations are heterogeneous, such a differentiated policy approach seems promising.

Acknowledgements

We would like to thank Jana Javornik Skrbinšek and Lars Alberth for their insightful comments and Corey Guitard for editorial assistance, which helped to improve this chapter.

Notes

[1] www.agefriendlyworld.org/cities-and-communities

[2] The federal government is primarily involved in income-related programmes (Banting, 1987). However, it has strong fiscal powers, resulting in transfers to provinces to finance social programmes like health care. With the amount provided to provinces being substantially reduced since the mid 1980s, the federal government has very limited tools to encourage the adoption and expansion of lifecourse approaches within health departments across the country.

References

Anxo, D., Bosch, G. and Rubery, J. (eds) (2010) *The welfare state and life transitions. A European perspective*, Cheltenham, Edward Elgar.

Banting, K.G. (1987) *The welfare state and Canadian federalism*, Montreal: McGill-Queen's University Press

Bonoli, G. (2007) 'Time matters: postindustrialization, new social risks, and welfare state adaptation in advanced industrial democracies', *Comparative Political Studies*, 40, 5, 495-520.

Boswell, C. (2009) 'Knowledge, legitimation and the politics of risk: the functions of research in public debates on migration', *Political Studies*, 57, 1, 165-86.

Boychuk, G.W. (2008) *National health insurance in the United States and Canada: race, territory, and the roots of difference*, Washington, DC: Georgetown University Press.

Clark, A., Georgellis, Y. and Sanfey, P. (2003) 'Scarring: the psychological impact of past unemployment', *Economica*, 68, 270, 221-41.

Dannefer, D. (2003) 'Cumulative advantage/disadvantage and the life course: cross-fertilizing age and social science theory', *The Journals of Gerontology*, 58B, 6, S327-37.

Edmondson, R. (2013) 'Cultural gerontology: valuing older people', in K. Komp and M. Aartsen (eds) *Old age in Europe. A textbook of gerontology*, Heidelberg: Springer, 113-30.

Elder, G., Jr (1994) 'Time, human agency, and social change: perspectives on the life course', *Social Psychology Quarterly*, 57, 1, 4-15.

Ervik, R. (2005) 'The battle of future pensions: global accounting tools, international organizations and pension reforms', *Global Social Policy*, 5, 1, 29-54.

Esping-Andersen, G. (2002a) 'A child-centered social investment strategy', in G. Esping-Andersen, D. Gallie, A. Hemerick and J. Myles (eds) *Why we need a new welfare state*, Oxford University Press: New York, 26-67.
Esping-Andersen, G. (2002b) 'Towards a god society, once again?', in G. Esping-Andersen, D. Gallie, A. Hemerick and J. Myles (eds) *Why we need a new welfare state*, Oxford University Press: New York, 1-25.
Esping-Andersen, G., Gallie, D., Hemerick, A. and Myles, J. (2002) *Why we need a new welfare state*, Oxford University Press: New York.
Federal/Provincial/Territorial Ministers Responsible for Seniors (FPT Seniors) (2007) *Age-friendly rural and remote communities: a guide*, Ottawa: FPT Seniors.
Flora, P. (1986) *Growth to limits: the Western European welfare states since World War II*, Berlin: De Gruyter.
Goffman, I. (1963) *Stigma: notes on the management of spoiled identity*, New York: Touchstone.
Gouldner, A.W. (2001) 'The future of intellectuals and the rise of the new class', in D.B. Grusky (ed), *Social stratification. Class, race and gender in sociological perspective*, Boulder, CO: Westview Press, 817-30.
Government of British Columbia (2011) *Seniors' healthy living: report on progress*, Vancouver, BC: Government of British Columbia.
Grenier, A. (2012) *Transitions and the lifecourse: challenging the constructions of 'growing old'*, Bristol: Policy Press.
Guillemard, A.M. (1980). *La vieillesse et l'Etat* [*Old age and the state*], Paris: Presses Universite de France.
Health Canada (Division of Aging and Seniors) (1998) *Principles of the national framework on aging: a policy guide*, Ottawa: Ministry of Public Works and Government Services Canada.
Hogwood, B.W. and Peters, B.G. (1982) 'The dynamics of policy change', *Policy Sciences*, 14, 3, 225-45.
Hudson, J. and Kuhner, S. (2009) 'Towards productive welfare? A comparative analysis of 23 OECD countries', *Journal of European Social Policy*, 19, 1, 34-46.
Immergut, E.M. (1990) 'Institutions, veto points, and policy results: a comparative analysis of health care', *Journal of Public Policy*, 10, 4, 391-416.
Jacobs, A.M. (2011) *Governing for the long term: democracy and the politics of investment*, Cambridge: Cambridge University Press.
Jenson, J. and Saint-Martin, D. (2003) 'New routes to social cohesion? Citizenship and the social investment state', *Canadian Journal of Sociology*, 28, 1, 77-102.
Komp, K. (2013) 'Political gerontology: ageing populations and the state of the state', in K. Komp and M. Aartsen (eds) *Old age in Europe. A textbook of gerontology*, Heidelberg: Springer, 59-78.
Kotlikoff, L.J. and Burns, S. (2005) *The coming generational storms: what you need to know about America's future*, Boston: MIT Press.
Laverty, K.J. (1996) 'Economic "short-termism": the debate, the unresolved issues, and the implications for management practice and research', *The Academy of Management Review*, 21, 3, 825-60.

Lindh, T. (2012) 'Social investment in the ageing populations of Europe', in N. Morel, B. Palier and J. Palme (eds) *Towards a social investment welfare state: ideas, policies and challenges*, Bristol: Policy Press, 261-84.

Loewenstein, G. and Thaler, R.H. (1989) 'Anomalies: intertemporal choice', *The Journal of Economic Perspectives*, 3, 4, 181-93.

Lynch, J. (2006) *Age in the welfare state: the origins of social spending on pensioners, workers, and children*, Cambridge: Cambridge University Press.

March, J.G. (1991) 'Exploration and exploitation in organizational learning', *Organization Science*, 2, 1, 71-87.

Marier, P. (2014) 'How should we administer population aging? A Canadian comparison', *International Journal of Canadian Studies*, 47, 101-122.

Marshall, V.W. and McMullin, J. (2009) 'The life course perspective and public policy formation: observations on the Canadian case', in G. Naegele (ed), *Soziale Lebenslaufpolitik* [*Social life-course politics*]. Wiesbaden: VS Verlag, 732–47.

McArthur, D. (2007) 'Policy analysis in provincial governments in Canada: from PPBS to network management', in L. Dobuzinskis, M. Howlett and D. Laycock (eds) *Policy analysis in Canada: the state of the art*, Toronto: Toronto University Press, 238-64.

McDaniel, S. and Bernard, P. (eds) (2011) 'Life course as a policy lens: challenges and opportunities', Special issue. *Canadian Public Policy*, 37(S1).

Morel, N., Palier, B. and Palme, J. (2012) 'Beyond the welfare state as we knew it?', in N. Morel, B. Palier and J. Palme (eds) *Towards a social investment welfare state: ideas, policies and challenges*, Bristol: Policy Press, 1-32.

Moulaert, T. and Biggs, S. (2013) 'International and European policy on work and retirement: reinventing critical perspectives on active ageing and mature subjectivity', *Human Relations*, 66, 1, 23-43.

Myles, J. (2002) 'A new social contract for the elderly?', in G. Esping-Andersen, D. Gallie, A. Hemerick and J. Myles, J. (eds) *Why we need a new welfare state*, Oxford University Press: New York, 130-72.

Nordhaus, W.D. (1975) 'The political business cycle', *The Review of Economic Studies*, 42, 2, 169-90.

Nygård, M. and Krüger, N. (2012) 'Poverty, families and the investment state. The impact of social investment ideas on family policy discourses in Finland and Germany', *European Societies*, 14, 5, 755-77.

O'Rand, A. (2002) 'Cumulative advantage theory in life course research', *Annual Review of Gerontology and Geriatrics*, 22, 14-30.

Organisation for Economic Co-operation and Development (2011) *Help wanted? Providing and paying for long-term care*, Paris: Organisation for Economic Co-operation and Development.

Peters, B.G. (1998) 'Managing horizontal government: the politics of co-ordination', *Public Administration*, 76, 2, 295-311.

Pierson, P. (1994) *Dismantling the welfare state? Reagan, Thatcher, and the politics of retrenchment*, Cambridge: Cambridge University Press.

Rochman, J. and Tremblay, D.-G. (2010) *Le soutien à la participation sociale des aînés et le programme 'villeamie des aînés' au Québec [Supporting the social participation of older people and the program 'Age-Friendly City' in Quebec]*. Working paper 2010-5 of the Alliance de recherche université-communauté, Montréal: Télé-université/ Université du Québec à Montréal.

Rose, R. (1990) 'Inheritance before choice in public policy', *Journal of Theoretical Politics*, 2, 3, 263-91.

Schneider, A.L. and Ingram, H. (1993) 'Social construction of target populations: implications for politics and policy', *American Political Science Review*, 87, 2, 334-47.

Settersten, R.A. and Mayer, K.U. (1997) 'The measurement of age, age structuring, and the life-course', *Annual Review of Sociology*, 23, 233-61.

Strandh, M. and Nordlund, M. (2008) 'Active labour market policy and unemployment scarring: a ten-year Swedish panel study', *Journal of Social Policy*, 37, 3, 357-82.

Tsebelis, G. (1999) 'Veto players and law production in parliamentary democracies: an empirical analysis', *American Political Science Review*, 93, 3, 591-608.

World Health Organization (2002) *Active ageing: a policy framework*, Geneva: WHO.

World Health Organization (2007) *Global age-friendly cities: a guide*, Geneva: WHO.

Part IV

DISCUSSION AND CONCLUSION

FOURTEEN

Discussion and conclusion

Stina Johansson and Kathrin Komp

Lifecourse perspectives on ageing populations

Population ageing is a global process, but the tempo and dynamics vary from country to country as well as within countries. For example, the rapidity of the population ageing process in China, one of the fastest in the world, has more consequences on the individual level than the slow transition in a country like Sweden, which has one of the slowest transitions of European countries (Chesnais, 1992; Kinsella and Phillips, 2005; Johansson and Cheng, 2014).

In Chapter Six of this volume, Turek, Perek-Bialas and Stypinska clarify how the integration of Poland into the European Union facilitated emigration, which became a mass phenomenon among younger cohorts after 2004. Mass emigration caused rapid population ageing, turning Poland and other post-socialist countries into the fastest-ageing societies in Europe. The process of population ageing affects both social structures and lifecourses. At the same time, changes in the lives of people impact on the processes of population ageing. In the introduction, we suggested a model that describes the existence of certain social mechanisms. In our conclusion, we are now able to give a more detailed answer to how such interactions between macro and micro levels can take place.

Knowledge about how the balance among age groups influences lifecourses and about the way that changes in lifecourses impact on demographic patterns of society are important for our understanding of society and the formulation of social policies that target social risks (Beck, 1992). This book illustrates events that have caused visible changes in demographics and lifecourses, including inventions in medicine and changes in health policies and social policies.

Population dynamics

People construct their lifecourses through choices and actions within the opportunities and constraints of history and social circumstances (Grenier, 2012). Motel-Klingebiel's Chapter Three in this volume describes substantial shifts for the individual, such as the increase in lifespan as mortality risks are postponed into later life, educational phases are prolonged, partnership and parenthood become increasingly conditional, regional mobility grows, and overall flexibilisation, pluralisation and individualisation become the order of the day. These institutionalised features of modern society intertwine as a structured trajectory within social contexts such as family, working life and the welfare system and as individual biographies.

Brown and Lynch's aggregated perspective (Chapter Two) demonstrates that births, deaths and moves are the driving forces behind a demographic transition like population ageing that structures our lives in a new way. When there are fewer children and more old people, the family structure has more vertical and fewer horizontal links, and this influences how lives are linked together. Fewer siblings, cousins and second cousins – but more grandparents and great-grandparents – might involve a shift of the emotional and financial interdependencies between generations, switching the focus from caring for children to caring for older individuals within families as well as in public welfare.

In addition, interesting historical examples of drastic changes in fertility rates exist. For example, Karisto and Haapola (Chapter Four) describe how Finland's baby boomers increased the need for day-care services and forced schools to operate in shifts. In each life stage, the baby boomers' presence strained the current system and led to the creation of new structures. But they do not seem to be more active than other generations at the same age. This was a surprise because some of them, like the educated elite and women, were visible as radical forerunners. Because of the size of that generation, smaller fractions also became visible in the public sphere and were thus able to make their mark on the social structures. This is a strong argument for the combination of macro and micro perspectives.

Aggregation: cumulative advantages and disadvantages

The model presented in the introductory chapter says that in any given demographic structure, individuals will find diverse paths through life, and at an aggregate level these will create a new structure. A theory used in Chapter Six and Chapter Seven to explore that correlation is the theory of cumulative advantages and disadvantages (CAD). This theory accounts for the differentiation of lifecourses as people age (Dannefer, 2003; Ferraro et al, 2009). An initial socioeconomic advantage for an individual tends to be cumulative throughout the individual's lifecourse, resulting in greater advantages in later life. Similarly, a disadvantaged position in the early stages of life will often eventually result in lower socioeconomic status as measured by education, income and occupation. Therefore, according to CAD, the intra-cohort inequalities tend to grow with time as the cohort ages. In modern Western societies, other aspects of diversity – including health, networks and family relations – are also found to be greater within older than within younger cohorts (Daatland and Biggs, 2006).

General trends

From the diverse material in this book, there is no doubt that education is an important factor for change. As a factor providing opportunities for individuals to adapt their lifecourse to, or to break free from, traditional lifestyles, higher education has, on an aggregate level, been shown to have an impact on macro-level structures. In Poland (Chapter Six), education was a crucial factor because it tended to be the well-educated who emigrated. Not only higher education, but the quality of education was important for the effects seen in later life. Even more important seems to be the effects that occur when women have access to higher education on a large scale, even if there is a contradictory trend in Portugal (Chapter Five). Well-educated women often choose to give birth later in life, and in the long run this will have an impact on demographic structures. Health is another characteristic that can limit or open up possibilities in people's lives and that also has a significant impact on macro structures and vice versa.

A system's sustainability is challenged by population ageing and the verticalisation of family structures, and the greater need for care in combination with the lower number of younger people available to support the system will raise the cost of the system. Part of a solution is to make 'young old' people productive either as consumers or as producers. We will come back to the question of how the social structures that are crystallised in family structures, labour markets and welfare institutions can create different opportunities for individual choice.

Population ageing: contradictory trends

Differing life histories will impact on the available choices for individuals and allow for various degrees of discretion in terms of financial freedom and choice of residence. Tensions will occur when more people do not experience the transitions in the standard lifecourse (for example, they remain single), or they experience them at different times in their lives (for example, youth unemployment), or they experience transitions that are not part of the standard lifecourse (for example, divorce and remarriage or long-term unemployment).

Decisions or plans are influenced by prior life experiences and events (see Franke's Chapter Nine; Elder, 1994), embedded over a long stretch of the lifetime in addition to age-related feelings that create a need for a new orientation. Different theoretical approaches have been used to understand what happens in later life. Cumming and Henry (1961) claim that older people increasingly perceive physical and cognitive limitations with age, but Atchley (1971) asserts that older people try to maintain their lifestyle, previous activities and behaviours even after retirement. Or is it a question of a socioemotional selectivity, that individuals become increasingly aware of their shrinking time-horizon and future perspectives (Carstensen et al, 1999; Lang and Carstensen, 2002; Carstensen, 2006)?

The first major increase in population ageing started with modernisation, and this has created an age group with unclear role opportunities in relation to working life and family obligations. This group is referred to as the 'young old'. Two contradictory trends occur in many countries, as people use their agency to stay in the workforce longer or to withdraw from it earlier.

Do people work longer?

Working life might change due to individuals' own planning for old age and/or planned structural contributions from employers and society. As Karisto and Haapola (Chapter Four) show, people who spent longer in education tend to stay longer in their working life. This is consistent with the conclusions of Hochguertel (2010), who found that people with higher qualification levels are more likely to stay in the labour market for longer.

Better health conditions and fewer family obligations also lead people to remain in the workforce for longer. For individuals, Franke argues in Chapter Nine that becoming self-employed is a strategy to choose, in order to join a group that reports a high job satisfaction and a motivation to work longer. A high sense of job identification means that fewer people will seek to retire early. A consequence of this on a structural level will be that more generations will coexist next to each other in the labour market.

Or do they look after their grandchildren?

In Chapter Ten, Thomese and Cong present phenomena like grandparenting and other forms of informal care as individual choices together with the conceptual notion of a third age – the age between working life and being a dependent care recipient.

On a personal level, people use their agency as grandparents to create a new lifestyle in the third age in countries where the two-generation family has been the most common. A complication is that there is an increase in so-called Janus generations (Hagestad and Herlofson, 2007), consisting of people with one or more generations above and below them. Any of these generations might be free from (other) work or family obligations, but they might also be working and caring for others. At the same time, the younger generations have become smaller and the older people in need of care have become more numerous. On an aggregated level, these changes affect the gender structure and the formation of care institutions.

Or do they make other choices?

Laslett (1991) argues against efforts to make this group of older people productive. Self-fulfilment is the only responsibility of older individuals, and they must make judgements that are necessary to sustain independence like those in Winterton and Warburton's description in Chapter Eight of people who have moved back to rural areas in Australia. In this case, older people's lifecourse trajectories impact on the demographic and social characteristics of rural places. Emigration of older community members will impact on their ability to maintain linked lives and their ability to relive and further create historical and social connections within rural spaces. However, the trend for younger cohorts to relocate to urban centres reduces the agency of older people, in that they become less able to access social support when it is needed.

Structures that influence lifecourses

Individual success reveals much about social structure and individual agency. Political changes that began in 1989 in Poland, as described by Turek, Perek-Bialas and Stypinska in Chapter Six, reshaped that society's structures and relations relatively quickly and had significant impacts on the population's individual lifecourses. Also, before the fertility rate decreased, women in particular spent more time in education. The formerly totally predictable communist welfare system disappeared and the society created opportunities for free choice. The integration of Poland into the European Union in 2004 also opened up a labour market outside the country. An educational boom and an emigration boom followed, as did unemployment. People of different ages made their own differing choices dependent on which stage in the lifecourse they had entered by that time. The inequalities between and within generations increased. Life became more unstructured and more difficult to categorise in stages. Instead of well-defined stages, there were in-betweens to be filled according to personal aspirations and future outlooks – or just for survival. A longer life gives several opportunities to aggregate both advantages and disadvantages. According to the theory of CAD, much of the later life situation is determined by early life events, position and assets. The theory predicts an increase of inequalities within cohorts as they age, but this pattern was not confirmed in Poland.

Market-oriented countries

The US, which is a less regulated society than most European countries, requires individuals to create their own safety and welfare plans during their lives. There is greater space for human agency. As expected, individuals with higher socioeconomic status are able to use their advantages to adopt protective strategies that enhance their wellbeing and reduce their likelihood of disease and mortality. Socioeconomic status is thus appreciably linked to access to health resources. Underutilisation of health care services influences premature mortality and poorer health with age, because early detection and intervention are positively associated with lower morbidity and mortality. Cumulative disadvantage is arguably the most powerful theoretical explanation for ethnic variation in economic resources, health and wellbeing in old age, and in turn, population ageing.

Yamashita, Melnyk, Keene, Monnat and Smedley (Chapter Seven) found that some ethnic groups like Hispanic immigrants in the US can come to play an important role as a potential future labour force because of their longer life expectancy than other groups, despite disadvantaged socioeconomic status in terms of education, income and employment. The rapidly increasing younger generation of Hispanics is a group of special interest. More attention must also be paid to the ethnically based cumulative disadvantages caused by immigration to countries with the pull factors. However, the US is relatively young compared to other developed nations and what is obvious in the US with regard to CAD might not be applicable to other contexts (nations), including other welfare regimes and family structures.

Family-oriented countries

A family-oriented pattern was found in Portugal, as described in Wall and Aboim's Chapter Five in this volume. This is not surprising in light of Anttonen and Sipilä's (1996) findings that care regimes in southern Europe are more family-oriented than in northern Europe. In the passage into later life, women are required to be more flexible and they appear to suffer greater uncertainty than men in this life stage. Also, family trajectories were more embedded in gender inequalities than occupational trajectories. Wall and Aboim found that family and work lifecourse regimes in Portugal seem to be independent of each other, a trend that also seemed to be replicated in younger generations. Family lifecourses were so strongly gendered that education and other structural and biographical variables, including work trajectories, seemed to be irrelevant and to have no palpable effect on what appears to be a phenomenon that cuts across different social groups. The conclusion holds true for all generations in Portuguese society. Advantages and disadvantages were not added in the way that was expected from the theory developed by Kohli (1986), yet they can be explained by the theory of welfare regimes.

The examples from the US and Portugal refer to two nations with different histories as democratic societies. Citizenship rights became an issue early in the history of the US. In Portugal before 1974, gender inequality and female responsibility for homemaking were actually written into the country's constitution. The norm of female caregiving and large families (given the absence of family planning and high infant mortality rates) was promoted by the state, the Catholic Church and women's organisations. CAD assumes a stability of advantageous and disadvantageous mechanisms over the lifecourse, but that might not necessarily be the case during significant changes in societies. What the Portuguese example shows is that old structures remain and shape individual agency long after a decision for structural change has been made.

State-oriented countries

In northern Europe, working life – the stage between education and retirement – has been the natural channel for the implementation of many welfare and gender-equality reforms. Working life is neither a homogeneous nor an unchanging institution. In Sweden, the success of pension reforms is dependent on workers' willingness to stay in the workforce longer. Thus significant changes must take place within the workplace to better fit conditions to an ageing workforce.

Stattin and Larsson stressed in Chapter Twelve how opportunities and constraints can either promote or limit older workers' ability to remain active in work as they age. Crucial factors include both personal initiatives in working life and a caring attitude among employers. Employers need to respond to the reality of population ageing with structured, proactive strategies to keep workers healthy and updated on current knowledge and skill requirements of competence, as well as by improving working conditions so that people can stay longer in the workforce (Siegrist and Wahrendorf, 2013).

People migrate within or between countries, and this is another kind of discontinuity in the lifecourse. When young or middle-aged people move, they can often catch up with a structure, an education, a labour market and a welfare structure. But what about when they migrate from one country to another in later life? Later life is often a result of investments from earlier life stages that are bound within a national structure. Whether the move means an advantage or a disadvantage depends on when in life one moves abroad and if the move is done by free will. Whether the welfare structure is well developed in the area one moves to is also important when moving within a country.

Welfare structures are often standardised and adapted to national norms. Johansson's Chapter Eleven on late-in-life migrants shows that there is a need for an overall flexibilisation, pluralisation and individualisation of welfare services. The need for pluralism in welfare is also the case for other minority groups. Johansson explains that for people who have not invested in the national welfare system built up in the country they migrate to, a decision to migrate can include a strong dependency on people whose life is linked to theirs – a kind of continuity even if there are many signs of discontinuity in their lives.

Gender equity?

Motel-Klingebiel (Chapter Three) argues that European societies' extensive efforts to increase female education and labour participation over the last decades have impacted on individual preferences and life ambitions. A main policy goal in many countries was the assimilation of male and female labour force participation, with the male breadwinner lifestyle as the norm. Such decisions dramatically changed the conditions and the possibilities for human agency.

For women, the stability of social structures, institutions, social relations and social norms are often important. From Poland we can see that mass reductions in employment due to privatisation and the destruction of supporting structures have been the main reasons for relatively low employment rates for women in the first decade after the political transformation.

Women became financially independent but not independent from caring responsibilities within their families. But why stress one generation with those double obligations when the number of generations has increased? Family roles in the ageing society will in any case be renegotiated, and the forms for such negotiation have to be invented on personal as well as institutional levels. When one generation is busy with paid work and childcare, new support roles might develop for the older generation as part of an intricate exchange system of services between generations. Thomese and Cong's chapter (Chapter Ten) details this trend in countries with a history of women's more or less equal participation in the labour market.

On the personal level, people use their agency as grandparents to create a new lifestyle in the third age in countries where the two-generation family has been the most common. But individuals' behaviours are largely shaped by social structures and cultures that existed long before. Traditional gender norms are often repeated, as exemplified in Chapter Five by Wall and Aboim. What happens with the new norms of gender equality established during modernity?

Staying longer in the workforce and caring for grandchildren seem to be two activities that are difficult to reconcile (Kohli and Künemund, 2013). It is also likely that both staying longer in working life as well as grandparenting will have consequences in relation to gender equality, and this is important to consider. Ambivalence is inherent in the complexity of social roles and interactions (Thomese and Cong in Chapter Ten), and people have to deal with three types of ambivalence when confronted with intergenerational norms: the simultaneous desire for autonomy and need for dependence on both sides; conflicting norms (for example, looking after oneself well versus being a burden on one's children); and conflicting solidarities, such as with one's parents and one's children where multiple perspectives and contexts are always involved. In late-modern societies, traditions and social contexts offer less guidance for behavioural choices, because such choices are seen as the responsibility of the individual (Van Tilburg and Thomese, 2011).

Families that can rely on care from grandparents have higher fertility rates and mothers who work longer, and these are structural changes. The question is whether the next generation should also be available for grandparenting. With later childbearing, it follows that the grandchildren will come later, making grandparenting more challenging. Family diversity will also increase. Thomese and Cong (Chapter Ten) show that divorces almost tripled in the Netherlands between 1950 and 2010. These changes indicate that there will be a huge variety in the ways people will spend their lives in what we call 'the third age'.

Old-age policies

Together with increased longevity, welfare institutions facilitated more complex and individualised lifecourses. Traditional policies for older people are pensions and social care specially designed for the old-age group. Riley and Riley (1994) argue that our currently age-differentiated society should transition to an age-integrated one. Traditional policies form a structure that people can trust when in difficult situations. These are helpful, but they create little room for one's own life planning. Incorporating lifecourse ideas into policy making requires a two-fold approach, as Komp and Marier argue in Chapter Thirteen. There is a need for policies that will strive to influence youths and middle-aged people to influence their lifecourses in a desired direction, and to guide lives towards empowerment, activation and self-help. The combination of policies specially designed for people in need of support and lifecourse-inspired policies ensures that effects are visible in the short and the long run, and that the situations of frail – as well as active – older people are addressed. Structures such as active-friendly and ageing-friendly cities belong to this perspective.

Diverse lifecourses: new opportunities and new risks

The risks that people now are confronted with are more abstract, diverse and difficult to recognise than the risks that motivated investments in present welfare institutions. There is a structural lag as populations grow older in a welfare structure based on risk calculations from the demographic structure that applied when they were young (Riley et al, 1994). People plan their lives differently, given the demographic structure and the welfare structure.

The convergence or homogeneity implicit in the transformation from agricultural to industrial society (First Modernity) is shown in the data collected in different countries and presented in this book. In contrast to that, diversity was found in the construction of gender roles and caring obligations as well as social stratification. This finding is consistent with actual modernisation theory, more precisely with the discussion about what has happened between what has been called a First and a Second Modernity (Beck and Grande 2010). In the period of Second Modernity, family institutions and institutions of welfare, care, and security must address a greater variety of older citizens due to greater mobility and greater dependency between countries.

In many of the country examples presented here, welfare systems with an imbalanced age structure lack transparency and predictability. This pinpoints the importance of building welfare structures that support an individual's desire to plan their own lifecourse. De-standardisation of present welfare solutions that are built on outdated risk predictions, especially age integration, would solve some of these problems, by creating more space for individual agency. One risk, however, is that different generations live in different conditions. Lindh et al (2005) discussed how justice between generations could be ensured in ageing societies. Deeper analyses done on the relation between welfare-state policies should not focus solely on economic outcomes for different generations and the effects that different regimes have on decisions regarding family formation. The role opportunities or places in the social structure must support people at the various stages of their lives – and because stages are more fluid and flexible, the support must also follow people's decisions in everyday life.

The ageing process offers options for renegotiation of gender roles with a variety of solutions. If the labour market was the arena for negotiating gender issues in the First Modernity, maybe the family is the arena for renegotiating gender issues in the Second Modernity. In the context of verticalisation, new types of inequalities can be created. A risk of increased economic, gender and ethnicity-related inequalities comes with ageing.

A special thought should be given to migration. People migrate between and within countries, and after migrating they have to follow a different lifecourse logic than the one they were born into. The role of young minorities as future caregivers for older populations needs to be better understood. Technological transition can change the personal life situation, because this enables individuals to maintain contacts with relatives and friends across the globe. But could it compensate for structures that marginalise people in their new homeland? Structures can change. Fertility is still the major driving force in the demographic transition. In some countries we can see the consequences of different fertility rates in different ethnic groups and how these can change the balance between majority and minority groups.

This book shows what structures do with people's agency and how people's agency can change gender, welfare and working-life structures. Open and democratic structures help people to use their agency, but outdated structures can constrain and marginalise people. The great challenge of the global era is to create structures that allow individual choice regardless of age, gender, ethnic affiliation, the generation born into, or place of residence. Knowledge about how demography and lifecourses intersect contributes to a better understanding of the transformation into a Second Modernity.

Acknowledgements

We would like to thank Fleur Thomese for comments on an early version that helped to improve this chapter.

References

Anttonen, A. and Sipilä, J. (1996) 'European social care services: Is it possible to identify models?', *Journal of European Social Policy*, 6, 2, 87-100.

Atchley, R.C. (1971) 'Retirement and leisure participation: Continuity or crisis?', *The Gerontologist*, 11, 1, 13-17.

Beck, U. (1992) *Risk society*, London: Sage Publications.

Beck, U. and Grande, E. (2010) 'Varieties of second modernity: The cosmopolitan turn in social and political theory and research', *The British Journal of Sociology*, 61, 3, 409-43.

Carstensen, L.L., Isaacowitz, D.M. and Charles, S.T. (1999) 'Taking time seriously: A theory of socioemotional selectivity', *American Psychologist*, 54, 3, 165-81.

Carstensen, L.L. (2006) 'The influence of a sense of time on human development', *Science*, 312, 5782, 1913-15.

Chesnais, J.-C. (1992) *The demographic transition. Stages, patterns, and economic implications*, Oxford: Oxford University Press.

Cumming, E. and Henry, W.E. (1961) *Growing old: The process of disengagement*, New York: Basic.

Daatland, S. and Biggs, S. (2006) *Aging and Diversity*, Bristol: Policy Press.

Dannefer, D. (2003) 'Cumulative advantage, and the life course: Cross-fertilizing age and social science knowledge', *Journal of Gerontology*, 58B, 6, 327-37.

Elder, G.H., Jr (1994) 'Time, human agency, and social change: Perspectives on the life course', *Social Psychology Quarterly*, 57, 1, 4-15.

Ferraro, K.P., Schippee, T.P. and Schafer, M.H. (2009) 'Cumulative inequality theory for research on aging and the life course', in V.L. Bengtson, M. Silverstein, D. Putney and D. Gans (eds) *Handbook of theories of aging*, New York: Springer, 413-34.

Grenier, A. (2012) *Transitions and the lifecourse: Challenging the constructions of 'Growing Old'*, Bristol: Policy Press.

Hagestad, G. and Herlofson, K. (2007) 'Micro and macro perspectives on intergenerational relations and transfers in Europe', in United Nations (ed) *United Nations expert group meeting on social and economic implications of changing population age structures*, New York: United Nations.

Hochguertel, S. (2010) *Self-employment around retirement age*. Tinbergen Institute Discussion Paper 10/067-3, Amsterdam: Tinbergen Institute.

Johansson, S. and Cheng, S. (2014) 'The old-age pension in China and Sweden' [online], *International Social Work*.

Kinsella, K. and Phillips, D.R. (2005) 'Global aging: The challenge of success', *Population Bulletin*, 60, 1, 5-42.

Kohli, M. (1986) 'Social organization and subjective construction of the life course', in A.B. Sorensen, F.E. Weinert and L.R. Sherrod (eds) *Human development and the life course: Multidisciplinary perspectives*, Hillsdale: Erlbaum, 271-92.

Kohli, M. and Künemund, H. (2013) 'The social connections of older Europeans', in J. Field, R.J. Burke and C.L. Cooper (eds) *The Sage handbook of aging, work and society*, London: Sage, 347-62.

Lang, F.R. and Carstensen, L.L. (2002) 'Time counts: Future time perspective, goals, and social relationships', *Psychology and Aging*, 17, 1, 125-39.

Laslett, P. (1991) *A fresh map of life*, Cambridge: Harvard University Press.

Lindh, T., Malmberg, B. and Palme, J. (2005) 'Generations at war or sustainable social policy in ageing societies', *Journal of Political Philosophy*, 13, 470-89.

Riley, M., Kahn, R.L. and Foner, A. (1994) *Age and structural lag: Society's failure to provide meaningful opportunities in work, family, and leisure*, New York: Wiley & Sons.

Riley, M. and Riley J.W. (1994) 'Age integration and the lives of older people', *The Gerontologist*, 34, 1, 110-5.

Siegrist, J. and Wahrendorf, M. (2013) 'Quality of work, wellbeing and retirement', in J. Field, R.J. Burke and C.L. Cooper (eds) *The Sage handbook of aging, work and society*, London: Sage, 324-26.

Van Tilburg, T.G. and Thomese, F. (2010) 'Societal dynamics in personal networks', in D. Dannefer and C.R. Phillipson (eds) *The Sage handbook of social gerontology*, London: Sage, 215-25.

Index

E

F

G

H

I